Horizons

Cahier d'activités écrites et orales

Horizons

Cahier d'activités écrites et orales

Joan H. Manley
Stuart Smith
John T. McMinn
Marc A. Prévost

Text Credits

Page 6 Document France Télécom—*Les pages jaunes* —édition 191; **22** Éditions Albert René; **47** "Les derniers cafés où l'on cause," *Francoscopie,* p. 207, 1993; **83** & **210** Trois Suisses; **137** *Elle,* no. 2404, août 1993; **170** "C'est l'histoire d'une vielle dame," *Jeune Afrique,* no. 1660, 1992; **174** "Apprenez à évaluer vos capacités professionelles," *Amina* magazine, no. 261, 1991; **266** "Préférence" par Claude-Emmanuel Abolo Bowole vu dans le livre *Poèmes de demain,* Editions Nouvelles du Sud, 1980.

Photo Credits

Page 187 Heinle & Heinle Image Resource Bank; **230** Mark Antmann / The Image Works; **236** Henri Cartier-Bresson / Magnum

Manufactured in the United States of America

ISBN 0-8384-7947-2

10 9 8 7 6 5 4 3 2 1

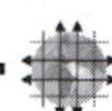

Table des Matières

Préface

The *Cahier d'activités écrites et orales* is divided into two parts. The ***Cahier d'activités écrites,*** on pages 1–176 in the front of the workbook / lab manual, provides you an opportunity to develop your writing skills in French and to practice the vocabulary and grammatical structures that you learn in class. The ***Cahier d'activités orales,*** on pages 179–266 in the back of the workbook / lab manual, and the accompanying *Lab Manual Tapes* give you the chance to improve your pronunciation and practice understanding spoken French. The *Cahier d'activités écrites et orales* supports the textbook directly. Except for the ***Chapitre de révision,*** there is a chapter in both the ***Cahier d'activités écrites*** and the ***Cahier d'activités orales*** with four ***Compétences*** corresponding to those in the textbook. You should always review all of the new words, phrases, and learning strategies or grammar rules presented in each ***Compétence*** in the *Horizons* textbook before beginning the corresponding section in either the ***Cahier d'activités écrites*** or the ***Cahier d'activités orales.*** Also remember that there are two sets of tapes that accompany *Horizons:* the *Text Tape* and the *Lab Manual Tapes.* The *Text Tape* contains activities marked with a cassette symbol in the textbook. Be sure that you have the *Lab Manual Tapes* when working in the ***Cahier d'activités orales.***

Writing the journal in the **Cahier d'activités écrites**

At the end of each ***Compétence*** in the ***Cahier d'activités écrites,*** you will write a journal entry. Each entry is a guided composition in which you combine all that you have learned in a global, communicative writing activity. As you begin each ***Compétence*** in class, look ahead in your workbook to see what you will be expected to communicate in written French after studying the vocabulary and the grammatical stuctures. This will help you stay focused on the real purpose of learning vocabulary and grammatical structures, which is communication. In class, note down expressions or sentences that you might need for your journal, and as you sit down to write your journal entry, reread the dialogues and readings in the chapter up to that point. This will give you examples of what to say. Try to be creative, but stick to what you know. Do not try to use vocabulary and structures that you have not yet studied in class, unless you feel confident that you understand them. If you do not have enough space to say all that you wish on the page in the workbook, you may write your journal entry on a separate sheet of paper.

Tips for success with the **Lab Manual Tapes**

It takes time, patience, and practice to understand French spoken at a normal conversational speed. Do not be surprised if at first you find it difficult to understand sections on the *Lab Manual Tapes.* Relax and listen to passages more than once. You will understand a little more each time. Remember that you will not understand everything, and that for particular activities, you are only expected to understand enough to answer specific questions. Read through listening exercises prior to listening to the tapes so that you know what you are listening for. If you find that you do not have enough time to process and respond to a question before the next one is asked, take advantage of the pause or stop button on your tape player to give yourself more time. Most importantly, stay patient and remember that you can always rewind and listen again.

Practice, patience, and persistence pay!

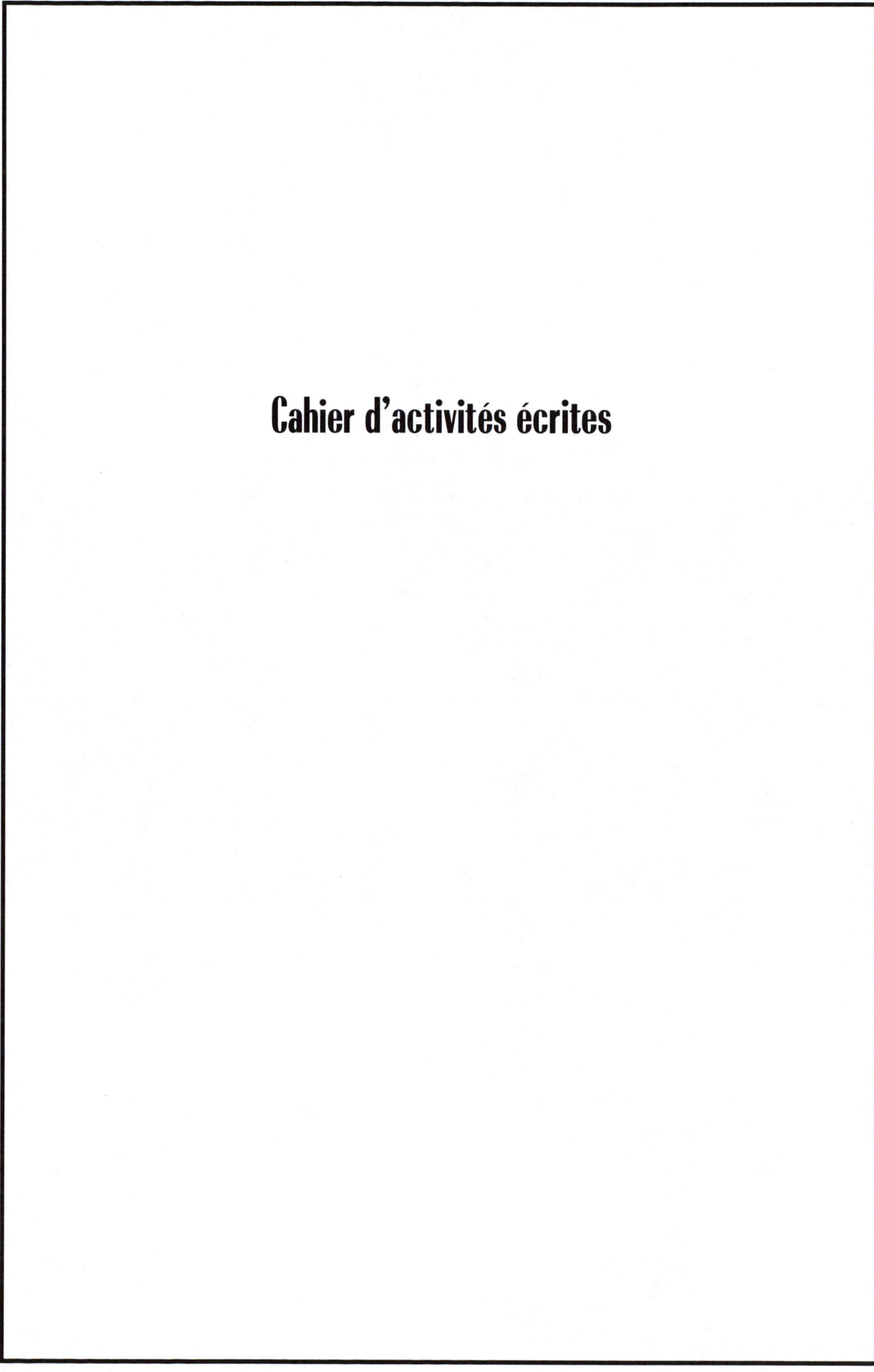

Cahier d'activités écrites

NOM ______________________ COURS ______________________

CHAPITRE PRÉLIMINAIRE
On commence!

COMPÉTENCE 1 Greeting people

At the end of each ***Compétence*** in the workbook, you will be asked to write a journal entry using the vocabulary and structures you have just practiced. The journal allows you to check whether you can combine all that you have studied to communicate in a real life situation in French. By the time you write your journal entry at the end of this ***Compétence***, you should be able to introduce yourself, meet others, ask how they are, and say good-bye.

A. Conversations. Complete the following conversations logically by filling in the missing words.

— Bonjour, monsieur.

— Bonjour, ______________________ .

— Comment ______________________ ?

— Je m'appelle Henri Prévost. Et ______________________ ?

— Je ______________________ Hélène Cauvin.

— Bonsoir, monsieur.

— ______________________, mademoiselle.

— Comment ______________________ ?

— Je vais très ______________________, merci. Et vous?

— Assez ______________________.

— Bonjour, je m'appelle Philippe. Et __________ ?

Tu ______________________ comment?

— Je suis Danielle.

— Salut, Jean-Pierre.

— ______________, Micheline. __________ va?

— __________ va. Et __________ ? Comment ça va?

— __________ mal.

B. Très bien, merci! How do you think these people would answer the question **Comment allez-vous?**

1. 

____

2. 

____

3. 

____

4. 

____

C. Qu'est-ce qu'on dit... ? How might you say good-bye to . . .

1. your friends until tomorrow?

____

2. someone you will see later in the day?

____

3. a relative you will visit next month?

____

D. Réponses. Write a logical response to the following questions or statements.

1. Bonjour, monsieur / madame / mademoiselle. ______________________________

2. Bonsoir, monsieur / madame / mademoiselle. ______________________________

3. Comment vous appelez-vous? ______________________________

4. Tu t'appelles comment? ______________________________

5. Salut! ______________________________

6. Comment allez-vous? ______________________

7. Comment ça va? ______________________

8. Je vais très bien. Et vous? ______________________

9. Au revoir! ______________________

10. À demain! ______________________

Sort the preceding list of expressions according to whether you can use them in informal situations, such as with another student **[avec un(e) étudiant(e)]** or in more formal situations, such as with a professor **[avec un professeur]**. Write each expression next to the appropriate heading. In some cases you can use them in both situations **[avec les deux]**.

avec un(e) étudiant(e): ______________________

____

____

____

avec un professeur: ______________________

____

____

____

avec les deux: ______________________

____

____

____

E. Les salutations familières. You might use the following phrases to talk to your instructor. What less formal expression could you use to address the student who sits next to you?

EXEMPLE Bonjour, monsieur. *Salut, Marc.*

1. Comment vous appelez-vous? ______________________

2. Comment allez-vous? ______________________

3. Je vais bien, et vous? ______________________

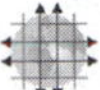

F. Une conversation. Here is a conversation between two students on the first day of classes. Rewrite it in more formal French, such as between two business associates. You may use any last names you wish.

— Bonjour, je m'appelle Alice. Et toi, tu t'appelles comment?
— Salut! Je suis Alain. Comment ça va?
— Ça va bien. Et toi?
— Ça va assez bien.
— Au revoir! À demain!
— Au revoir!

____

____

____

____

____

____

____

____

If you have access to Système-D software, you will find the following phrases there.
PHRASES: Greetings; Introducing; Leaving; Describing health

Journal. Write both roles of a logical conversation in which you:

- greet a classmate from your French class
- introduce yourself and ask his/her name
- ask how he/she is and answer his/her question about how you are
- say good-bye

VOUS: ____

L'ÉTUDIANT(E): ____

VOUS: ____

L'ÉTUDIANT(E): ____

VOUS: ____

L'ÉTUDIANT(E): ____

VOUS: ____

L'ÉTUDIANT(E): ____

NOM ______________________ COURS ______________________

COMPÉTENCE 2 Spelling and counting

By the time you write your journal entry at the end of this ***Compétence,*** you should be able to spell out words and count from zero to thirty.

A. Les accents. In French, accents may indicate how a word is pronounced, and sometimes the presence or absence of an accent changes a word's meaning entirely. For example, the word **ou** means *or,* whereas the accented word **où** means *where.* With the exception of the **cédille,** which occurs on the letter **c (ç),** you will find accents only on vowels. Look over the accent-vowel combinations below and do the exercises that follow.

e + accent aigu:	é	écouter	répéter	étudier
e + accent grave:	è	bibliothèque	lève	grève
a + accent grave:	à	là-bas	au-delà	
u + accent grave:	ù	où		
e + accent circonflexe:	ê	tête	fête	forêt
a + accent circonflexe:	â	pâté	âne	mât
i + accent circonflexe:	î	dîner	gîte	île
o + accent circonflexe:	ô	hôpital	hôtesse	rôti
u + accent circonflexe:	û	piqûre	mûr	sûr
e + tréma:	ë	Noël	Joël	
i + tréma:	ï	naïf	Haïti	

An **accent circonflexe** frequently indicates that an **s** has been dropped from the spelling of a word. Knowing this will help you recognize the meaning of more words. Can you find the French equivalents of the following English words in the example words above?

(meat) paste: ______________ hospital: ______________

mast: ______________ hostess: ______________

forest: ______________ roast: ______________

When writing in French, pay close attention to accents, since a misplaced accent can change the pronunciation or the meaning of a word. With practice, you will learn to determine where the accents should go on a word and how it should then be pronounced. In the meantime, learn accents as part of the spelling of words. To get started, copy the following sentences, making sure to place the accents where they belong.

1. Mon père va à l'hôtel où il travaille avec Frédéric Ponçoux.

____

2. Nous préférons parler français à la bibliothèque et écouter les cassettes là-bas.

____

3. Ces enfants naïfs rêvent de dîner avec le président de la République française.

____

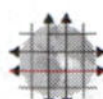

B. Ça s'écrit comment? Explain to a student from France how to spell the English equivalents of the following French words.

EXEMPLES hôpital **En anglais, *hospital* s'écrit sans accent circonflexe et avec un s.**
biologie **En anglais, *biology* s'écrit avec un y.**

1. philosophie ______________________________

2. mariage ______________________________

3. forêt ______________________________

4. intellectuel ______________________________

5. adresse ______________________________

C. Des adresses. You are giving the names and addresses of some hotels you are going to be staying at while in Paris. Complete each conversation logically by filling in the missing words. Spell out all numbers.

1.

Hôtel Ritz
15, Place Vendôme
75041 Paris Cedex 01
(01) 42 60 38 30
Tx Réservat.: RITZ RES 670 112 F
Tx Messages: RITZ MES 220 262 F
Messages télécopieur : Télétax (01) 42 60 23 71
Réservations télécopieur : (01) 42 86 00 91
★★★★
Restaurant Grill «ESPADON»
Salons privés pour réceptions
Bars - Health Club
Piscine - Ritz Club
Salon de coiffure

— Hôtel Ritz, ______________________________, place Vendôme.

— Vendôme, ça s'écrit avec un ______________________________ circonflexe?

2.

HÔTEL DE LA TRÉMOILLE
★★★★
14, r. de la Trémoille - 75008 PARIS
Télex : 640344 F - Fax : (01) 40 70 01 08
(01) 47 23 34 20/ (01) 47 23 75 12

— Hôtel de la Trémoille, ______________________________ rue de la Trémoille.

— Trémoille, ça s'écrit ______________________________?

— T - R - E - accent ______________________________ - M - O - I - L - L - E.

NOM ______________________ COURS ______________________

D. C'est combien? You are shopping in Quebec, where they use Canadian dollars. Give the price of the following items by spelling out the numbers.

1. 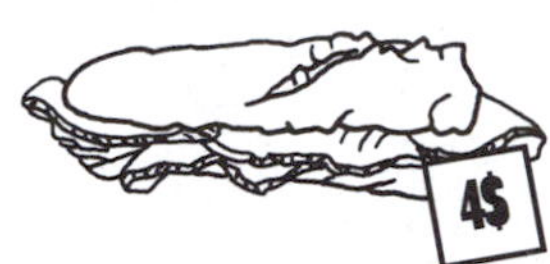

2. 

3. 

4. 

5. 

6. 

1. Un sandwich, c'est ______________________ dollars.

2. Une calculatrice, c'est ______________________ dollars.

3. Un tee-shirt, c'est ______________________dollars.

4. Une plante, c'est ______________________ dollars.

5. Une cassette vidéo, c'est ______________________ dollars.

6. Un disque compact, c'est ______________________ dollars.

E. Problèmes de maths. Complete the following math problems by filling in the missing words. Spell out all the numbers.

1. — Combien font sept et ______________________?

   — Sept et ______________________ font vingt et un.

2. — ______________________ font six ____________ sept?

   — Six ______________ sept font treize.

3. — Combien font ________________ moins treize?

   — ____________________ moins treize font dix-sept.

4. — Combien ________________ vingt ____________ douze?

   — Vingt ________________ douze ______________ huit.

5. — Combien font huit et ______________________?

   — Huit et ________________ font vingt-cinq.

F. L'Union européenne. France is one of the countries in the European Union. Spell out the numbers in parentheses to give its relative importance. France has . . .

1. (23) ______________________________ pour cent de la superficie *(area)*
2. (17) ______________________________ pour cent de la population
3. (21) ______________________________ pour cent de la production agricole
4. (19) ______________________________ pour cent des chômeurs *(of the unemployed)*

G. Pays francophones. French is spoken in many countries around the world. Guess the populations (rounded to the nearest million) of these countries where French is spoken. Write out a number from the list in each blank. You can find these countries on the maps inside the front and back covers of the textbook. The correct populations are given at the bottom of the page.

2, 13, 10, 27, 6, 9, 28, 8, 7

EXEMPLE le Canada: vingt-sept millions

1. la Belgique: ____________________ millions
2. la Suisse: ____________________ millions
3. la Mauritanie: ____________________ millions
4. le Mali: ____________________ millions
5. le Sénégal: ____________________ millions
6. Haïti: ____________________ millions
7. la Côte-d'Ivoire: ____________________ millions
8. l'Algérie: ____________________ millions

SYSTÈME-D

If you have access to Système-D software, you will find the following phrases there.
PHRASES: Introducing; Asking for information

Journal. Your professor is taking attendance and asks you what your name is. He/She then asks how you spell your last name. Write a logical conversation.

PROFESSEUR: ____

VOUS: ____

PROFESSEUR: ____

VOUS: ____

Correct populations for ***G. Pays francophones*** (rounded to the nearest million): Canada 27,000,000; Belgium 10,000,000; Switzerland 7,000,000; Mauritania 2,000,000; Mali 8,000,000; Senegal 9,000,000; Haiti 6,000,000; Ivory Coast 13,000,000; Algeria 28,000,000

NOM ______________________ COURS ______________________

COMPÉTENCE 3 Talking about your schedule

By the time you write your journal entry at the end of this *Compétence,* you should be able to describe your schedule, explaining the days and times you are at the university and when you work.

A. Quelle heure est-il? Write the time for each clock in complete sentences, spelling out all numbers.

1. 

____

2. 

____

3. 

____

4. 

____

5. 

____

6. 

____

7. 

____

8. 

____

B. À quelle heure? At what time during the day do you usually do the following things?

EXEMPLE get up *à sept heures et demie du matin*

1. go to your French class ______________________
2. go home ______________________
3. eat dinner ______________________
4. go to bed ______________________

C. Vous êtes à la maison? Write sentences in French stating whether you are generally at home at the following times on Mondays.

EXEMPLE 1:20 P.M. **Le lundi, je suis à la maison à une heure vingt de l'après-midi. / Le lundi, je ne suis pas à la maison à une heure vingt de l'après-midi.**

1. 9:10 A.M. ____________________

2. 4:45 P.M. ____________________

3. noon ____________________

4. 8:30 P.M. ____________________

5. 12:15 A.M. ____________________

6. 10:40 A.M. ____________________

D. Mon emploi du temps. Fill in the days of the week in the left column on the following daily planner. The first one has been done as an example.

JOUR	MATIN	APRÈS-MIDI	SOIR
lundi			

Now go back and indicate when you work on the weekly planner by writing in **Je travaille.** Also indicate when you are in class by writing **Je suis en classe.**

E. Et vous? Complete the following sentences with the appropriate days. Remember to use **le** to say you do something *on* a particular day in general. If you do not work, leave the second sentence blank.

1. Je suis en cours de français ____________________.

2. Je travaille ____________________.

3. Je ne travaille pas ____________________.

4. Je ne suis pas en classe ____________________.

NOM ______________________ COURS ______________________

F. Quels sont les devoirs pour demain? Which classroom instructions match each drawing? Write the appropriate letter in the blank under the corresponding illustration.

a. Faites les devoirs dans le livre.

b. Écoutez les cassettes.

c. Lisez la page 17.

d. Apprenez les mots de vocabulaire aux pages 26 et 27 pour le prochain cours.

1. 

____

2. 

____

3. 

____

4. 

____

G. Questions. You are talking to some of your classmates as you are leaving your next French class and they ask you the following questions. Answer each one with a complete sentence in French.

1. Quelle heure est-il maintenant?

____

2. C'est quel jour, aujourd'hui?

____

3. C'est quel jour, demain?

____

4. La bibliothèque ferme à minuit aujourd'hui?

____

5. La bibliothèque ouvre à sept heures demain matin?

____

6. La bibliothèque ferme à quelle heure le samedi?

___

7. Quels sont les devoirs pour le prochain cours de français?

___

8. Les devoirs sont à quelle page dans le cahier d'activités écrites?

___

9. Les mots de vocabulaire sont à la page 16 dans le livre?

___

10. Le prochain cours de français, c'est demain?

___

SYSTÈME-D *If you have access to Système-D software, you will find the following phrases there.*
PHRASES: Telling Time; VOCABULARY: Studies, courses; Time expressions; Time of day; Days of the week; DICTIONARY: The verb **être**

Journal. Write a paragraph describing your weekly schedule. What days and times are you in class? When do you work? When are you at **(à)** the library? When are you at home? You may begin your paragraph with one of the following phrases to say whether you are busy this semester/trimester. If you are female, include the extra **e** on the word **occupé(e)** *(busy)*. If you are male, do not.

Ce semestre/trimestre je suis très occupé(e)...

Ce semestre/trimestre je ne suis pas très occupé(e)...

___

NOM ______________________ COURS ______________________

COMPÉTENCE 4 Getting acquainted in class

By the time you write your journal at the end of this ***Compétence,*** you should be able to ask your professor for clarification in French, and you should also be able to give a little personal information about yourself.

A. Les instructions en classe. What did the professor say to these students? Write the labels below the matching illustrations.

Allez au tableau.
Écoutez la question.
Répondez à la question.
Écrivez la réponse au tableau.

Ouvrez votre livre à la page 23.
Prenez une feuille de papier et un stylo.
Donnez-moi votre feuille de papier.
Fermez votre livre.

1. 

____

2. 

____

3. ______________________

4. 

____

5. ______________________

6. 

____

7. ______________________

8. 

____

B. Des instructions logiques. Using vocabulary you have learned, list as many words as you can that logically complete the following commands.

Écoutez...	Lisez...	Ouvrez...
______	______	______
______	______	______
______	______	______
______	______	______

Prenez...	Écrivez...	Faites...
______	______	______
______	______	______
______	______	______
______	______	______

C. Comment? Using phrases you learned in ***Compétences 3*** and ***4,*** tell or ask your professor the following.

1. Ask him/her how to say *book* in French.

______

2. Ask him/her to repeat something.

______

3. Tell him/her that you don't understand.

______

4. Ask him/her what the word **prenez** means.

______

5. Ask him/her how **prenez** is written.

______

6. Tell him/her that you don't know the answer.

______

7. Ask him/her what the homework is for the next class.

______

NOM ________________ COURS ________________

D. Moi... Complete the following sentences, providing information about yourself.

1. J'habite ________________.

   Je n'habite pas ________________.

2. Je parle ________________.

   Je ne parle pas ________________.

3. Je suis ________________.

   Je ne suis pas ________________.

4. Je pense que le français est ________________.

E. Une interview. Answer the following questions with complete sentences in French.

1. Comment vous appelez-vous?

____

2. Vous êtes américain(e)?

____

3. Vous habitez à Paris maintenant?

____

4. Vous habitez seul(e)?

____

5. Vous êtes de New York?

____

6. Vous travaillez beaucoup?

____

7. Vous parlez espagnol?

____

8. Le français est difficile ou facile?

____

F. Qui suis-je? Using the French actress Catherine Deneuve's description of herself as an example, tell how two other famous Americans or Canadians would describe themselves. Have them say their name, their nationality, what city they are from, and what city they live in now.

EXEMPLE *Je m'appelle Catherine Deneuve. Je suis française. Je suis de Paris et j'habite à Paris maintenant.*

1. ______________________________

____

2. ______________________________

____

If you have access to Système-D software, you will find the following phrases there.
PHRASES: Introducing; Telling Time; VOCABULARY: Studies, courses; Time expressions; Time of day; Days of the week; Nationality; DICTIONARY: The verb **être**

Journal. Using everything you have learned in the ***Chapitre préliminaire,*** write two paragraphs introducing yourself. Include the following information.

- In paragraph 1, tell your name, where you are from originally, where you live now, and with whom you live.
- In paragraph 2, describe your schedule this semester, telling which days you are in class and at what times. Then, say whether you work, where, which days, and at what times.

____

____

____

____

____

____

____

____

____

____

____

____

____

NOM ______________________ COURS ______________________

CHAPITRE 1
À l'université

COMPÉTENCE 1 Identifying people

By the time you write your journal entry at the end of this ***Compétence,*** you should be able to identify friends and classmates and tell a little about them.

A. **Qui est-ce?** You are introducing the people pictured below. Copy the following sentences next to the appropriate picture.

Ce sont mes amis.
C'est un ami.
C'est une amie.
Elle est étudiante.
Il est étudiant.
Elle est française.
Ils sont américains.
Il est canadien.
Il est beau.
Elle est belle.
Il est sportif.
Elle est sportive.
Ils sont étudiants.
Ils sont jeunes.
Ils sont sympathiques.

B. Et vous? Circle the word that someone should use if asking you the following questions. Then answer each one in the space provided.

1. Vous êtes étudiant / étudiante ?

____

2. Vous êtes canadien / canadienne ?

____

3. Vous êtes français / française ?

____

4. Vous êtes américain / américaine ?

____

C. Questions. A student who sits on the other side of the room in your French class sees you in the library and asks the following questions. Answer them with complete sentences.

1. Ton professeur de français, c'est un homme ou une femme?

____

2. Et ton cours de français, c'est à quelle heure?

____

3. Nous sommes dans le même cours, n'est-ce pas?

____

D. Les mots apparentés. Guess the meaning of each cognate in italics, writing your answer in the blank.

1. ______________________ Je comprends *généralement.*

2. ______________________ *Normalement,* le cours de français est facile.

3. ______________________ Les examens sont *probablement* difficiles.

4. ______________________ Je suis *frustré(e).*

5. ______________________ Je suis *fatigué(e).*

6. ______________________ Je suis *occupé(e).*

Now go back and circle the numbers of the preceding statements that are true for you in your French class.

NOM ______________________ COURS ______________________

E. **Cours d'été.** As you read the following prospectus for French courses for foreign students at a French university, circle the cognates that you encounter. You are not expected to understand every word, but the cognates should help you understand a lot.

SESSION DU PRINTEMPS

Du 10 mai au 19 juin

Les étudiants et étudiantes doivent s'inscrire à un minimum de 6 crédits (équivalent d'un plein cours) jusqu'à un maximum de 12 crédits. Les cours de trois crédits suivants (en français ou en anglais selon le cas) sont offerts*:

Archéologie de la Méditerranée

Histoire de l'art: La Renaissance; l'art français du XXe siècle

Commerce (6 crédits): Le commerce international

Écrivains anglais de la Méditerranée

Beaux-arts: Le dessin; l'histoire du cinéma français

Français: Le roman français moderne

Géographie: L'Union européenne

Histoire du monde méditerranéen moderne

Introduction interdisciplinaire à la culture européenne de la période suivant la Renaissance

Musique et culture populaires

Science politique: L'Union européenne

Français semi-intensif (3 crédits): S'adresse aux étudiants qui désirent le suivre de concert avec un ou plusieurs cours offerts lors de la session du printemps.

LE PROGRAMME INTENSIF DE FRANÇAIS

(12 crédits)

Le programme intensif de français est destiné aux étudiants qui désirent apprendre le français ou améliorer leurs connaissances dans cette langue. Au début de la session, ils doivent se soumettre à un test de classement qui permet de déterminer le niveau qui répond le mieux à leurs besoins.

*Programmation sujette à changement

Now use cognates to help you find the following information.

1. What is the minimum number of credits a student can take? _______

2. What is the maximum? _______

3. What courses could you recommend for . . .

someone interested in history?

____

someone interested in art?

____

someone interested in music?

____

F. Voilà ce qui arrive. Reread the story on pages 30–31 of the textbook. Then complete the paragraph using the following choices.

ANNETTE	suis	*Vous ne comprenez pas*
ARRIVE	comprend	la situation
elle ne parle pas	pense	des sœurs jumelles	sauvée

David ____________ au musée des Beaux-Arts et il voit Yvette. Il dit: «Salut, Annette» parce qu'il ____________ que c'est son amie Annette. Yvette répond avec difficulté parce qu' ____________ très bien français. Elle dit: «____________. Je ne suis pas Annette. Je ____________ Yvette.» David ne ____________ pas. Finalement, ____________ arrive et Yvette est ____________. David comprend ____________. Annette et Yvette sont ____________.

SYSTÈME-D *If you have access to Système-D software, you will find the following phrases there.*
PHRASES: Describing people; Introducing; VOCABULARY: Nationality; Studies, courses; DICTIONARY: The verb **être**

Journal. Using what you have learned in this ***Compétence,*** write five sentences introducing and telling something about a classmate from your French class. You may start your paragraph with:

C'est mon ami(e)... Nous sommes dans le même cours de français. Il/Elle est...

____

____

____

____

____

____

____

____

____

____

NOM ______________________ COURS ______________________

COMPÉTENCE 2 Describing people

By the time you write your journal entry at the end of this ***Compétence,*** you should be able to describe a person's personality and compare two individuals.

A. Qui est-ce? Look at the illustrations and decide whether each adjective describes André, Nathalie, or both. Write a sentence using each adjective under the appropriate picture. Be sure to put adjectives describing Nathalie in the feminine form. The first one has been done as an example.

amusant(e), ennuyeux (ennuyeuse), timide, extraverti(e), optimiste, pessimiste, dynamique, paresseux (paresseuse), agréable, désagréable, beau (belle)

André

____

____

____

____

____

____

Nathalie

Nathalie est amusante.

____

____

____

____

____

B. Tout le contraire. Is it true that opposites attract? One of David's friends is attracted to Annette, but they are not at all alike. Read what he says about himself, then complete the description of Annette, saying that she is the opposite.

Je suis petit et sportif. J'aime *(I like)* bien le sport mais je n'aime pas beaucoup les cours à l'université. Pour moi, les profs sont un peu ennuyeux. En classe, je suis un peu paresseux. Je travaille assez mais pas beaucoup.

Annette *est grande et intellectuelle.* Elle n'aime pas le sport mais elle aime beaucoup les cours à l'université. Pour elle, les profs ______________________.

En classe, elle ______________________.

Elle travaille ______________________.

C. Astérix et Obélix. First impressions can be misleading, but what impressions do these pictures give you of the famous French comic characters **Astérix** and **Obélix?** Complete the following comparisons with **plus, moins,** or **aussi.**

Astérix

Obélix

EXEMPLE Astérix est plus petit qu'Obélix.

1. Astérix est ______________ grand qu'Obélix.
2. Astérix est ______________ dynamique qu'Obélix.
3. Astérix est ______________ pessimiste qu'Obélix.
4. Astérix est ______________ extraverti qu'Obélix.
5. Astérix est ______________ beau qu'Obélix.
6. Astérix est ______________ jeune qu'Obélix.

D. Meilleurs amis. Write three sentences describing personality traits that you and your best friend have in common.

EXEMPLE Nous sommes optimistes.

1. ______________________________
2. ______________________________
3. ______________________________

Now write three sentences explaining how your friend differs from you.

EXEMPLES Il/Elle est plus extraverti(e).
Il/Elle est moins intellectuel(le).

1. ______________________________
2. ______________________________
3. ______________________________

NOM ______________________ COURS ______________________

E. Comparaisons. Write sentences with the following adjectives, comparing yourself now to the way you were five years ago.

EXEMPLE optimiste *Je suis plus optimiste maintenant. / Je suis moins optimiste maintenant. / Je suis aussi optimiste maintenant.*

1. dynamique ______________________
2. jeune ______________________
3. paresseux (paresseuse) ______________________
4. sportif (sportive) ______________________
5. bête ______________________

F. Une présentation. David is introducing Annette to a friend. Complete their conversation with the correct form of **être.**

DAVID: Jean-Luc, c' __________ mon amie Annette Clark. Annette, c' __________ mon ami Jean-Luc. Il __________ aussi étudiant à l'université de Nice. Nous __________ dans le même cours de mathématiques.

JEAN-LUC: Bonjour!

ANNETTE: Bonjour!

JEAN-LUC: Tu __________ étudiante?

ANNETTE: Oui, je __________ à Nice pour étudier.

Et toi, tu __________ de Nice?

JEAN-LUC: Oui, je __________ d'ici.

Now imagine that David is introducing both Annette and Yvette to two friends, Jean-Luc and Bruno. Complete the following conversation, making all necessary changes.

DAVID: Jean-Luc, Bruno, ce __________ mes amies Annette et Yvette Clark. Annette et Yvette, ce __________ mes amis Jean-Luc et Bruno. Ils __________ aussi étudiants à l'université de Nice. Nous __________ dans le même cours de mathématiques.

JEAN-LUC ET BRUNO: Bonjour!

ANNETTE ET YVETTE: Bonjour!

JEAN-LUC: Vous __________ étudiantes?

ANNETTE: Moi, je ______________ à Nice pour étudier mais Yvette n'______________ pas étudiante. Et vous, vous ______________ de Nice?

JEAN-LUC: Oui, nous ______________ d'ici.

G. Questions. Answer the following questions about your French class with complete sentences. Replace any subject nouns with the appropriate pronoun in your answers.

1. Vous êtes en classe le vendredi après-midi?

____

2. Le professeur est américain?

____

3. Les étudiants sont bêtes?

____

4. Les étudiants sont sympathiques?

____

SYSTÈME-D *If you have access to Système-D software, you will find the following phrases there.* PHRASES: Describing people; Comparing and contrasting; Linking ideas; VOCABULARY: Personality; Nationality; GRAMMAR: Present tense; DICTIONARY: The verb **être**

Journal. Imagine that you are looking through your photo album with a classmate and you come across pictures of two of your close friends. Using what you have learned in this ***Compétence*** and your journal entry for ***Compétence 1,*** write a paragraph identifying them and describing and comparing their personalities, using at least five traits.

EXEMPLE Ce sont mes amis André et Sophie. André est étudiant à l'université mais Sophie n'est pas étudiante. Ils sont très sympas mais André est un peu pessimiste. Sophie est beaucoup plus optimiste. Sophie est très intelligente et André est intelligent aussi, mais il est un peu paresseux...

____

____

____

____

____

____

____

____

COMPÉTENCE 3 Talking about the university

By the time you write your journal entry at the end of this ***Compétence,*** you should be able to describe the campus and courses at your university.

A. Préférences. Express your feelings about these courses, activities, and places at your university, by writing them in the appropriate category.

LE FRANÇAIS les mathématiques *l'histoire* la chimie
la littérature les cours de commerce **la biologie**
les cours à huit heures du matin les boums le campus les devoirs
les examens *la bibliothèque* les étudiants les activités en groupe

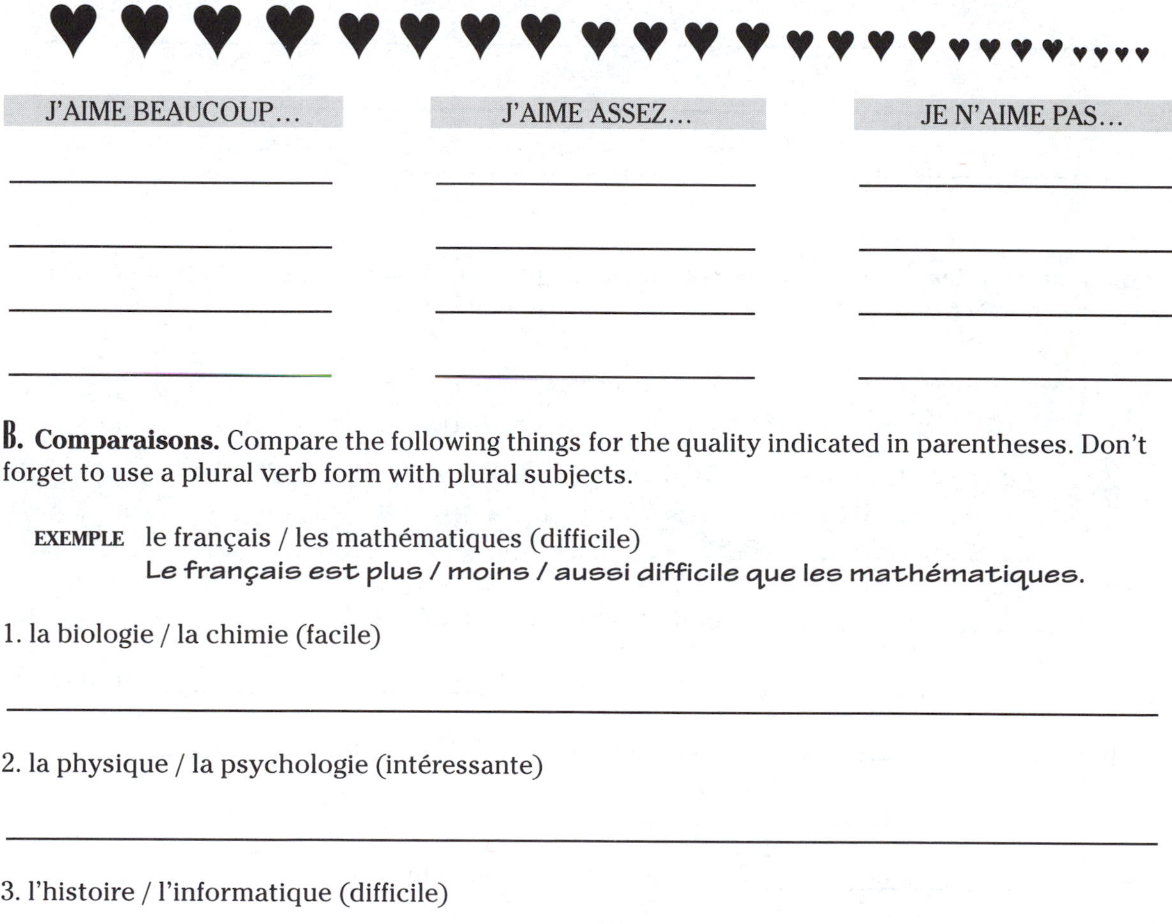

J'AIME BEAUCOUP...	J'AIME ASSEZ...	JE N'AIME PAS...
____________	____________	____________
____________	____________	____________
____________	____________	____________
____________	____________	____________

B. Comparaisons. Compare the following things for the quality indicated in parentheses. Don't forget to use a plural verb form with plural subjects.

EXEMPLE le français / les mathématiques (difficile)
Le français est plus / moins / aussi difficile que les mathématiques.

1. la biologie / la chimie (facile)

____

2. la physique / la psychologie (intéressante)

____

3. l'histoire / l'informatique (difficile)

____

4. les exercices en groupe en classe / les exercices dans le cahier (amusants)

____

5. les boums / les devoirs (ennuyeuses)

____

C. Mon université. Complete these questions about your university by filling in the correct form of the definite article: **le, la, l', les.**

1. __________ université est grande?
2. __________ cours sont faciles?
3. __________ professeurs sont sympathiques?
4. __________ campus est agréable?
5. __________ bibliothèque est moderne?
6. __________ étudiants sont intelligents?

Now answer each question, using the appropriate pronouns **il, elle, ils,** or **elles** to replace the subject nouns. The first one has been done as an example.

1. *Oui, elle est grande. / Non, elle n'est pas grande. / Non, elle est petite.*
2. ______________________________
3. ______________________________
4. ______________________________
5. ______________________________
6. ______________________________

D. Comment sont les cours? Two students are talking at a university in France. Complete their conversation by writing the logical words from the list in the blanks.

HEURES DU MATIN	intéressant	*ennuyeux*	
ne comprends pas	comment	n'est-ce pas	**est-ce que**
le cours	du tout	sympathique	est

— ______________ sont les cours à l'université?

— J'aime bien ______________ de français. Il est ______________. Je n'aime pas ______________ le cours de maths. Il est un peu ______________ et je ______________.

— ______________ les examens sont difficiles?

— Oui, très difficiles.

— Comment ______________ le prof de français?

— Il est très ______________.

— Le professeur, c'est monsieur Prévost, ______________?

— Oui, et le cours est à huit ______________.

NOM ______________________ COURS ______________________

E. Deux universités. Look at the illustrations and decide whether each statement is more true **à l'université A** or **à l'université B.**

l'université A

l'université B

EXEMPLE Le campus est grand.
Le campus est plus grand à l'université B.

1. La bibliothèque est grande.

____

2. Les étudiants sont sympathiques.

____

3. Le campus est beau.

____

4. Le sport est important.

____

5. L'atmosphère est agréable.

____

F. Des questions. You are thinking about attending one of the universities pictured in ***E. Deux universités.*** Using **est-ce que,** write questions asking . . .

EXEMPLE whether the courses are difficult?
Est-ce que les cours sont difficiles?

1. whether the library is pleasant?

____

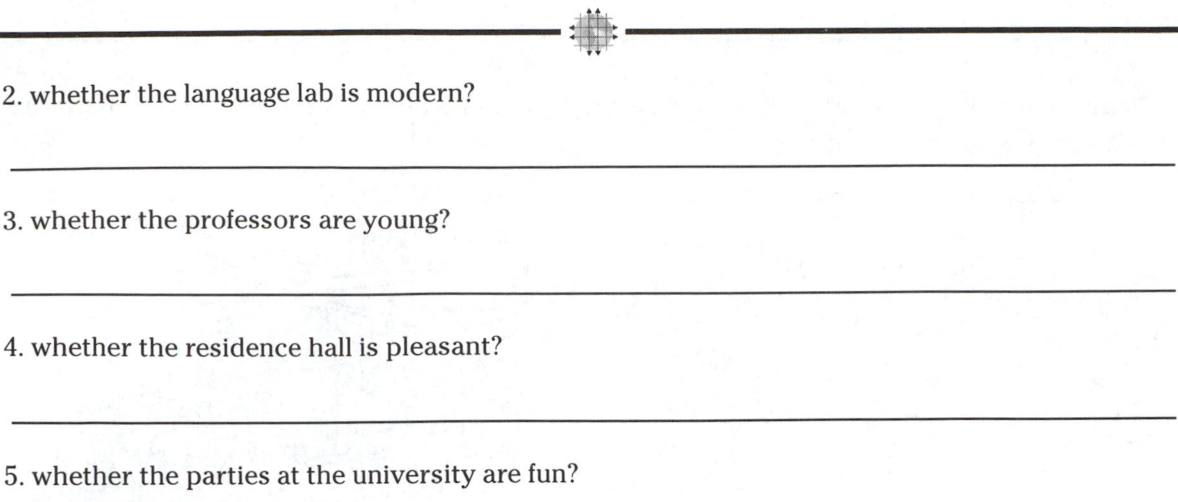

2. whether the language lab is modern?

3. whether the professors are young?

4. whether the residence hall is pleasant?

5. whether the parties at the university are fun?

If you have access to Système-D software, you will find the following phrases there.
PHRASES: Describing people; Telling time; VOCABULARY: Studies, courses; Days of the week; Time expressions; Personality

Journal. Write a journal entry describing your courses this semester. Answer the following questions in your composition.

- Qu'est-ce que vous étudiez?
- Quels jours et à quelle heure sont les cours?
- Quels cours est-ce que vous aimez? Quels cours est-ce que vous n'aimez pas?
- Comment sont les cours?
- Comment sont les professeurs et les étudiants?

NOM ______________________ COURS ______________________

COMPÉTENCE 4 Saying what's in the neighborhood

By the time you write your journal entry at the end of this ***Compétence,*** you should be able to describe your campus and tell what's in the surrounding neighborhood.

A. Qu'est-ce que c'est? Identify each place or thing pictured, as in the example.

EXEMPLE

C'est un cinéma.

1.

____

2.

____

3.

____

4.

____

5.

____

6.

____

7.

____

B. Sur le campus. Write a sentence saying whether there are the places or things pictured in ***A. Qu'est-ce que c'est?*** on campus **(sur le campus)** or in the university neighborhood **(dans le quartier universitaire).**

EXEMPLE *Oui, il y a un cinéma sur le campus. / Oui, il y a un cinéma dans le quartier universitaire. / Non, il n'y a pas de cinéma dans le quartier universitaire.*

1. ____________________
2. ____________________
3. ____________________
4. ____________________
5. ____________________
6. ____________________
7. ____________________

C. Qu'est-ce qu'il y a dans le quartier? According to these individuals' leisure activities, what sort of place might they ask about? Write logical questions, as in the example.

EXEMPLE J'aime beaucoup le tennis.
Est-ce qu'il y a des courts de tennis dans le quartier?

1. J'aime beaucoup les films étrangers. ____________________
2. J'aime beaucoup l'exercice aérobic. ____________________
3. J'aime beaucoup le théâtre. ____________________
4. J'aime beaucoup les livres. ____________________
5. J'aime beaucoup le cappuccino. ____________________

D. À l'université. Name as many things as you can in these places. Be sure to use the correct form of the indefinite article **(un, une, des).**

1. Sur le campus, il y a ____________________

____________________.

2. Dans le quartier universitaire, il y a ____________________

____________________.

3. En cours de français, il y a ____________________

____________________.

NOM ______________________________ COURS ______________________________

Now name something that there is not in each place, but that you would like to have. Remember that after **ne... pas, un, une,** and **des** become **de.**

1. Sur le campus, il n'y a pas ______________________________.

2. Dans le quartier universitaire, il n'y a pas ______________________________.

3. En cours de français, il n'y a pas ______________________________.

E. Quel article? Complete each question with the correct form of the definite article **(le, la, l', les)** or the indefinite article **(un, une, des).** Then answer each question with a complete sentence.

1. Est-ce qu' il y a ________ examen au prochain cours de français?

____

2. Est-ce que ________ examens de français sont faciles ou difficiles?

____

3. Est-ce qu'il y a ________ devoirs pour ________ prochain cours de français?

____

4. Est-ce que ________ devoirs sont dans ________ cahier ou dans ________ livre?

____

F. Qui est-ce? Write sentences describing the following people using **c'est, ce sont, il/elle est,** or **ils/elles sont** with the indicated words.

EXEMPLE

David et Annette / étudiants / à Nice

1.

une jeune étudiante / en classe / très intelligente / dynamique

2.

une famille / américains / à la maison / sympas

EXEMPLE *Ce sont David et Annette. Ils sont étudiants. Ils sont à Nice.*

1. ______________________________

____

2. ______________________________

____

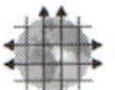

G. Qui est-ce? Using **c'est, il est,** or **elle est,** write four sentences describing someone in your class. At the end, use **c'est** to identify the person you are describing.

If you have access to Système-D software, you will find the following phrases there.
PHRASES: Describing people; VOCABULARY: City; Store

Journal. Write a journal entry describing your campus and the surrounding neighborhood. In your composition, answer the following questions.

- Est-ce que vous aimez le campus?
- Qu'est-ce qu'il y a sur le campus?
- Qu'est-ce que vous aimez sur le campus? Qu'est-ce que vous n'aimez pas?
- Comment sont les endroits *(places)* sur le campus?
- Comment est le quartier universitaire?
- Qu'est-ce qu'il y a dans le quartier universitaire?
- Qu'est-ce que vous aimez dans le quartier? Qu'est-ce que vous n'aimez pas?

NOM ______________________ COURS ______________________

CHAPITRE 2

Après les cours

COMPÉTENCE 1 Talking about your free time

By the time you write your journal entry at the end of this ***Compétence,*** you should be able to tell how you like to spend your free time and invite a friend to do something.

A. Qu'est-ce que vous pensez? What do you think about the following activities? Express your opinion by writing each activity in one of the indicated categories.

SORTIR AVEC DES AMIS rester à la maison *travailler sur l'ordinateur*
DORMIR lire faire du jogging regarder la télé

C'EST AMUSANT / INTÉRESSANT.	C'EST ENNUYEUX.
______________________	______________________
______________________	______________________
______________________	______________________
______________________	______________________

B. Voudriez-vous...? For each of the following activities, say whether you would like to do it, or, if you prefer doing something else, express your preference.

EXEMPLE rester à la maison ce soir
Je voudrais bien rester à la maison ce soir. / Je préfère aller au cinéma ce soir.

1. jouer au basket demain

____

2. faire les devoirs après les cours

____

3. aller danser en boîte ce week-end

____

4. dîner au restaurant demain soir

____

5. regarder la télé ce soir

____

C. Est-ce que vous aimez...? Look at the following pictures and state whether you like or dislike doing the things shown. Start each sentence with **J'aime...** or **Je n'aime pas...**

1. 

2. 

3. 

1. ______________________________

2. ______________________________

3. ______________________________

4. 

5. 

6. 

4. ______________________________

5. ______________________________

6. ______________________________

7. 

8. 

9. 

7. ______________________________

8. ______________________________

9. ______________________________

NOM ______________________________ COURS ______________________________

D. Invitations. Annette is making plans with two different friends. Finish logically what they say.

1. — Tu voudrais jouer au tennis?

— Non, je ______________________________ faire du jogging.

2. — Tu voudrais aller au cinéma ce soir?

— Oui, je veux bien. ______________________________?

— À huit heures, d'accord?

— Oui, ______________________________.

E. Projets. Choose four activities you would like to do during your free time this week. Indicate with whom, on what day, and at what time you want to do each.

	ACTIVITÉ	AVEC QUI?	QUEL JOUR?	À QUELLE HEURE?
EXEMPLE	aller au cinéma	avec Kim	samedi soir	à huit heures
	________	________	________	________
	________	________	________	________
	________	________	________	________
	________	________	________	________

F. On sort? Choose two of the activities you listed in ***E. Projets*** and write two conversations in which you invite the person in question to go out, as in the example.

EXEMPLE aller au cinéma avec Kim samedi soir à huit heures

— *Kim, tu es libre samedi soir? Tu voudrais aller au cinéma avec moi?*

— *Oui, je voudrais bien. Vers quelle heure?*

— *Vers huit heures, d'accord?*

— *D'accord. À samedi.*

— *Au revoir!*

1. ______________________________

2. ______________________________

If you have access to Système-D software, you will find the following phrases there.
PHRASES: Sequencing events

Journal. Using what you have learned in this ***Compétence,*** write a paragraph describing what you like to do before and after class **(avant les cours, après les cours)** each day you have class.

EXEMPLE Le lundi, j'aime faire les devoirs avant les cours. Après les cours, j'aime...

NOM ________________ COURS ________________

COMPÉTENCE 2 Telling what you and others do

By the time you write your journal entry at the end of this ***Compétence,*** you should be able to tell what you and those you know do regularly.

A. Talents et connaissances. Are you musical? Athletic? How well do you do the following things?

EXEMPLE

Je joue assez bien / assez mal au volley. / Je joue au volley comme ci comme ça. Je ne joue pas au volley.

Très Bien assez bien
comme ci comme ça
assez mal **très mal**

1. 

2. 

3. 

1. ________________
2. ________________
3. ________________

4. 

5. 

6. 

4. ________________
5. ________________
6. ________________

B. Chacun ses goûts. What do the following people like to do in their free time?

EXEMPLE Moi, j'*aime beaucoup lire.*

1. Mes amis et moi, nous ________________.
2. Moi, j' ________________.
3. Mon meilleur *(best)* ami ________________.
4. Les membres de ma famille ________________.

C. Un sondage. How active are you and your friends? Say how often the indicated people do the following things on the weekend, choosing one of the options provided. Write a complete sentence for each question. Remember to conjugate the verb!

TOUJOURS souvent *quelquefois*
RAREMENT **ne... jamais**

1. mes amis / regarder la télévision le week-end

____

2. moi, je / jouer au golf le week-end

____

3. ma meilleure *(best)* amie / écouter la radio le week-end

____

4. moi, je (j') / inviter des amis à la maison le week-end

____

5. les étudiants de l'université / travailler le week-end

____

D. Et vous? Use the adverbs given to make statements about yourself.

PARLER (ANGLAIS / FRANÇAIS / ???) bricoler ??? *chanter*
DANSER travailler **JOUER AU TENNIS / AU GOLF / AU ???**
jouer du piano / de la guitare / de la batterie
inviter des amis à la maison **rester à la maison**
??? écouter la radio

1. assez bien ____

2. souvent ____

3. ne... jamais ____

4. quelquefois ____

5. assez mal ____

NOM ________________________ COURS ________________________

E. La famille d'Annette. Annette is talking to a new friend about her family. Complete her statements with the correct conjugated form of the verb in parentheses.

Ma famille ________________ (habiter) à Los Angeles. Mon père *(father)* et ma mère *(mother)* ________________ (être) à la retraite *(retired)*. Ils ne ________________ (travailler) pas. Mon père ________________ (rester) souvent à la maison. Il ________________ (regarder) la télé et il ________________ (bricoler). Ma mère préfère sortir et elle ________________ (inviter) souvent des amies à la maison. Elles ________________ (parler) et elles ________________ (jouer) au bridge. Ma mère ________________ (aimer) la musique. Elle ________________ (danser) et elle ________________ (chanter) très bien. Ma sœur Yvette ________________ (travailler) dans un club de gym. Elle ________________ (aimer) beaucoup le sport et elle ________________ (jouer) très bien au tennis.

Moi, j' ________________ (habiter) à Nice maintenant parce que j'________________ (étudier) à l'université de Nice. Yvette ________________ (être) ici à Nice maintenant. Nous ________________ (aimer) être ensemble. Le soir, nous ________________ (dîner) ensemble et après nous ________________ (inviter) des amis à sortir.

F. Et toi? Complete the questions so that a classmate could ask them of you. Then answer each question in the space provided. Be careful, not all the verbs need to be conjugated!

1. Qu'est-ce que tu ________________ (étudier)?

____

2. Tu ________________ (être) plutôt intellectuel(le) ou plutôt sportif (sportive)?

____

3. Est-ce que tu ________________ (aimer) lire?

____

4. Qu'est-ce que tu aimes ______________________ (faire) après les cours?

____

5. Tes *(your)* amis et toi, vous ______________________ (aimer) sortir ensemble *(together)?*

____

6. Vous ______________________ (dîner) souvent ensemble?

____

7. Vous ______________________ (regarder) la télé ensemble?

____

SYSTÈME-D

If you have access to Système-D software, you will find the following phrases there. PHRASES: Weighing alternatives; Expressing an opinion; VOCABULARY: Time expressions; Leisure; Sports

Journal. Using what you have learned in this ***Compétence,*** write a paragraph describing how you typically spend your time on the weekend.

EXEMPLE Le vendredi soir, je reste souvent à la maison parce que je suis fatigué(e). Quelquefois, j'aime sortir avec des amis. Le samedi matin...

____

____

____

____

____

____

____

____

____

____

____

NOM ______________________ COURS ______________________

COMPÉTENCE 3 Talking about your day

By the time you write your journal entry at the end of this ***Compétence,*** you should be able to tell how you and people you know typically spend their day and ask for further information from someone such as *who, what, when, where,* and *why.*

A. L'emploi du temps de Gisèle. Look at the weekly schedule of David's friend Gisèle below. Then answer the questions that follow in complete sentences.

	LUNDI	MARDI	MERCREDI	JEUDI	VENDREDI
MATIN 8h 10h 12h	en cours	en cours	en cours	en cours	en cours
APRÈS-MIDI 1h 3h 5h	bibliothèque avec David et Thomas	bibliothèque avec David et Thomas	travailler		travailler
SOIR		Star Trek			

1. Combien de jours par semaine *(per week)* est-ce que Gisèle est en cours?

____

2. Quels jours est-ce que Gisèle est en cours?

____

3. Où est-ce qu'elle prépare ses *(her)* cours le lundi après-midi?

____

4. Avec qui est-ce qu'elle prépare quelquefois ses cours?

____

5. Quand est-ce qu'ils préparent les cours ensemble?

____

6. Qu'est-ce que Gisèle aime regarder à la télévision?

____

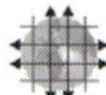

B. Et vous? Answer the questions about your schedule by selecting the most appropriate response from each box.

TOUS LES JOURS (SAUF…) le lundi, le mardi…
toute la journée DE ??? HEURES À ??? HEURES
le matin **l'après-midi** le soir le week-end ???

1. Quand est-ce que vous êtes à l'université?

____

2. Quand est-ce que vous êtes en cours?

____

3. Quand est-ce que vous passez beaucoup de temps à la maison?

____

4. Quand est-ce que vous préparez les cours?

____

CHEZ MOI chez mon ami(e) ??? *au restaurant (universitaire)*
DANS UN FAST-FOOD au café **á la bibliothèque** ???

5. Où est-ce que vous aimez mieux préparer les cours?

____

6. Où est-ce que vous déjeunez le plus souvent?

____

SEUL(E) avec ma famille *avec mon ami(e)…* avec ???

7. Avec qui est-ce que vous aimez préparer les cours?

____

8. Avec qui est-ce que vous aimez déjeuner?

____

9. Avec qui est-ce que vous aimez passer beaucoup de temps?

____

C. Une lettre. Annette is writing to her former French teacher in California about her new experiences in Nice. Complete her statements with the correct form of the indicated verb. Pay attention to the spelling change verbs!

Chère madame Filloux,

Je ______________ (être) très contente ici à Nice. J' ______________ (aimer) beaucoup mes cours et l'université. Les étudiants ______________ (être) sympas et les cours ______________ (être) intéressants. Je ______________ (être) à l'université tous les jours sauf le week-end. Le matin, je ______________ (préparer) mes cours à la bibliothèque. Je ______________ (préférer) travailler avec une amie. Nous ______________ (commencer) à travailler vers neuf heures et l'après-midi, je ______________ (être) en cours.

Je ne ______________ (passer) pas tout mon temps à l'université, bien sûr. J' ______________ (aimer) sortir avec mes amis Gisèle, Thomas et David. Nous ______________ (aimer) aller au cinéma et nous ______________ (manger) souvent ensemble. Quelquefois, nous ______________ (déjeuner) ensemble dans un fast-food et d'autres fois nous ______________ (dîner) ensemble au restaurant. J' ______________ (aimer) mieux aller au restaurant!

Yvette ______________ (être) ici et nous ______________ (passer) beaucoup de temps ensemble. Elle ______________ (être) très sportive et elle ______________ (aimer) beaucoup jouer au tennis. Moi, je n'aime pas beaucoup ______________ (jouer) avec elle parce qu'elle ______________ (gagner) toujours. Quelquefois, nous ______________ (voyager) le week-end pour voir un peu la France.

Amitiés,

Annette

D. Un père trop curieux. Read the following dialogue between a nosy father and his son, who is planning to go out this evening. Based on the son's responses, complete the father's questions by supplying the appropriate question word and **est-ce que.**

LE PÈRE: ______________________________ tu fais ce soir?

LE FILS: Je dîne en ville avec des amis.

LE PÈRE: ______________________________ vous dînez?

LE FILS: Au restaurant L'Étoile, sur la place. C'est un bon restaurant!

LE PÈRE: Et ______________________________ vous allez payer ça?

LE FILS: Avec ma nouvelle carte de crédit. Après, nous allons au cinéma. Il y a un grand classique ce soir.

LE PÈRE: Ah! ______________________________ le film commence?

LE FILS: À sept heures et demie. Après le film nous allons chez d'autres amis.

LE PÈRE: ______________________________ tu ne restes pas à la maison?

LE FILS: Parce que je n'aime pas rester à la maison le week-end!

SYSTÈME-D

If you have access to Système-D software, you will find the following phrases there.
PHRASES: Linking ideas; VOCABULARY: Time expressions; Days of the week

Journal. Using what you have learned in this ***Compétence,*** write a paragraph describing your day-to-day activities during the week, saying when and where you do these things.

EXEMPLE Le lundi et le mercredi je travaille à Parmer's Nursery le matin...

____

____

____

____

____

____

____

____

____

NOM ______________________ COURS ______________________

COMPÉTENCE 4 Ordering at the café

By the time you write your journal entry at the end of this ***Compétence,*** you should be able to say what you like to eat and drink at a café.

Au Bar Monaco. Look at the menu below and do exercises **A** and **B.**

A. L'article indéfini. Fill in the blank with the correct indefinite article **(un, une, des).** Then indicate whether the information given is **vrai** or **faux** by circling **V** or **F.**

1. _____ café au lait coûte *(costs)* vingt francs.

V F

2. _____ eau minérale coûte huit francs.

V F

3. _____ thé au citron coûte dix-huit francs.

V F

4. _____ coca coûte onze francs.

V F

5. _____ sandwich au jambon coûte vingt-deux francs.

V F

6. _____ bière Carlsberg coûte vingt-quatre francs.

V F

7. _____ sandwich au camembert coûte treize francs.

V F

—Bar Monaco—

..... *Nos boissons*.....

—Chaudes—

Café express	10 F
Café au lait	20 F
Café décaféiné	14 F
Thé (avec lait ou citron)	18 F
Chocolat	16 F

—Froides—

Orangina	10 F
Coca Cola	12 F
Schweppes tonic	10 F
Limonade	8 F
Eau minérale	6 F

—Vins—

Verre de rouge	9 F
Verre de blanc	7 F

—Bières—

Kanterbrau demi	9 F
Carlsberg	24 F
Heineken	22 F
Kronenbourg 1664	15 F

..... *Nos sandwichs* .....

Jambon de pays	22 F
Saucisson sec	17 F
Pâté de campagne	14 F
Gruyère, camembert	13 F

B. C'est combien? Look at what various people have ordered at the Bar Monaco and determine the total bill.

EXEMPLE Un verre de vin rouge et un verre de vin blanc? *Ça fait seize francs.*

1. Un café décaféiné et un Orangina? ______________________

2. Un Schweppes et une Heineken? ______________________

3. Un sandwich au saucisson et un demi de Kanterbrau? ______________________

4. Un café au lait et un café décaféiné? ______________________________

5. Une Kronenbourg et un coca? ______________________________

C. Je voudrais un/une/des… / Non, je n'aime pas le/la/les… Look at the following pictures and say either that you'd like to have the item shown or that you don't like it. Use **Je voudrais…** or **Je n'aime pas…** and the appropriate article. Notice the use of the articles in the example.

EXEMPLE

Je voudrais un café. / Je n'aime pas le café.

1. ______________________________

2. ______________________________

3. ______________________________

4. ______________________________

5. ______________________________

D. Il faut payer! Here is a list of the amounts various clients owe at the café. Indicate in numerals how much each one owes.

EXEMPLE quarante-huit francs *48 F*

1. soixante-quatre francs ____________
2. soixante-quatorze francs ____________
3. quatre-vingt-un francs ____________
4. trente-trois francs ____________
5. soixante-quinze francs ____________
6. trente-six francs ____________
7. quatre-vingt-dix-neuf francs ____________
8. cinquante-sept francs ____________
9. quarante-deux francs ____________
10. cinquante-quatre francs ____________
11. vingt-cinq francs ____________
12. quatre-vingt-huit francs ____________

NOM ______________________________ COURS ______________________________

E. Allons au café! Look at the menu for the Bar Monaco on page 45. Order something to eat and drink for yourself and a friend. For number 3, determine how much you owe, how much your friend owes, and how much you owe in total.

1. Pour moi, ______________________________ et ______________________________.

2. Pour mon ami(e), ______________________________ et ______________________________.

3. Pour moi, ça fait ______________________________ et pour mon ami(e), ça fait ______________________________. Alors *(so)*, au total, ça fait ______________________________.

F. Le café. The café is perhaps the most enduring of images associated with France. Even so, as you will find when you read this short passage, this French institution has undergone a great change in the past century. First, skim the article to find two cognates ending in **-é** where English would have *-ed.* Write the cognates in the blanks on the left. Then write their English equivalents in the blanks on the right.

1. ____________________ ____________________

2. ____________________ ____________________

Now read the article and put an **X** next to the best answer(s) to the following questions.

1. Since 1980, the number of cafés in France has declined by a little more than:

____ 10% ____ 30% ____ 50%

2. In the article, which of the following are cited as possible causes for the decline in café patrons?

____ a population shift to the suburbs, where there are fewer cafés

____ a poor economy

____ an increase in the amount of time doing sports

Les derniers cafés où l'on cause

Il ne reste plus en France que 70 000 cafés, contre 107 000 en 1980, 200 000 en 1960 et plus de 500 000 en 1910. On peut distinguer trois causes à ces disparitions: le déplacement d'une partie de la population des centres-villes vers les banlieues où la densité des cafés est moins élevée, la crise économique qui a touché certaines régions et surtout le changement d'attitude à l'égard des loisirs. Le temps passé au café est remplacé par celui consacré à la télévision ou à des activités spécifiques. Enfin, la multiplication des fast-foods a porté un coup décisif aux cafés, le hamburger ayant remplacé le sandwich, en particulier pour les jeunes. Avec le café, c'est un outil privilégié de la convivialité qui disparaît, en même temps qu'un mode de vie.

G. Vos préférences. A friend wants to know what you like to eat and drink. Answer her questions. To say *I have* a certain food or drink, use **Je prends... (Le matin, je prends un café.)**

1. Est-ce que tu aimes le café?

2. Est-ce que tu aimes mieux le café ou le thé?

3. Est-ce que tu prends un café le matin d'habitude?

4. Est-ce que tu aimes le coca? l'eau minérale?

5. Est-ce que tu prends souvent un coca au déjeuner *(at lunch)?*

6. Qu'est-ce que tu prends quand tu déjeunes dans un fast-food? un sandwich? un hamburger? une salade? des frites? un coca?

SYSTÈME-D

If you have access to Système-D software, you will find the following phrases there.
PHRASES: Expressing an opinion; VOCABULARY: Time expressions; Food; Drinks; Meals

Journal. Using what you have learned in this ***Compétence,*** write a short paragraph about your preferences in drinks in the morning **(le matin)** and at lunch **(au déjeuner)**, and about your preferences in fastfoods. Use your answers to the questions in ***G. Vos préférences*** to guide you.

EXEMPLE Je n'aime pas beaucoup le café, mais le matin, je prends souvent un thé.

NOM ______________________ COURS ______________________

CHAPITRE 3
Un nouvel appartement

COMPÉTENCE 1 Telling where you live

By the time you write your journal entry for this ***Compétence,*** you should be able to describe where you live in French.

A. Une maison. Fill in each blank to identify the room.

B. Dans quelle pièce? Write sentences to tell in which room you generally do the following activities.

EXEMPLE travailler sur l'ordinateur
Je travaille sur l'ordinateur dans ma chambre ou dans le salon. / Je ne travaille pas sur l'ordinateur à la maison.

1. manger ______________________
2. préparer le dîner *(dinner)* ______________________
3. regarder la télé ______________________
4. préférer faire mes devoirs ______________________
5. parler au téléphone ______________________
6. aimer faire la sieste *(to take a nap)* ______________________
7. écouter la radio ______________________

C. Au grand magasin. Answer the questions about where different departments are located in this department store. Use the French way of counting floors in your responses. Remember to use **au** to say *on which floor.*

1. À quel étage se trouve le salon de beauté?

____

2. À quel étage se trouve l'entrée *(entrance)* du magasin *(store)?*

____

3. À quel étage se trouvent les articles de sport?

____

4. À quel étage se trouvent les parfums et les vêtements d'hommes?

____

5. À quel étage se trouve l'agence de voyages?

____

D. Et vous? Answer the following questions about your living situation with complete sentences.

1. Est-ce que vous habitez dans un appartement, dans une maison ou dans une chambre à la résidence universitaire?

____

2. Habitez-vous avec un(e) camarade de chambre?

____

3. Est-ce que vous habitez en ville, en banlieue ou à la campagne?

____

4. Comment est votre appartement / votre chambre / votre maison?

____

5. Est-ce que vous aimez l'appartement / la maison / la résidence où vous habitez? Pourquoi ou pourquoi pas?

____

6. Est-ce que vous habitez loin de l'université ou est-ce que l'université est tout près?

____

7. À quel étage est-ce que vous préférez habiter? au rez-de-chaussée? au premier étage? au deuxième étage?

____

E. L'arrivée de Robert. Read the following passage describing Robert's arrival at Thomas's apartment, paying close attention to the verbs. Even if you haven't seen certain **–er** verbs before, you should be able to identify them. As you read, list six **–er** verbs from the passage. The first one has been done as an example.

Robert consulte les instructions dans la lettre de Thomas et vérifie l'adresse. Il lit: «Mon appartement se trouve 38, rue Dauphine. C'est un grand immeuble avec une porte bleue. Je suis au deuxième étage.»

«Oui, c'est bien là», pense-t-il. Il entre dans l'immeuble et monte l'escalier. Arrivé à la porte de l'appartement, il sonne. Quelques instants après, une jolie jeune femme vient lui ouvrir.

— Euh... Bonjour mademoiselle, je suis Robert. C'est bien ici que Claude et Thomas habitent? demande Robert.

— Claude, c'est moi. Mais...

Robert, bien surpris, l'interrompt...

— Claude, c'est vous? Euh... Mais vous êtes une femme!

1. *consulter*

2. ______________________

3. ______________________

4. ______________________

5. ______________________

6. ______________________

F. En contexte. Some words can have different meanings, depending on the context. Read the following sentences from a description of where a student lives and circle the meaning of the boldfaced words.

1. *fairly*	*enough*		Mon appartement est **assez** loin de l'université.
2. *only*	*lonely*	*alone*	Le **seul** inconvénient, c'est que l'ascenseur tombe souvent en panne *(breaks down).*
3. *well*	*very*		C'est **bien** sympa.
4. *still*	*always*		J'habite **toujours** avec ma famille.

If you have access to Système-D software, you will find the following phrases there.
PHRASES: Describing objects; Comparing and contrasting; VOCABULARY: Rooms; House; City

Journal. Write a paragraph describing where you live. In your paragraph, explain:

- whether you live in a house, an apartment, or a dormitory and whether it is very far from the university.
- whether you live in town, in the suburbs, or in the country.
- what your house, apartment or dormitory is like (new, old, big, small, pleasant, unpleasant, convenient, expensive, pretty, ugly, etc.).
- whether you like where you live or, if not, what sort of place you would like to have **(je voudrais avoir).**
- what rooms there are in your house or apartment (unless you live in a dormitory).
- with whom you live.
- on what floor your room is.
- where you like to spend a lot of time when you are home.

NOM ______________________ COURS ______________________

COMPÉTENCE 2 Talking about your possessions

By the time you write your journal entry for this ***Compétence,*** you should be able to describe your belongings in French.

A. Qu'est-ce qu'ils ont? Look at the pictures of Claude's room and of that of his younger brother Paul. Write sentences saying which brother has each of the following items and which one does not. Remember that **un, une,** and **des** change to **de** after a negated verb.

la chambre de Claude

la chambre de Paul

EXEMPLE des disques compacts
Claude a des disques compacts, mais Paul n'a pas de disques compacts.

1. une télé ______________________
2. un vélo ______________________
3. un chat ______________________
4. un chien ______________________
5. une chaîne stéréo ______________________
6. un magnétoscope ______________________

B. Où? Refer to the illustrations in ***A. Qu'est-ce qu'ils ont?*** to answer the following questions about Claude's and Paul's rooms.

Dans la chambre de Claude…

1. Qu'est-ce qu'il y a sur le lit? ______________________
2. Qu'est-ce qu'il y a sous le lit? ______________________
3. Qu'est-ce qu'il y a entre la porte et le bureau? ______________________
4. Où est la chaîne stéréo? ______________________

Dans la chambre de Paul…

1. Qu'est-ce qu'il y a derrière l'aquarium? ______________________

2. Est-ce que tous *(all)* les vêtements sont dans le placard ou est-ce qu'il y a des vêtements sur le lit? ______________________

____

3. Qu'est-ce qu'il y a derrière la porte du placard? ______________________

C. Qu'est-ce qu'ils ont? Robert is talking to Thomas about what they have. Complete the following statements or questions with the verb **avoir** and the name of the pictured item.

EXEMPLE

Dans ma chambre, je (j')…
Dans ma chambre, j'ai un ordinateur.

1. Dans le salon, nous…

2. Thomas, tu…?

1. ______________________

2. ______________________

3. Claude et toi, vous…?

4. Claude…

3. ______________________

4. ______________________

NOM ______________________ COURS ______________________

5. Devant ma fenêtre, je (j')...

6. Claude et toi, vous...?

5. ____

6. ____

D. Camarades de chambre. Two friends are thinking about becoming roommates. Complete their conversation with the correct form of **avoir.**

— Est-ce que tu voudrais partager l'appartement avec mon camarade de chambre et moi?

Nous ____________ beaucoup de place *(space).*

— Vous ____________ combien de chambres?

— Deux, mais j'____________ une grande chambre avec deux lits.

— Tu ____________ des animaux?

— Moi, je n'____________ pas d'animaux mais mon camarade de chambre ____________ un chat. Pourquoi? C'est un problème?

— Oui, je (j') ____________ des allergies.

E. Et toi? A friend is asking you about your belongings. Complete each question with **ton, ta,** or **tes.** Then answer the question, using **mon, ma,** or **mes.**

1. Est-ce que ________ chambre est grande ou petite?

____

2. Dans quelle pièce de la maison est-ce que tu préfères faire ________ devoirs?

____

3. Est-ce que ________ amis sont souvent chez toi?

____

4. Est-ce que ________ quartier est agréable?

____

5. Est-ce que ________ chaîne stéréo est dans ________ chambre ou dans le salon?

____

6. Quel est ________ disque compact préféré?

____

F. Des descriptions. Complete the descriptions of the following people you know using a descriptive adjective and the verb **être.** Then name one thing they have, using **avoir.**

SPORTIF(–IVE)	matérialiste		
idéaliste	INTELLECTUEL(LE)		
optimiste	sérieux (sérieuse)		
???	**marié(e)**	grand(e)	**TIMIDE**
sympa	*pessimiste*	???	

BEAUCOUP DE LIVRES	
beaucoup d'amis	
beaucoup de problèmes	???
beaucoup de choses	**un vélo**
une grande famille	des cours intéressants
???	**BEAUCOUP D'AMBITION**

EXEMPLE Mon/Ma camarade de chambre *est très sportif/sportive. Il/Elle a un vélo.*

1. Mon meilleur ami ______________________________.
2. Ma meilleure amie ______________________________.
3. Mon professeur de français ______________________________.
4. Les étudiants de la classe de français ______________________________ ______________________________.
5. Moi, je ______________________________.

SYSTÈME-D

If you have access to Système-D software, you will find the following phrases there.
PHRASES: Describing objects; VOCABULARY: House; Bedroom; Telling time

Journal. Write a paragraph in French describing your room. Tell:

- what your room is like (large or small? pleasant or unpleasant? pretty or ugly?)
- what there is in your room
- whether you have any pets

____
____
____
____
____
____

NOM ______________________ COURS ______________________

COMPÉTENCE 3 Describing your house

By the time you write your journal entry for this ***Compétence,*** you should be able to describe in French the furnishings in your house.

A. Les meubles. Label in French the objects indicated in each room.

1. ______________________
2. ______________________
3. ______________________
4. ______________________

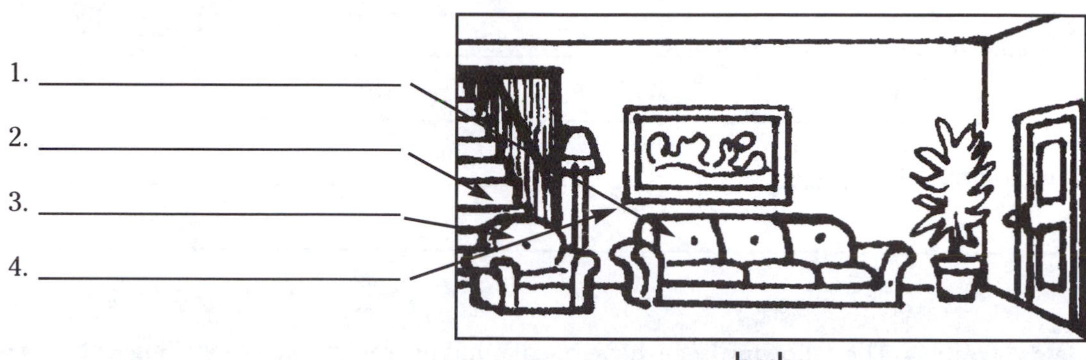

la salon

1. ______________________
2. ______________________
3. ______________________

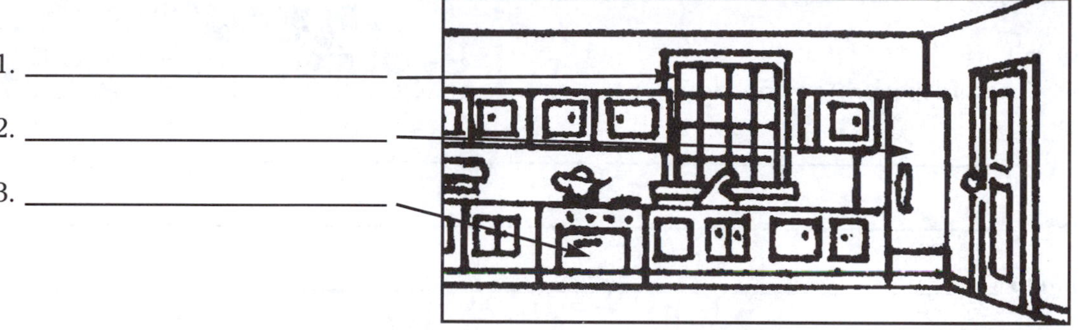

la cuisine

1. ______________________
2. ______________________
3. ______________________
4. ______________________

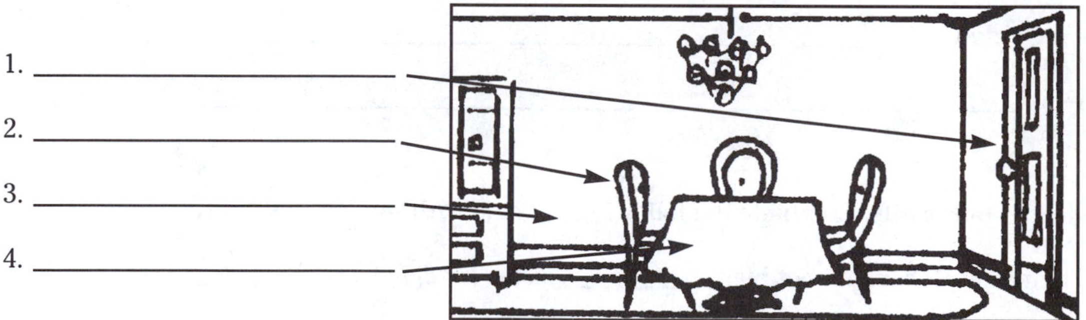

la salle à manger

1. ______________________
2. ______________________
3. ______________________
4. ______________________

la chambre

B. Et vous? Write sentences naming at least three items your family has in each of these rooms.

1. Dans notre salon, nous avons ______________________________

____.

2. Dans notre cuisine, nous avons ______________________________

____.

3. Dans notre salle à manger, nous avons ______________________________

____.

4. Dans ma chambre, j'ai ______________________________

____.

C. Des objets retrouvés. The following items have been found near your classroom. Suggest who the owners might be, indicating possession with **de**.

LE PROFESSEUR	
les étudiants	*l'université*

EXEMPLE le livre
C'est le livre du professeur.

1. la chaise ______________________________
2. les livres ______________________________
3. l'ordinateur ______________________________
4. les disques compacts______________________________
5. la cassette vidéo ______________________________
6. les bureaux______________________________

D. Les adjectifs possessifs. Complete the following passage with **son, sa, ses, leur,** or **leurs.**

Claude, Thomas et Robert aiment bien ________ voisins *(neighbors)* et ________ appartement, mais Claude n'aime pas trop ________ chambre parce que ________ fenêtres sont très petites.

Thomas et Robert n'aiment pas les animaux de ________ camarade de chambre Claude. Ils pensent que ________ animaux sont embêtants parce que ________ chien aime dormir sur le canapé et ________ chats dorment sur la table de la cuisine.

NOM ______________________ COURS ______________________

E. Chez nous. Rewrite the paragraphs in the preceding activity so that Robert is talking about himself and his roommates. The first part has been done as an example.

Claude, Thomas et moi aimons bien nos voisins... ______________________

____

____

____

____

____

____

F. De qui parlez-vous? About whom might you make the following statements? Give the names of people using **de** to show possession.

EXEMPLES Leur maison est agréable. *La maison de mes amis Marc et Laura est agréable.*
Je n'aime pas sa musique. *Je n'aime pas la musique de Michael Jackson.*

1. Leur maison n'est pas loin de chez moi.

____

2. Ses cours sont intéressants.

____

3. Leurs enfants sont embêtants.

____

4. J'aime bien ses films.

____

5. Je n'aime pas leur musique.

____

G. Adjectifs possessifs. Sometimes when speaking a foreign language, you cannot remember a word or a verb form and you have to rephrase what you want to say using what you know. Rephrase the following statements using the verb **être** with a possessive adjective, as in the examples.

EXEMPLES Vous avez une très belle maison. *Votre maison est très belle.*
Ils ont un appartement agréable. *Leur appartement est agréable.*

1. J'ai un joli canapé. ______________________

2. Tu as une grande cuisine. ______________________

3. Vous avez des murs blancs? ______________________________

4. Nous avons une très belle vue. ______________________________

5. Il a un chien bête. ______________________________

6. Elle a un chien sympa. ______________________________

7. Ils ont des tableaux bizarres. ______________________________

SYSTÈME-D *If you have access to Système-D software, you will find the following phrases there.*
PHRASES: Describing objects; Expressing an opinion;
VOCABULARY: House; Furniture; Bedroom; Living room; Rooms

Journal. Using the paragraphs about your house and your room that you wrote in your journal for ***Compétences 1*** and ***2,*** write a more detailed description of your house, including the furniture that you have in each room.

NOM ______________________ COURS ______________________

COMPÉTENCE 4 Giving your address and phone number

By the time you write your journal entry for this ***Compétence,*** you should be able to give personal information about yourself, such as your address and telephone number, in French.

A. Des renseignements personnels. When renting a hotel room or a car on trips abroad, you may be asked to fill out forms containing personal information. Fill out the following registration form, supplying the requested information.

Hôtel Vieux Québec

Fiche d'inscription pour voyageurs étrangers.

Nom de famille: ______________________

Prénom(s): ______________________

Domicile légal:

______________________ (rue)

______________________ (ville)

______________________ (pays)

Numéro de passeport: ______________________

ou de carte d'identité: ______________________

Nationalité: ______________________

B. Quel, quelle, quels ou quelles? If a hotel clerk were filling out the fiche **d'inscription** from ***A. Des renseignements personnels*** for you, what questions with **quel(le)(s)** might he/she ask you? Note that the word **domicile** is masculine.

EXEMPLES *Quel est votre nom de famille?*
Dans quelle ville habitez-vous?

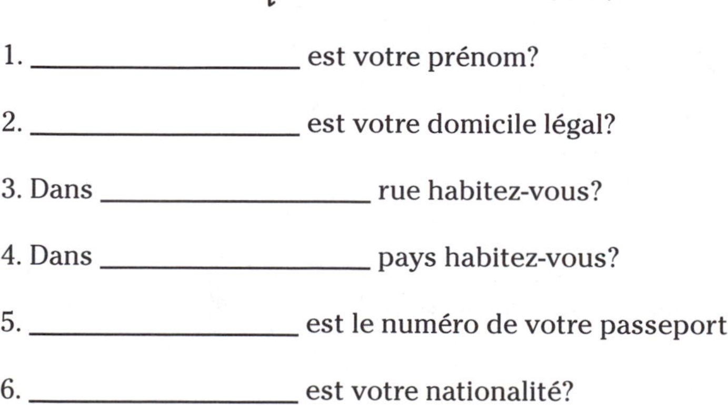

1. ______________ est votre prénom?
2. ______________ est votre domicile légal?
3. Dans ______________ rue habitez-vous?
4. Dans ______________ pays habitez-vous?
5. ______________ est le numéro de votre passeport?
6. ______________ est votre nationalité?

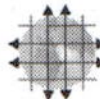

C. Phrases utiles. What useful questions with **quel(le)(s)** that you have already seen could you ask to find out the following?

EXEMPLE la date *Quelle est la date?*

1. les devoirs pour le prochain cours ______
2. l'heure ______
3. le jour de la semaine ______

D. Où est-ce que je mets ça? A friend is helping you move in. As you point to different items, tell your friend where to put them. Use **ce, cet, cette,** or **ces** in your answers, as in the example.

EXEMPLE la table *Mets (Put) cette table dans la salle à manger.*

1. le lit ______
2. les chaises ______
3. le canapé ______
4. la commode ______
5. les vêtements ______
6. le fauteuil ______
7. la chaîne stéréo ______

E. Vous composez... Look at the following listings for services in Montreal and give the phone number you would dial for the indicated services. Write out the numbers as words.

Renseignements Trains
Gare centrale
935, rue Lagauchetière Ouest
Via Rail (CN)
871-1331

Maison du tourisme
2, place Ville-Marie
Montréal (Québec)
H3B 2C9
873-2015

Renseignements Avions
Aéroport international de Montréal (Dorval)
Transports Canada
636-5921

Télégrammes
Télécommunications CNCP
740, rue Notre-Dame Ouest
Service de 24 heures pour envoi de télégrammes et câblogrammes.
861-7311

Urgences—Santé
Centre de référence du Grand Montréal
du lundi au vendredi de 8h30 à 16h45:
931-2292
en tout temps:
842-4242

NOM ______________________ COURS ______________________

1. Pour des renseignements touristiques, vous composez *(dial)* le...

____

2. Pour envoyer un télégramme, vous composez le...

____

3. Pour une urgence médicale en tout temps, vous composez le...

____

4. Pour avoir des renseignements sur les avions, vous composez le...

____

5. Pour avoir des renseignements sur les trains, vous composez le...

____

F. À quelle distance? Using the following distance chart, give the distance between the indicated American and Canadian cities and Montreal or Quebec. Spell out the numbers.

	MONTRÉAL		QUÉBEC	
Ville	Km	Durée	Km	Durée
BOSTON	512	(5h)	618	(6h)
BUFFALO	607	(6h)	866	(8h30)
CHICAGO	1 333	(13h15)	1 592	(16h)
DETROIT	904	(9h)	1 164	(11h30)
HALIFAX	1 295	(13h)	1 056	(10h30)
NEW YORK	608	(6h)	834	(8h15)

EXEMPLE Quelle est la distance entre Boston et Montréal?
Cinq cent douze kilomètres.

Quelle est la distance entre...

1. Boston et Québec? ______________________
2. Buffalo et Québec? ______________________
3. Chicago et Québec? ______________________
4. Halifax et Montréal? ______________________
5. New York et Montréal? ______________________

G. Devinette. Read the following riddle to figure out the national holiday of the countries named. Write out the date of each country's national holiday in the space provided.

> À Haïti, la fête nationale, c'est le jour de l'an *(New Year's Day)*. Les Canadiens célèbrent six mois après les Haïtiens et deux semaines avant les Français. En Suisse, c'est exactement un mois après les Canadiens. Les Belges ont leur fête nationale une semaine après les Français et trois semaines après les Canadiens.

La date de la fête nationale à Haïti, c'est ______________________.

Au Canada, c'est ______________________.

En France, c'est ______________________.

En Suisse, c'est ______________________.

En Belgique, c'est ______________________.

Quelle est la date de la fête nationale aux États-Unis?______________________.

SYSTÈME-D *If you have access to Système-D software, you will find the following phrases there.* PHRASES: Writing a letter (informal); Expressing an opinion; VOCABULARY: Numbers; City; Store

Journal. A friend is thinking about moving in with you. Write a note in French, giving your telephone number and address, including the area code. Also explain some of the good aspects of your living situation, including some information about your neighborhood. At the top right corner of your note, write out today's date.

____

Cher / Chère...

NOM ____________________ COURS ____________________

CHAPITRE 4
En famille

COMPÉTENCE 1 Talking about your family

By the time you write your journal entry for this ***Compétence,*** you should be able to name family members and tell a little about them in French.

A. Ma famille. A friend is describing his family. Complete his descriptions with the words for the appropriate family members.

Ce sont mes ____________________, mon père et ma mère.

Ils sont entre mon ____________________ Jérôme et moi.

Mon autre ____________________ Alain est derrière mon père, et c'est son

ex-____________________ Marianne derrière ma ____________________. Ils

sont divorcés maintenant.

Voici mes grands-parents, mon ____________________ et ma

____________________. Derrière mes grands-parents,

c'est mon oncle et ma ____________________. Ils

sont avec mes deux cousins, leur ____________________

et leur ____________________.

B. La parenté. A friend is showing you pictures of the following family members. Write a question asking your friend to clarify her relationship to each one.

EXEMPLE Voilà mon neveu. *C'est le fils de ton frère ou de ta sœur?*

1. Voilà ma grand-mère. ____
2. Voilà ma nièce. ____
3. Voilà ma tante Marie. ____
4. Voilà mon oncle Antoine. ____
5. Voilà mon grand-père. ____

C. Des familles. Imagine what the indicated persons might say to explain who the family members in each picture are.

Je m'appelle Didier.

EXEMPLE Je m'appelle Didier. Sur la photo, c'est ma mère et mon petit frère. Nous sommes avec nos grands-parents.

Moi, je m'appelle Alice Pérez.

1. ______________________________

____

____

____

____

Je m'appelle Martin.

2. ______________________________

____

____

____

____

Je m'appelle André Serin.

3. ______________________________

____

____

____

____

D. Des présentations. Write sentences introducing different family members to the person(s) indicated. Use the expressions **Je te présente... / Je vous présente...** Also give a piece of information about the family member you are presenting.

EXEMPLE à votre professeur
Je vous présente ma cousine, Suzanne Forestier. Elle habite à Montréal où elle étudie à l'université Laval.

1. à un(e) ami(e) ____________________

____

2. à vos camarades ____________________

____

3. à votre petit(e) ami(e) ____________________

____

4. au père d'un(e) ami(e) ____________________

____

E. Voisins. Robert runs into Claude again, the woman who lives downstairs, and he is trying to find out a little more about her. Complete their conversation logically.

— Bonjour, mademoiselle! Excusez-moi pour l'autre jour! Permettez-moi de me présenter.

Je ____________________ Robert Martin.

Et vous êtes Claude...

— Oui, Claude Lange. Enchantée, Robert!

— Euh... vous avez des enfants?

— Oui, j'habite ici avec mon ____________________ André

et ma ____________________ Annick.

— Alors, vous êtes ____________________?

— Non, non, je suis divorcée. Mon ex-____________________ est remarié et il habite à

Trois-Rivières avec sa nouvelle ____________________.

F. Questions. Answer each question with a complete sentence in French.

1. Vous êtes combien dans votre famille?

____

2. Où habite votre famille?

____

3. Est-ce que vous passez beaucoup de temps chez vos parents?

____

4. Combien de tantes et d'oncles avez-vous?

____

5. Combien de cousins avez-vous?

____

6. Est-ce que vos frères et vos sœurs sont mariés?

____

SYSTÈME-D *If you have access to Système-D software, you will find the following phrases there.* PHRASES: Describing people; VOCABULARY: Family members; Personality; Leisure; Sports

Journal. Write a paragraph describing your family. In your description explain:

- how many there are in your immediate family
- where different family members live and what their personalities are like
- whether your brothers and sisters are married or divorced and whether they have any children
- with whom you prefer to spend a lot of time and what you like to do together

____

____

____

____

____

____

____

____

____

NOM ______________________ COURS ______________________

COMPÉTENCE 2 Describing people and things

By the time you write your journal entry for this *Compétence,* you should be able to give physical descriptions of people and tell how old they are in French.

A. Qui est-ce? Copy each description next to the person it best describes.

Il a environ soixante-dix ans.
Il a environ quarante-cinq ans.
Il a les cheveux noirs.
Il n'a pas beaucoup de cheveux.
Il a une moustache.
Il n'a pas de moustache.
Il a l'air triste.
Il a l'air content.

Elle a environ cinquante ans.
Elle a environ quatre-vingts ans.
Elle a les cheveux blonds et courts.
Elle a les cheveux gris.
Elle a l'air sympa.
Elle a l'air un peu snob et désagréable.
Elle porte une robe élégante.
Elle porte des lunettes.

André

____

____

____

____

Vincent

____

____

____

____

Valérie

____

____

____

____

Marie

____

____

____

____

B. Des personnes célèbres. Write a few sentences describing the physical attributes and age of the following celebrities. Make sure that adjectives agree with the nouns they describe.

1. Tom Cruise: ____

____

2. Julia Roberts: ____

____

Now name and describe a celebrity whom you like.

____

____

C. Couleurs. Answer the following questions with a complete sentence.

1. De quelles couleurs sont les vêtements que vous portez aujourd'hui?

____

2. De quelle couleur sont vos yeux?

____

D. Monsieur Bonvivant. Complete the following paragraph about Monsieur Bonvivant's possessions by putting the correct form of each adjective in the appropriate blank. One adjective from each pair goes before the noun and the other goes after it.

EXEMPLE Monsieur Bonvivant a deux *grosses* voitures *allemandes*. (allemand, gros)

1. En ville, il a une ____________ maison ________________. (grand, ultra-moderne)

2. Á la campagne, il a une ______________ maison ______________. (autre, rustique)

3. Sa femme porte beaucoup de ______________ vêtements ______________. (élégant, joli)

4. Quand il est en voyage, il achète toujours beaucoup de ______________ jeux

__________________ pour ses enfants. (électronique, petit)

5. Ce sont de ______________ enfants ________________. (beau, intelligent)

6. Il voyage souvent aux USA, alors il a beaucoup de ______________ amis

__________________. (américain, vieux)

NOM ______________________ COURS ______________________

E. Descriptions. Write sentences saying whether the adjectives in parentheses describe each noun. Pay attention to the placement of the adjectives. Remember that **un, une,** and **des** do not change to **de** after **être** when it is negated.

EXEMPLE un quartier (vieux, moderne, agréable)
Ce n'est pas un vieux quartier.
C'est un quartier moderne.
C'est un quartier agréable.

1. des vêtements (chers, très élégants, laids)

____

____

____

2. un ordinateur (petit, grand, moderne)

____

____

____

3. une ville (grande, américaine, canadienne)

____

____

____

4. un tableau (beau, vieux, intéressant)

____

____

____

5. une femme (jeune, jolie, blonde)

____

____

____

F. Mes possessions. Describe the things that you have. If you do not have something mentioned, tell what kind you would like to have using **Je voudrais avoir...**

EXEMPLE un chien *J'ai un petit chien sympa. / Je voudrais avoir un grand chien noir.*

1. une maison ____________________
2. une chambre ____________________
3. une voiture ____________________
4. une chaîne stéréo ____________________
5. une cuisine ____________________
6. un fauteuil ____________________

SYSTÈME-D *If you have access to Système-D software, you will find the following phrases there.* PHRASES: Describing people; VOCABULARY: Colors; Hair colors; Numbers; GRAMMAR: **Avoir** expressions; Present tense; Adjective agreement; Adjective position

Journal. Write a portrait of two members of your family in French. Give each person's name and age and tell what he or she looks like. Also describe each person's personality, using adjectives that you have learned in previous chapters.

NOM ______________________ COURS ______________________

COMPÉTENCE 3 Saying where you go in your free time

By the time you write your journal entry for this ***Compétence,*** you should be able to tell in French where you go in your free time and suggest activities to your friends.

A. Où va-t-on? Say where one goes to do each of the activities in the left column. Write complete sentences as in the example.

EXEMPLE *Pour écouter de la musique, on va à un concert.*

écouter de la musique	à la plage
prendre un verre	à la piscine
manger	au restaurant
voir une exposition	au café
faire du shopping	au centre commercial
acheter des livres	à un concert
jouer avec son chien	à la librairie
nager	au musée
prendre un bain de soleil	au parc

____

____

____

____

____

____

____

____

B. Où allez-vous? Where do you go in your city to do these things? Complete each sentence with a specific place as in the example.

EXEMPLE Pour acheter des livres, *je vais à la librairie Bookstop.*

1. Pour retrouver mes amis, ______________________.
2. Pour acheter des vêtements, ______________________.
3. Pour passer un après-midi tranquille, ______________________.
4. Pour passer une soirée romantique, ______________________.

C. La préposition *à*. Complete the following passage with the appropriate form of **à** and the definite article **le, la, l'** or **les.** Use the contracted forms when necessary.

Yannick est toujours très occupé. Pendant la semaine, il va tous les jours __________ école *(school)*. À midi, il va __________ café manger avec ses amis. Après, ils vont ensemble __________ bibliothèque où ils lisent et préparent leurs devoirs. Ensuite, ils rentrent ________ maison. Quand le vendredi soir arrive, Thomas et Yannick aiment aller ________ cinéma ou __________ parc. Le samedi, Yannick va _________ centre commercial avec sa petite amie pour faire du shopping. Le dimanche matin, toute la famille va ________ église et le dimanche à midi, ils vont __________ restaurant, parce que la maman de Yannick n'aime pas faire la cuisine ce jour-là.

Now imagine that you are Yannick and a friend asks you the following questions. Answer each one with a complete sentence according to the information given in the preceding paragraph.

1. Où vas-tu avec tes amis à midi?

____

2. Et après le café, où allez-vous?

____

3. Quel jour est-ce que ta famille va au restaurant?

____

D. Où vont-ils? Complete the following sentences, telling how often the indicated people go to the places shown.

SOUVENT	quelquefois	rarement	**ne... jamais**

EXEMPLE Mes grands-parents... 1. Mes amis et moi, nous... 2. Moi, je...

EXEMPLE Mes grands-parents vont rarement au théâtre.

1. ____

2. ____

NOM ______________________ COURS ______________________

3. Mon/Ma meilleur(e) ami(e)... 4. Ma famille... 5. Mes parents...

3. ______________________

4. ______________________

5. ______________________

E. Dans quel endroit? Tell a French friend where people do the following things where you live. Write sentences using the pronoun **on.**

EXEMPLE trouver *(to find)* des magazines français
On trouve des magazines français à la librairie Barnes & Noble. /
On ne trouve pas de magazines français ici.

1. manger bien

____

2. acheter de jolis vêtements

____

3. rencontrer *(to meet)* des gens intéressants

____

4. passer *(to show)* des films étrangers

____

5. jouer au football

____

6. parler français

____

7. aller danser

____

F. Des projets. It's Friday night and you are making plans with a friend. Write a response to your friend's questions by making suggestions with the **nous** form of the the verb.

EXEMPLE Alors, on va au cinéma ce soir ou on regarde une cassette vidéo à la maison?
Allons au cinéma. / Regardons une cassette vidéo à la maison.

1. On regarde un film français ou un film américain?

____

2. On invite d'autres étudiants de la classe de français?

____

3. On mange avant?

____

4. Et demain, on reste à la maison ou on va au parc?

____

If you have access to Système-D software, you will find the following phrases there.
PHRASES: Inviting; Telling time; Sequencing events; VOCABULARY: Leisure; Restaurant; City; Time of day; GRAMMAR: Imperative; DICTIONARY: The verb **aller**

Journal. You are making plans with a French-speaking friend to do something next Wednesday or Thursday evening. Write him or her a note asking if your friend would like to go out with you and suggest a place to eat and somewhere to go afterward. Explain what you usually do on that day, where you go, what time you usually return home, and what time you prefer to go out.

____

____

____

____

____

____

____

____

____

____

____

NOM ______________________ COURS ______________________

COMPÉTENCE 4 Telling what you are going to do

By the time you write your journal entry for this ***Compétence,*** you should be able to talk about your plans for tomorrow, this weekend, and the near future in French.

A. Le week-end. Answer the following questions about your typical Saturday with complete sentences in French.

1. À quelle heure est-ce que vous quittez la maison généralement?

____

2. Est-ce que vous déjeunez souvent au restaurant le samedi?

____

3. Où est-ce que vous passez la journée le samedi?

____

4. Est-ce que vous allez souvent boire un café avec des amis?

____

5. Avec qui est-ce que vous passez la soirée?

____

6. À quelle heure est-ce que vous rentrez chez vous généralement?

____

B. Et samedi prochain? Say whether you are going to do each of the things you wrote in ***A. Le week-end*** next Saturday.

EXEMPLE Samedi prochain, je vais quitter la maison vers... heures.

1. ____
2. ____
3. ____
4. ____
5. ____
6. ____

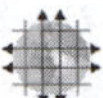

C. Projets pour la journée. Alice is talking about what her family is going to do today. Fill in each blank with the correct form of **aller** followed by the logical infinitive from the list. The first one has been done as an example.

D'abord, je *vais quitter* la maison pour aller au supermarché. Vers dix heures la famille ______________ pour Deauville où nous ______________ vers midi.

LOUER
faire
prendre

Vincent et moi, nous ______________ un bain de soleil à la plage. On ______________ un bateau et Éric ______________ du ski nautique.

RENTRER
boire
passer
ALLER

Le soir, Vincent ______________ avec moi chez des amis où nous ______________ la soirée. Éric ______________ quelque chose avec ses amis au café. Vincent et moi ______________ tard à la maison.

NOM ______________________ COURS ______________________

D. Mes projets d'avenir. Write a complete sentence in French telling something you are going to do at each of the following times. Use **aller** followed by a different infinitive for each one.

1. Ce soir? ______________________
2. Ce week-end? ______________________
3. La semaine prochaine? ______________________
4. Le mois prochain? ______________________
5. L'année prochaine? ______________________

E. Compléments d'objets directs. Answer the following questions, replacing the underlined direct objects with a pronoun.

EXEMPLE Où est-ce que vous retrouvez vos amis pour prendre un verre?
Je les retrouve souvent au café Les Amis pour prendre un verre.

1. Est-ce que vous invitez souvent vos amis chez vous?

____

2. Généralement le samedi, est-ce que vous passez la soirée seul(e), en famille ou avec des amis?

____

3. Où est-ce que vous passez votre temps libre?

____

4. Est-ce que vous visitez souvent les musées?

____

5. Trouvez-vous les expositions d'art intéressantes ou ennuyeuses?

____

6. À quel restaurant est-ce que vous retrouvez souvent vos amis pour dîner?

____

7. Qui prépare le dîner chez vous?

____

8. Est-ce que vous regardez souvent la télé quand vous mangez?

____

F. Une soirée entre amis. Rewrite the following paragraph, replacing the underlined direct objects with pronouns to make it sound less repetitive. The first part has been done as an example.

Ce soir, Alice et Vincent vont passer la soirée chez leurs amis, Jérôme et Sophie. Jérôme et Sophie aiment inviter <u>Alice et Vincent</u> à dîner. Quand ils sont ensemble, ils aiment parler anglais. Jérôme parle assez bien <u>anglais</u> mais Sophie parle <u>anglais</u> avec un accent. De temps en temps, Jérôme et Sophie retrouvent Alice et Vincent au restaurant mais ils préfèrent inviter <u>Alice et Vincent</u> à leur appartement. Sophie prépare le dîner le plus souvent mais quelquefois Jérôme prépare <u>le dîner</u>.

Ce soir, Alice et Vincent vont passer la soirée chez leurs amis, Jérôme et Sophie.

Jérôme et Sophie aiment *les* inviter à dîner. ____________________

____

____

____

____

____

____

If you have access to Système-D software, you will find the following phrases there.
PHRASES: Telling time; Sequencing events; Linking ideas; VOCABULARY: Leisure; Time expressions; Time of day; GRAMMAR: Future with **aller;** Direct objects; DICTIONARY: The verb **aller**

Journal. Write a paragraph in French explaining what you are going to do next weekend. Tell what you are going to do on Saturday or Sunday morning, afternoon, and evening. Give as many details as you can about what time you are are going to do each activity and with whom.

____

____

____

____

____

____

____

____

____

NOM ______________________________ COURS ______________________________

CHAPITRE 5
Les projets

COMPÉTENCE 1 Buying clothing

By the time you write your journal entry for this *Compétence,* you should be able to describe clothing in French.

A. Les vêtements. Label the following pieces of clothing in French.

1. ______________________ 3. ______________________ 5. ______________________

2. ______________________ 4. ______________________ 6. ______________________

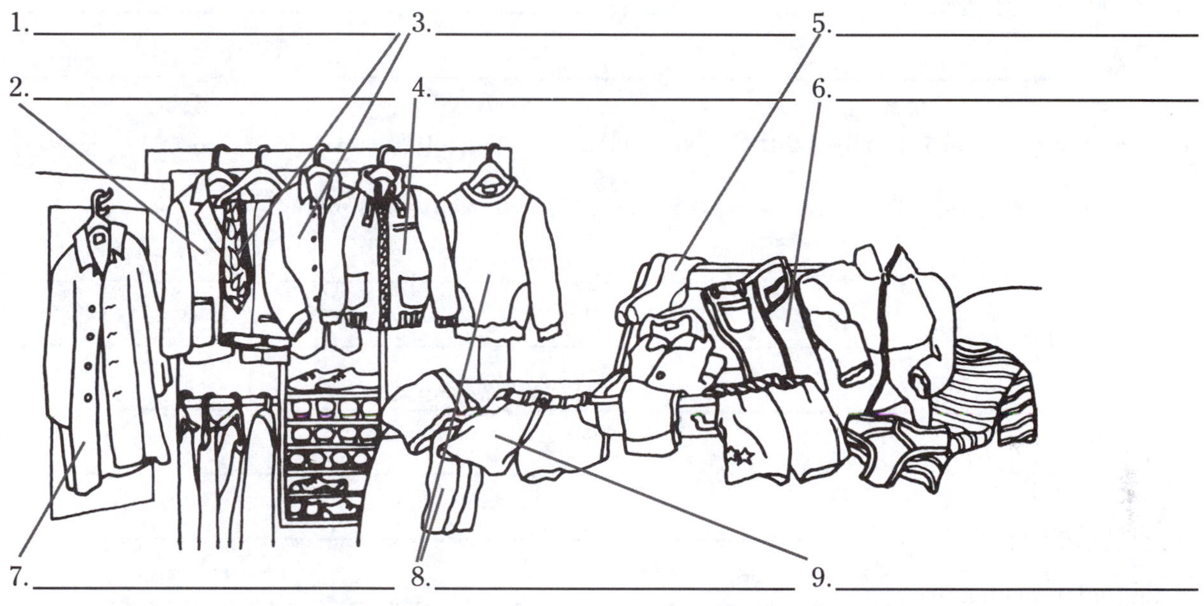

7. ______________________ 8. ______________________ 9. ______________________

1. ______________________ 3. ______________________ 5. ______________________

2. ______________________ 4. ______________________ 6. ______________________

7. ______________________ 8. ______________________ 9. ______________________

B. Que portent-ils? Using the verb **porter,** tell what these people are wearing.

1. 
2. 
3. 
4. 

1. Alice ____
2. Claude ____
3. Véronique ____
4. Paul ____.

C. Que mettez-vous? Describe your clothing in the following situations.

EXEMPLE Pour aller à la plage, **je mets un maillot de bain / un bikini.**

1. Pour aller à une soirée élégante, ______________________________.
2. Pour aller au travail, ______________________________.
3. Pour aller en classe, ______________________________.
4. Pour sortir avec mes amis le vendredi soir, ______________________________.
5. En décembre ou en janvier, ______________________________.
6. En juillet ou en août, ______________________________.

D. Comprenez-vous? Read the following page from the French department store **Trois Suisses** and find how to say the following italicized things in French. Remember that it is not necessary to understand every word to find the answers.

1. T-shirt HANES: *short sleeves* ______________________________
2. Chemise chambray STRUGGLE'S: *light or dark* ______________________________,

   buttoned chest pockets ______________________________

   long sleeves ______________________________
3. Gilet ACROSS en jean: *metal buttons* ______________________________

   four chest sizes ______________________________
4. Jean COMPLICES: *fitted* ______________________________

A. T-shirt HANES
Ample et en pur coton pour l'uni, en 75% coton, 25% polyester pour le chine, pour aborder l'été agréablement. Imprimé devant et très bien fini par bord-côtés double à l'encolure ras-de-cou et doubles surpiqûres aux emmanchures, base et bas des manches courtes.
Marine: 243.5451
Gris chine: 243.5453
4 tours de poitrine (en cm):

78–86	89,00 F
87–96	99,00 F
97–106	109,00 F
107–116	119,00 F

B. Chemise Chambray
STRUGGLE'S
Chambray clair ou foncé ? À vous de choisir pour assortir à vos jeans. 2 poches poitrine boutonnées. Manches longues à patte capucin. Pans arrondis. Finition par doubles surpiqûres. En 100% coton.
Bleu ciel: 273.5101
Bleu foncé: 273.5104
5 encolures:

37–38	149,00 F
39–40, 41–42	159,00 F
43–44, 45–46	169,00 F

C. Gilet ACROSS en Jean
Doublure fantaisie qui lui donne tout son cachet. 2 poches passepoilées. 1 patte de serrage au dos. 5 boutons métal. Entièrement surpiqué. En 100% coton.
Stone bleached: 013.6310
Stone washed: 013.6314
4 tours de poitrine (en cm)

84–88, 92–96	229,00 F
100–104	249,00 F
108–112	269,00 F

D. Jean COMPLICES
Taillé comme un authentique jean 5 poches et agrémente de nombreuses vignettes tissées devant et dos. Braguette à boutons. Largeur bas 19 cm. Coupe large. En 100% coton.
Stone bleached: 113.7763
Stone washed: 113.7767
8 tours de ceinture (en cm)

72, 76	249,00 F
80, 84, 88	269,00 F
92, 96, 100	289,00 F

E. On achète des vêtements. You are buying some clothes. Complete the following conversation with the salesperson in a logical way.

LA VENDEUSE: Bonjour, monsieur / madame / mademoiselle. Comment est-ce que je peux vous aider?

VOUS: ____

LA VENDEUSE: Vous faites quelle taille?

VOUS: ____

LA VENDEUSE: Quelle couleur est-ce que vous préférez?

VOUS: Je préfère quelque chose en ______________________________.

Est-ce que je peux essayer ______________________________?

LA VENDEUSE: Mais bien sûr! Voilà la cabine d'essayage.

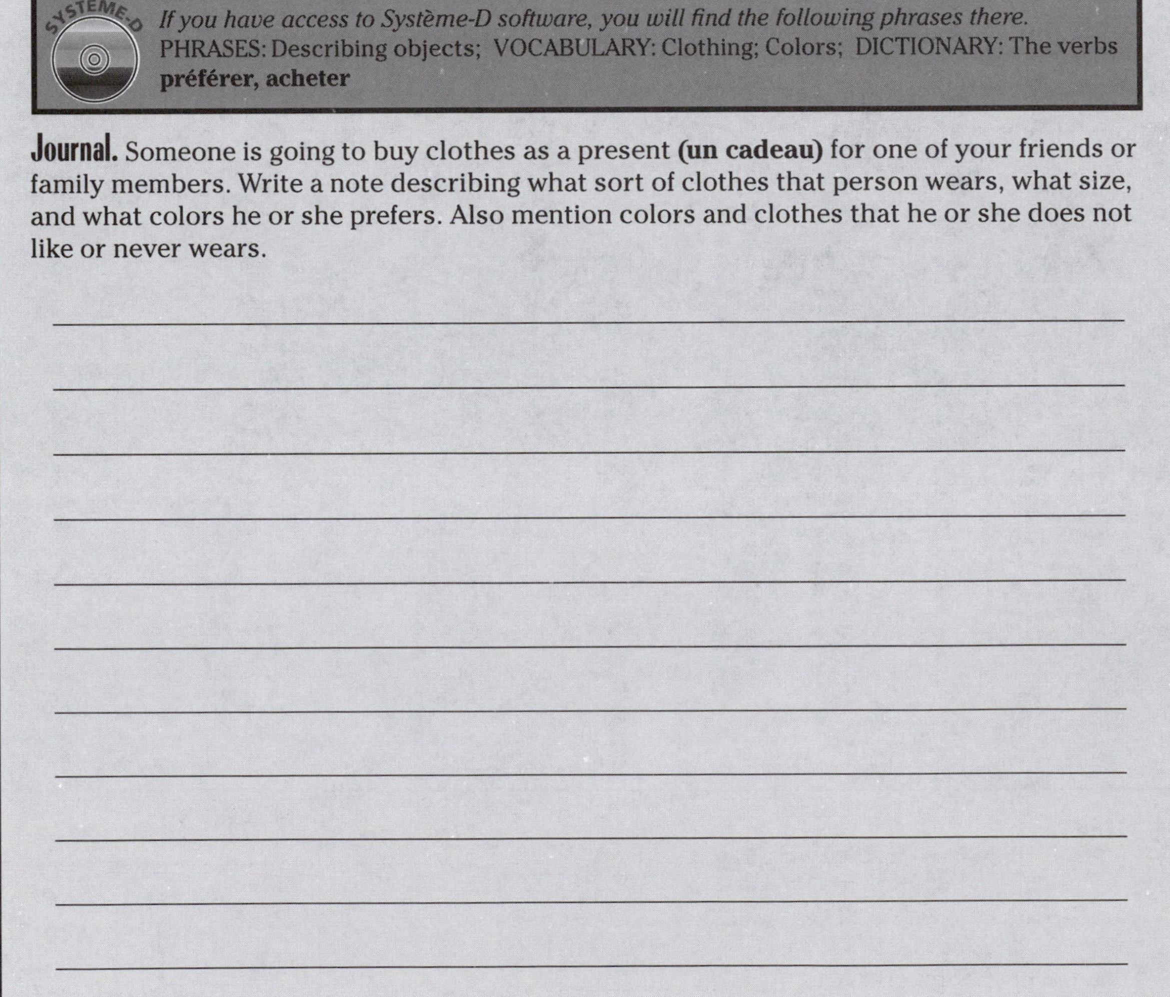

If you have access to Système-D software, you will find the following phrases there.
PHRASES: Describing objects; VOCABULARY: Clothing; Colors; DICTIONARY: The verbs **préférer, acheter**

Journal. Someone is going to buy clothes as a present **(un cadeau)** for one of your friends or family members. Write a note describing what sort of clothes that person wears, what size, and what colors he or she prefers. Also mention colors and clothes that he or she does not like or never wears.

NOM ______________________ COURS ______________________

COMPÉTENCE 2 Deciding what to do

By the time you write your journal entry for this ***Compétence,*** you should be able to describe the weather in different seasons and say what people do in French.

A. Quel temps fait-il? In which place and in what season is the pictured weather common? Write complete sentences describing the weather depicted in each illustration.

EN ALASKA EN HIVER? au Texas en été?
au printemps en France? EN SUISSE EN AUTOMNE?

1.

2. 

3. 

4. 

1. ____
2. ____
3. ____
4. ____

B. Quoi faire? The weather can change your plans. Complete the following sentences saying what you intend to do according to the indicated weather conditions. Use the expression **avoir l'intention de.**

RESTER À LA MAISON aller au cinéma *travailler*
??? FAIRE DU BATEAU ??? faire du ski (nautique)
partir en week-end **passer la journée à la plage**
??? ne rien faire

1. S'il fait mauvais demain, ______________________________.
2. S'il fait du soleil demain, ______________________________.
3. S'il pleut ce week-end, ______________________________.
4. S'il fait beau ce week-end, ______________________________.
5. S'il neige beaucoup cet hiver, ______________________________.

C. Et chez vous? Describe the weather where you live at the indicated times.

1. en été ____________________

2. en hiver ____________________

3. au printemps ____________________

4. en automne ____________________

5. aujourd'hui ____________________

D. Quand? Complete the following sentences with a weather expression.

1. Je préfère passer la journée au lit quand ____________________.

2. J'ai beaucoup d'énergie quand ____________________.

3. J'aime le temps quand ____________________.

4. Je ne fais rien quand ____________________.

E. Un après-midi. Complete the following conversation between Alice and Vincent by filling in each blank with the correct form of **faire.**

— Où sont les enfants? Qu'est-ce qu'ils ______________ cet après-midi?

— Cathy ______________ du shopping avec son amie et les deux garçons ______________ du vélo.

— Et nous, on ______________ quelque chose en ville cet après-midi ou on reste à la maison?

— Nous ne ____________________ pas assez d'exercice récemment. Allons au parc pour ______________ une promenade.

F. Qu'est-ce qu'ils font? Alice is talking about what different family members often do. Complete her sentences using an expression with **faire.**

1. 2. 3. 4.

BOULANGERIE

1. Vincent et moi ____________________.

2. Éric ____________________.

NOM ______________________ COURS ______________________

3. Vincent ______________________.

4. Moi, je ______________________.

5. 6. 7. 8.

5. Les enfants ______________________.

6. Éric et Vincent ______________________.

7. Nous ______________________.

8. Vincent ______________________.

G. De quoi as-tu envie? Write complete sentences, telling two things you feel like doing and two things you need to do. Use the expressions **avoir envie de** and **avoir besoin de.**

FAIRE LA LESSIVE faire un voyage *faire les devoirs* faire de l'exercice FAIRE UNE PROMENADE faire du ski **faire du shopping** faire le ménage **FAIRE DU CAMPING** *faire du sport* faire du jogging

1. ______________________
2. ______________________
3. ______________________
4. ______________________

H. Suggestions. You are talking to two children. Respond to their statements, using the command form of the indicated verb in either the **tu** or the **vous** form, according to the situation. Replace the underlined direct objects with **le, la, l',** or **les.**

EXEMPLES Je n'aime pas ce sandwich.
manger *Ne le mange pas!*

Nous avons envie de voir ce film à la télévision.
regarder *Regardez-le!*

1. J'ai besoin de faire mes devoirs.

faire ______________________

2. Nous avons envie d'inviter nos amis à la maison.

inviter ______________________

3. Nous n'aimons pas du tout cette musique que vous écoutez!

ne pas écouter ______________________________

4. Je n'aime pas faire la vaisselle.

ne pas faire ______________________________

5. Est-ce que nous avons besoin de faire nos lits?

faire ______________________________

SYSTÈME-D

If you have access to Système-D software, you will find the following phrases there. PHRASES: Describing weather; Advising; Writing a letter (informal); VOCABULARY: Clothing; Seasons; Leisure; Sports; DICTIONARY: **Faire** expressions; Present tense; Future with **aller**

Journal. Write notes to two friends who are coming to visit you, one in the summer and the other in the winter. Describe what people do for fun during each season, what the weather is like, and what type of clothes they are going to need.

NOM ______________________ COURS ______________________

COMPÉTENCE 3 Saying what you did

By the time you write your journal entry for this ***Compétence,*** you should be able to tell in French what you did yesterday or last weekend.

A. Qu'est-ce qu'ils ont fait? Look at the following pictures and say what the weather was like and what certain people did recently. Use the **passé composé.**

1. Vincent...

2. 
Éric...

3. 
Alice...

4. 
Les enfants...

1. ____

2. ____

3. ____

4. ____

B. Déjà fait! Alice made a list of things for Vincent and the children to do for her before she returns today, and they have already done them. Look at Alice's list and write what Vincent and the children did, using the **passé composé** of the indicated verbs and the adverb **déjà.**

À faire aujourd'hui...

(Éric) faire les courses
(les enfants) faire le ménage
(Vincent et Éric) acheter une valise (*suitcase*)
(Vincent) faire la lessive
(Vincent) téléphoner à l'agence de voyages
(Vincent) trouver un hôtel pour ce week-end

EXEMPLE Éric a déjà fait les courses.

____

____

____

____

____

____

____

____

C. La dernière fois. Write complete sentences telling when you last did the activities pictured.

HIER la semaine dernière *il y a trois jours* l'année dernière IL Y A LONGTEMPS ne... jamais ???

1. 2. 3. 4.

1. ____________________
2. ____________________
3. ____________________
4. ____________________

D. Vous l'avez fait? Tell whether you did the following things at the indicated times.

1. dîner au restaurant (hier soir)

____

2. dormir jusqu'à dix heures (ce matin)

____

3. prendre l'autobus (la semaine dernière)

____

4. voir un bon film (le mois dernier)

____

5. acheter un livre (récemment)

____

E. Hier. Answer the following questions about your day yesterday. Write complete sentences.

1. À quelle heure est-ce que vous avez quitté la maison?

____

2. Est-ce que vous avez pris l'autobus?

____

3. Combien de temps est-ce que vous avez passé en classe?

____

4. Où est-ce que vous avez mangé?

____

5. Est-ce que vous avez fait de l'exercice?

____

F. Un peu d'histoire canadienne. Review a little Canadian history by finding the correct ending to each sentence and putting the verb in the **passé composé.** The first one has been done as an example. You may need to refer to the culture note on pages 120–121 of the textbook.

En 1534, Jacques Cartier, navigateur français,...
En 1608, Samuel de Champlain...
Entre 1642 et 1701, les Iroquois...
Entre 1756 et 1763, la guerre *(war)* de Sept Ans...
En 1763, la France...
Sous les Anglais, la Nouvelle-France...

opposer les Anglais et les Français.
faire la guerre *(war)* contre les Français.
prendre possession du Canada (la Nouvelle-France) au nom de François Ier de France.
fonder la ville de Québec.
céder ses territoires canadiens à l'Angleterre.
prendre le nom de «Canada».

En 1534, Jacques Cartier, navigateur français, a pris possession du Canada (la Nouvelle-France) au nom de François Ier de France. ____________________

____

____

____

____

____

____

____

____

____

____

____

____

____

____

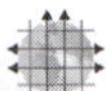

G. La journée d'Alice. Alice is talking about her day last Sunday. Complete the following paragraph by putting the verbs in parentheses in the **passé composé.**

Dimanche dernier, j'____________________ (dormir) jusqu'à huit heures et demie. Le matin, je __________________ (ne pas faire) grand-chose. Vincent et moi __________________ (prendre) le petit déjeuner avec les enfants et après, Vincent et les enfants ________________ (faire) une promenade. Moi, j'___________________ (préferer) rester à la maison. J'__________________ (faire) la vaisselle et j'________________ (lire) le journal. Vers onze heures, j'____________________ (téléphoner) à mon amie Sophie pour l'inviter à déjeuner avec Vincent et moi. Nous ______________________________ (retrouver) Sophie et son mari en ville où nous ____________________ (manger) dans un excellent restaurant. Après le déjeuner, Vincent et moi__________________ (faire) des courses et nous _______________ (prendre) l'autobus pour rentrer à la maison. Nous __________________ (passer) la soirée à la maison. Nous __________________ (voir) un bon film à la télé et après, Vincent et les enfants ___________________ (jouer) avec quelque chose sur l'Internet. Moi, j'___________________ (mettre) mon jogging et j'________________ (faire) de l'exercice.

SYSTÈME-D *If you have access to Système-D software, you will find the following phrases there.* PHRASES: Describing weather; Sequencing events; Linking ideas; VOCABULARY: Leisure; Sports; City; GRAMMAR: Compound past tense

Journal. Write a paragraph telling what the weather was like last weekend and what you did. If you wish to say *I went, I stayed, I went out* or *I arrived,* use **je suis allé(e), je suis resté(e), je suis sorti(e),** or **je suis arrivé(e),** rather than using **avoir** to form the past tense, as you have learned to do with other verbs. Females must also add an extra **e** to the end of the past participle of these four verbs, unlike those formed with **avoir.** You will learn more about these verbs in the next ***Compétence.***

____

____

____

____

____

____

____

____

NOM ______________________ COURS ______________________

COMPÉTENCE 4 Telling where you went

By the time you write your journal entry for this ***Compétence,*** you should be able to tell where you went and what you did in French.

A. Une excursion. Answer the following questions about the last time you went to another city for the weekend.

1. Où est-ce que vous êtes allé(e)?

____

2. Quel jour êtes-vous parti(e)?

____

3. Est-ce que vous y êtes allé(e) en avion?

____

4. À quelle heure êtes-vous arrivé(e)?

____

5. Est-ce que vous êtes descendu(e) dans un hôtel?

____

6. Est-ce que vous êtes allé(e) chez des amis ou chez des parents?

____

7. Combien de jours êtes-vous resté(e)?

____

8. Quel jour êtes-vous rentré(e)?

____

B. Le dernier cours. Using the verb **être** as the auxiliary, say whether the following people did the things indicated in parentheses the last day you went to French class.

EXEMPLE Je... (partir tôt)
Je suis parti(e) tôt. / Je ne suis pas parti(e) tôt.

1. Tous les étudiants... (aller en cours de français)

____

2. Je... (arriver en retard *[late]*)

____

3. Nous… (aller au laboratoire de langues)

____

4. Le professeur… (sortir de la salle de classe pendant le cours)

____

5. Je… (partir à la maison après le cours)

____

6. Les autres étudiants… (rester sur le campus après le cours)

____

7. Moi, je… (rentrer à la maison pour faire les devoirs)

____

C. La journée d'Éric. Complete the following passage about what Éric did yesterday by supplying the correct form of the appropriate auxiliary verb **avoir** or **être.**

Éric ________ commencé sa journée à 7h30. D'abord, il ________ fait du jogging dans le quartier et après, il ________ rentré à la maison où il ________ pris son petit déjeuner. Ensuite, il ________ allé en ville. L'après-midi, il ________ joué au football avec des amis pendant une heure. Tout le monde ________ parti à 5h30 pour rentrer à la maison. Hier soir, une amie ________ invité Éric à dîner chez elle. Alors Vincent, Alice et les autres enfants ________ dîné en ville et ils ________ allés au cinéma. Toute la famille ________ rentrée très fatiguée à 11h du soir.

D. Tu as passé un bon week-end? Two friends are talking about the weekend. Complete their conversation by putting the verbs in parentheses into the **passé composé.** Be careful to distinguish which verbs take **avoir** as their auxiliary and which ones require **être.**

— Alors, tu ____________________ (passer) un bon week-end?

— Oui, très bon. Je (J') ____________________ (aller) à la plage avec ma petite amie et ses parents.

— Quand est-ce que vous ____________________ (partir)?

— Nous ____________________ (partir) vendredi et nous ____________________ (rentrer) hier.

— Vous ____________________ (descendre) dans un hôtel?

— Non, nous ____________________ (faire) du camping.

E. Où sont-ils allés? Using the indicated verbs, explain what Alice and Vincent Pérez did today. Make sure you choose the correct auxiliary, **avoir** or **être.**

EXEMPLE Alice
quitter la maison, faire une promenade, rentrer à la maison

1. Vincent
rester à la maison, travailler sur l'ordinateur, pleuvoir toute la journée

2. Vincent et Alice
aller chez des amis, parler, boire un verre de vin, partir

3. Vincent et Alice
rentrer, monter dans leur appartement

EXEMPLE Ce matin, **Alice a quitté la maison vers 7h30. Elle a fait une promenade et elle est rentrée à la maison.**

1. Cet après-midi, ____

____.

2. Ce soir, ____

____.

3. Vers minuit, ____

____.

F. Et vous? Answer the following questions in complete sentences.

1 Est-ce que vous êtes sorti(e) avec vos amis récemment?

____

2. À quelle heure est-ce que vous avez quitté la maison ce matin?

____

3. À quelle heure est-ce que vous êtes rentré(e) hier soir?

____

4. Où est-ce que vous êtes allé(e) le week-end dernier? Est-ce que vous êtes resté(e) à la maison?

____

5. Est-ce que vous êtes parti(e) en week-end récemment?

____

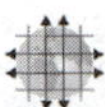

If you have access to Système-D software, you will find the following phrases there.
PHRASES: Describing objects; Requesting something; Writing a letter (formal); VOCABULARY: Clothing; Colors; Traveling; Days of the week; GRAMMAR: Compound past tense; Verbs with auxiliary **être**

Journal. You stayed at a hotel in France where you left a few pieces of clothing in your room. Write a letter to the hotel asking them to send them to you. In your letter include the following information:

- how long you stayed at the hotel and in which room
- when you arrived and when you left
- what pieces of clothing you forgot **(oublier),** giving their color

The last part of the letter has been written for you.

Monsieur, Madame,

____

____

____

____

____

____

____

____

____

____

____

Si vous trouvez les vêtements décrits ci-dessus, je vous prie de les envoyer à l'adresse suivante:

____

____

____

Vous pouvez mettre les frais postaux sur ma carte de crédit __________ numéro __________.

Je vous remercie d'avance de votre gentillesse et, en attendant votre réponse, je vous prie,

Monsieur, Madame, d'accepter l'expression de mes sentiments les plus distingués.

____

NOM ______________________ COURS ______________________

CHAPITRE 6
Les invitations

COMPÉTENCE 1 Talking about movies

Dans le journal à la fin de cette ***Compétence,*** vous allez parler de la dernière fois que vous êtes allé(e) au cinéma.

A. Quel genre de film? Identifiez le genre des films suivants. Commencez chaque phrase avec **C'est...**

1. 
2. 
3. 
4. 

1. ______________________
2. ______________________
3. ______________________
4. ______________________

B. Quels genres aimez-vous? Exprimez *(Express)* votre opinion sur chaque genre de film en utilisant l'un des verbes et l'un des adjectifs dans les listes.

AIMER préférer *détester**

VIOLENTS bêtes *amusants* ennuyeux ??? INTÉRESSANTS

EXEMPLE les films policiers *Je déteste les films policiers. Ces films sont souvent violents.*

1. les films d'aventures ______________________

____

2. les films de science-fiction ______________________

____

3. les films d'amour ____

____

4. les films d'épouvante ____

____

5. les drames psychologiques ____

____

6. les dessins animés ____

____

C. Films américains. Trouvez dans la liste suivante le titre original des films dont *(about which)* votre ami français vous parle. Précisez le genre de ces films et, si vous les avez vus, dites comment vous les avez trouvés et si vous les recommandez à vos amis.

The Fugitive	*Lethal Weapon*	*Star Wars: The Empire Strikes Back*
The Sword and the Stone	*Regarding Henry*	*Honey, I Shrunk the Kids*

EXEMPLE *Chérie, j'ai rétréci les gosses* (Honey, I Shrunk the Kids) Non, je ne l'ai pas vu. C'est une comédie. / Oui, je l'ai vu. C'est une comédie. Je l'ai trouvé bête (amusant, intéressant, ennuyeux) et je (ne) le recommande (pas) à mes amis.

1. *À propos d'Henry* (______________________________) ______________

____

____

2. *L'Empire contre attaque* (______________________________) ______________

____

____

3. *L'Arme fatale* (______________________________) ______________

____

____

4. *Merlin l'enchanteur* (______________________________) ______________

____

____

5. *Le Fugitif* (______________________________) ______________

____

____

D. Une cassette vidéo. Répondez aux questions suivantes avec des phrases complètes.

1. Est-ce que vous louez souvent des cassettes vidéo?

____

2. Avec qui est-ce que vous regardez souvent des cassettes vidéo chez vous?

____

3. Quel genre de film est-ce que vous préférez? Et vos amis?

____

____

4. Est-ce que vous préférez voir un film au cinéma où l'écran *(screen)* est plus grand ou à la maison où on peut *(can)* parler et manger plus facilement pendant le film?

____

5. Quel film avez-vous loué récemment?

____

6. Est-ce que vous avez vu ce film chez vous ou chez un(e) ami(e)?

____

7. Comment est-ce que vous avez trouvé le film? intéressant? ennuyeux? bête? amusant?

____

E. Ma biographie. On fait un film biographique de votre vie *(life)*. Répondez aux questions suivantes en français.

1. Quel genre de film est-ce? un drame? une comédie? un film d'amour? un film d'aventures? un film d'épouvante?

____

2. Quel acteur / quelle actrice joue le premier rôle *(leading role)?*

____

3. Y a-t-il d'autres personnages *(characters)* importants dans le film? Quels acteurs interprètent leurs rôles?

____

____

____

4. Quelle est la meilleure partie du film: le commencement, le milieu ou la fin *(the beginning, middle or end)?* Pourquoi?

5. Quelle est la partie du film la plus ennuyeuse? Pourquoi?

If you have access to Système-D software, you will find the following phrases there.
PHRASES: Expressing an opinion; VOCABULARY: Time expressions; Time of day

Journal. Décrivez la dernière fois que vous êtes allé(e) au cinéma. Dans votre description, répondez aux questions suivantes.

- Quand est-ce que vous y êtes allé(e) et avec qui?
- À quel cinéma êtes-vous allé(e), et qu'est-ce que vous avez vu?
- Comment avez-vous trouvé le film? Pourquoi?

NOM ______________________ COURS ______________________

COMPÉTENCE 2 Planning an outing

Dans le journal à la fin de cette ***Compétence,*** vous allez inviter un(e) ami(e) à faire quelque chose et vous allez répondre à une invitation.

A. On vous invite à... Imaginez que votre petit(e) ami(e) vous invite à faire les choses suivantes. Acceptez ou refusez chaque invitation.

EXEMPLE Tu veux aller au centre commercial avec moi cet après-midi?
Oui, je veux bien. /
Non, je regrette mais je ne peux pas. Je dois travailler aujourd'hui.

1. Tu as envie d'aller prendre un verre au café?

____

2. Est-ce que tu voudrais faire la cuisine ce soir?

____

3. On va voir le nouveau film d'Al Pacino?

____

4. Tu veux aller à l'église avec ma famille ce week-end?

____

5. Tu es libre pour aller au musée jeudi matin?

____

B. Invitons des gens! Invitez les personnes indiquées à faire les choses illustrées.

1. 
2. 
3. 
4. 

1. votre petit(e) ami(e) ____
2. votre mère ____
3. des camarades de classe ____
4. des amis ____

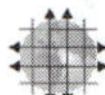

C. Pourquoi pas? Alice explique que les personnes suivantes ne peuvent pas faire la première chose illustrée parce qu'elles doivent faire la seconde chose. Complétez ses phrases en utilisant les verbes **vouloir, pouvoir** et **devoir.**

EXEMPLE Vincent et moi *voulons aller à la plage mais nous ne pouvons pas parce que je dois aller acheter des vêtements pour notre fils.*

1. Éric ____
____
____
____.

2. Vincent et moi ____
____
____
____.

3. Les enfants ____
____
____
____.

D. Impossible! Expliquez que les personnes indiquées ne peuvent pas faire les choses qu'elles veulent parce qu'elles doivent faire autre chose. Complétez les phrases suivantes en utilisant votre imagination.

ALLER AU CINÉMA ???
faire une boum
FAIRE UNE PROMENADE
regarder la télévision
louer une cassette vidéo **aller au café**
aller au centre commercial **???**

FAIRE LA LESSIVE faire le ménage
faire des devoirs
??? faire de l'exercice
faire la cuisine ALLER EN VILLE
préparer un examen

EXEMPLE Mon frère *veut aller au cinéma mais il ne peut pas. Il doit préparer un examen.*

NOM ______________________ COURS ______________________

1. Je ____

____.

2. Mes camarades de classe ____

____.

3. (au professeur) Vous ____

____.

4. (à votre meilleur[e] ami[e]) Toi, tu ____

____.

E. Au café. Alice est au café avec sa famille et elle demande à chacun ce qu'il va prendre. Complétez leur conversation avec le verbe **prendre.**

— Les enfants, vous ______________________ un chocolat ou un coca?

— Nous ______________________ un coca.

— Et toi, Vincent, tu ______________________ une eau minérale ou un demi?

— Je ______________________ un demi. Et toi, Alice, qu'est-ce que tu vas

______________________?

— Je vais ______________________ un café.

Maintenant, Alice commande pour la famille. Qu'est-ce qu'elle dit au garçon? Complétez ses phrases.

Les enfants ____.

Mon mari ____.

Et moi, je ____.

F. Et vous? Répondez aux questions suivantes avec des phrases complètes.

1. La dernière fois que vous êtes allé(e) à l'université, est-ce que vous avez pris votre voiture, l'autobus, ou est-ce que vous y êtes allé(e) à pied?

____

2. Quand est-ce que vous avez appris à conduire *(to drive)* une voiture? L'année dernière? Il y a deux / trois / ??? ans? Vous n'avez pas encore appris?

____

3. Est-ce que vous prenez souvent l'autobus? Quand est-ce que vous l'avez pris la dernière fois?

4. Quand vous êtes dans une grande ville comme Paris ou New York, est-ce que vous prenez quelquefois le métro?

5. Quels moyens de transport n'avez-vous jamais pris? Pourquoi?

If you have access to Système-D software, you will find the following phrases there.
PHRASES: Writing a letter (informal); Inviting; Accepting and declining; Apologizing
VOCABULARY: Leisure; City; Time expressions; Time of day

Journal. Écrivez deux paragraphes à des ami(e)s. Dans le premier paragraphe, invitez votre ami(e) à faire quelque chose. Donnez tous les détails importants comme le jour et l'heure. Dans le deuxième paragraphe, répondez à l'invitation d'un(e) autre ami(e). Refusez l'invitation en donnant une excuse et suggérez quelque chose d'autre pour une autre fois.

NOM ______________________________ COURS ______________________________

COMPÉTENCE 3 Describing childhood memories

Dans le journal à la fin de cette ***Compétence,*** vous allez décrire des souvenirs d'enfance.

A. Mon enfance. Dites ce que vous faisiez dans votre famille pour célébrer les fêtes suivantes quand vous étiez petit(e).

FAIRE UN PIQUE-NIQUE faire un barbecue *aller à l'église*
ALLER VOIR UN DÉFILÉ faire une fête dîner au restaurant
ne rien faire de spécial inviter des amis chez nous **aller voir nos grands-parents**
OUVRIR DES CADEAUX ??? aller au feu d'artifice *(fireworks)*

EXEMPLE Pâques

1. Noël

2. la Saint-Valentin

EXEMPLE *On allait à l'église. / On ne célébrait pas Pâques.*

1. ____

2. ____

3. le réveillon du jour de l'an

4. un anniversaire

5. la fête nationale

3. ____

4. ____

5. ____

B. Au présent et au passé. Écrivez trois phrases. Dites si vous faites chaque chose souvent actuellement *(at present),* si vous l'avez faite hier et si vous la faisiez quand vous étiez petit(e).

EXEMPLE manger dans des fast-foods
Maintenant, je ne mange pas souvent dans des fast-foods.
Hier, je n'ai pas mangé dans un fast-food.
Quand j'étais petit(e), je mangeais souvent dans des fast-foods.

1. regarder des dessins animés ______________________________

____

____

2. prendre l'autobus ______________________________

____

____

3. faire du shopping ______________________________

____

____

C. Monsieur Monotone. Pauvre monsieur Monotone fait la même chose depuis *(since)* des années. Voici ce qu'il a fait hier. C'est exactement ce qu'il faisait il y a dix ans. Récrivez la description de sa journée d'hier pour décrire ses occupations de tous les jours il y a dix ans en mettant les verbes à l'imparfait.

Avant de sortir ce matin, monsieur Monotone **a pris** un café et il **a mangé** un croissant. Il **a quitté** la maison à 7h45 et il **a pris** l'autobus à 7h52 à l'arrêt d'autobus devant son immeuble. Quand il **est arrivé** au travail, il **est entré** dans son bureau et il **a commencé** à travailler sans parler à personne. Il **est resté** devant son ordinateur toute la journée jusqu'à 16h55, quand il **a quitté** son bureau pour rentrer à la maison. De retour à la maison, il **a préparé** son dîner, il **a mangé** et il **a pris** un bain. Après son bain, il **a regardé** la télé pendant une heure avant de se coucher *(going to bed)*.

Avant de sortir le matin, monsieur Monotone prenait un café...

____

____

____

____

____

____

____

____

____

____

____

NOM ______________________ COURS ______________________

D. En sortant de chez moi. Décrivez la situation hier quand vous êtes sorti(e) de chez vous en répondant aux questions suivantes.

1. Quelle heure était-il?

____

2. Est-ce que vous étiez en retard?

____

3. Où est-ce que vous alliez?

____

4. Est-ce que vous vouliez rester à la maison?

____

5. Quel temps faisait-il?

____

6. Qu'est-ce que vous aviez envie de faire?

____

E. Situations. Décrivez la situation quand vous avez vu les personnes dans les illustrations. Utilisez les verbes indiqués.

EXEMPLE Alice… (être, faire, entrer)
Alice était en ville.
Elle faisait des courses.
Elle entrait dans un magasin.

1. Éric et vous… (être, faire, porter)

____

____

____

2. Alice et Vincent… (être , jouer, porter)

____

____

____

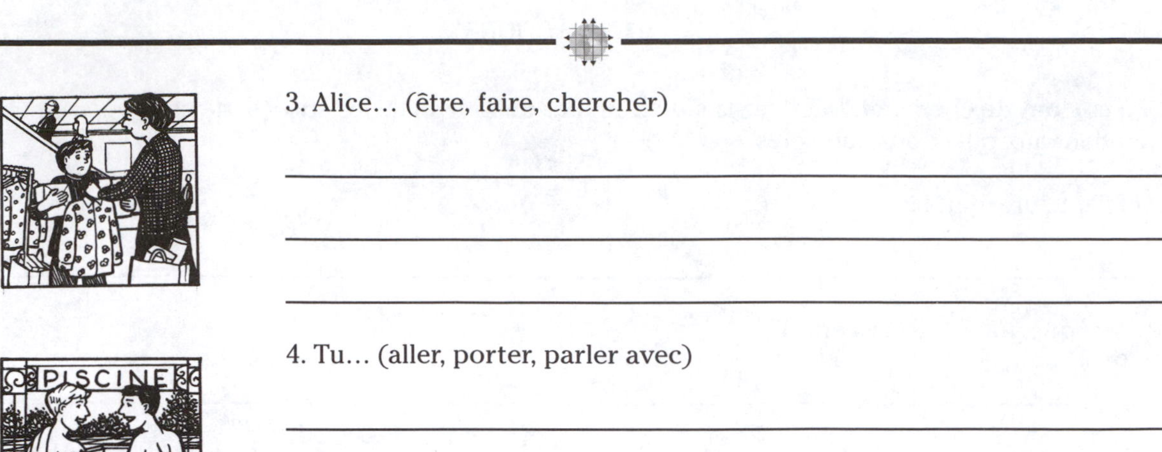

3. Alice… (être, faire, chercher)

4. Tu… (aller, porter, parler avec)

If you have access to Système-D software, you will find the following phrases there.
PHRASES: Linking ideas; VOCABULARY: Family members

Journal. Parlez de comment votre famille célébrait les fêtes et les anniversaires quand vous étiez jeune. Quelles fêtes célébriez-vous et qu'est-ce que vous faisiez?

NOM ______________________ COURS ______________________

COMPÉTENCE 4 Narrating what happened

Dans le journal à la fin de cette ***Compétence,*** vous allez raconter *(tell)* une histoire au passé.

A. Une sortie. Répondez aux questions suivantes à propos de la dernière fois que vous avez retrouvé des amis au restaurant pour dîner.

1. Est-ce que vos amis étaient déjà au restaurant quand vous êtes arrivé(e)?

____

2. Quelle heure était-il quand vous êtes arrivé(e) au restaurant?

____

3. Est-ce que vous aviez faim quand vous êtes arrivé(e) au restaurant?

____

4. Après le repas, êtes-vous parti(e) tout de suite parce que vous étiez fatigué(e) ou est-ce que vous êtes resté(e) au restaurant parce que vous vouliez parler avec vos amis?

____

5. Quelle heure était-il quand vous avez quitté le restaurant?

____

B. Leur journée. Mettez les phrases suivantes au passé. Mettez le verbe qui décrit ce qui a eu lieu *(took place)* au passé composé et mettez le verbe qui décrit les circonstances ou la situation à l'imparfait.

EXEMPLE Il pleut quand Vincent va au parc pour faire du jogging ce matin.
Il pleuvait quand Vincent est allé au parc pour faire du jogging ce matin.

1. Alice va au travail parce qu'elle a beaucoup de choses à faire.

____

2. Éric mange beaucoup au petit déjeuner parce qu'il a très faim.

____

3. Vincent veut aller voir un film, alors il achète un *Pariscope.*

____

4. Vincent et les enfants vont au cinéma Rex parce qu'il y a un bon film d'aventures.

____

5. Alice reste à la maison parce qu'elle est fatiguée après sa longue journée au travail.

____

C. Une soirée. Éric parle de ce qu'il a fait hier soir. Reliez *(combine)* les phrases des deux colonnes dans un ordre logique pour recréer sa soirée. Utilisez des mots comme **et, mais, quand, parce que, alors** et **comme** *(since).*

LA SCÈNE / LA SITUATION	LES ACTIONS
Ma petite amie Michèle voulait sortir.	Nous sommes allés au cinéma.
Il était six heures et demie.	J'ai retrouvé Michèle au cinéma.
Le film était un peu bête et il y avait beaucoup de violence.	Beaucoup de gens sont partis avant la fin.
Je voulais partir aussi.	Nous avons décidé de rester.
Après le film nous avions faim.	Nous avons dîné dans un petit restaurant.
Le dîner était excellent.	J'ai beaucoup mangé.
Ni Michèle ni moi ne voulions rentrer.	Nous avons beaucoup parlé.
Il était minuit.	Nous sommes rentrés.

Hier soir, ma petite amie Michèle voulait sortir, alors nous sommes allés au cinéma...

____

____

____

____

____

____

____

____

____

____

____

____

____

NOM ______________________________ COURS ______________________________

D. Une interview. Alice raconte *(is telling about)* l'interview d'une candidate pour un poste avec sa compagnie. Récrivez le paragraphe suivant en mettant les verbes au passé composé ou à l'imparfait.

Quand j'**entre** dans le bureau, elle **est** déjà là. C'**est** une jeune femme agréable mais elle **a** l'air très nerveuse. Elle **porte** un très beau tailleur et il **est** évident qu'elle **veut** ce poste. Je l'**invite** à entrer dans mon bureau et nous **commençons** à parler. Elle **est** belge et elle **va** bientôt terminer ses études à Bruxelles où elle **veut** travailler dans notre nouveau bureau. Elle **parle** non seulement le français, mais aussi l'anglais, le néerlandais et un peu d'allemand. Nous **faisons** une partie de l'interview en anglais et son accent **est** excellent. Nous **parlons** plus d'une heure et je **suis** presque certaine que je **vais** l'engager *(hire her),* mais je ne **peux** rien dire parce qu'il y **a** encore deux autres candidats.

Quand je suis entrée dans le bureau, elle était déjà là.

____

____

____

____

____

____

____

____

____

____

____

E. Un autre point de vue. La candidate qu'Alice a interviewée parle à une amie. Complétez leur conversation en mettant les verbes entre parenthèses au passé composé ou à l'imparfait.

— Alors, tu ________________ (avoir) ton interview aujourd'hui? C'________________ (être) à quelle heure?

— C'________________ (être) à neuf heures, mais je (j') ________________ (penser) que c'________________ (être) à huit heures et demie et je (j') ________________ (arriver) trop tôt. Je (J') ________________ (devoir) attendre *(to wait)* plus d'une demi-heure.

— Tu ________________ (mettre) ton nouveau tailleur?

— Non, je ____________________ (ne pas pouvoir) trouver la jupe alors je (j') ____________________ (mettre) mon vieux tailleur. Je (J') ____________________ (avoir) l'air affreuse *(horrible)*.

— Comment __________________ (être) la personne avec qui tu __________________ (parler)?

— Elle ____________________ (être) très sympa, mais c'____________________ (être) une Américaine et je (j') ____________________ (devoir) parler anglais avec elle. Je suis sûre qu'elle ____________________________ (ne rien comprendre) avec mon mauvais accent!

— Et elle, elle _________________ (avoir) un accent quand elle _________________ (parler) français?

— Oui, un peu. Mais je suis certaine que je (j') ____________________ (faire) mauvaise impression.

If you have access to Système-D software, you will find the following phrases there.
PHRASES: Sequencing events; Describing weather; VOCABULARY: Leisure; Sports;
GRAMMAR: Compound past tense; Past imperfect

Journal. Décrivez une sortie *(outing)* récente avec des amis. Dans votre paragraphe, utilisez le passé composé pour dire ce que vous avez fait et l'imparfait pour décrire la situation.

____

____

____

____

____

____

____

____

____

____

____

____

____

NOM ______________________ COURS ______________________

CHAPITRE 7
La vie quotidienne

COMPÉTENCE 1 Telling about relationships

Dans le journal à la fin de cette ***Compétence,*** vous allez parler des relations personnelles et des qualités que vous trouvez importantes chez un(e) partenaire.

A. Des définitions. Écrivez les mots de vocabulaire présentés à la page 234 du livre qui correspondent aux définitions suivantes.

1. Une personne qui n'est pas encore mariée est ______________________.

2. Une femme qui a perdu *(has lost)* son mari est ______________________.

3. Quand on tombe amoureux de façon soudaine, ça s'appelle le ______________________.

4. Si on a terminé légalement son mariage, on est ______________________.

5. Un homme et une femme mariés qui n'habitent plus ensemble sont ______________________.

B. Et vous? Répondez aux questions suivantes avec une phrase complète.

1. Êtes-vous célibataire, fiancé(e), marié(e), séparé(e), divorcé(e) ou veuf (veuve)?

____

2. Est-ce que vous tombez facilement amoureux (amoureuse)?

____

3. Quelles sont les qualités les plus importantes pour vous chez un(e) partenaire? Sa personnalité? Son apparence physique? Son éducation? Sa classe sociale? Sa religion? Sa situation économique? Son passé?

____

____

4. Combien d'enfants voulez-vous avoir?

____

5. Pour vous, est-ce que votre carrière est plus importante, aussi importante ou moins importante que le mariage et la famille?

____

____

6. Est-ce que les sentiments jouent un rôle très important dans votre vie?

____

7. Que doit-on faire pour être heureux *(happy)* dans la vie?

____

C. Les verbes et les noms. Parcourez *(skim)* la lecture *Il n'est jamais trop tard!* aux pages 236–237 du livre et trouvez un verbe de la même famille que les noms suivants. Si vous n'êtes pas certain(e) de la forme de l'infinitif d'un verbe conjugué, consultez un dictionnaire.

EXEMPLE un habitant **habiter**

1. un retour ____________________
2. l'admiration ____________________
3. un arrêt d'autobus ____________________
4. la ressemblance ____________________
5. une décision ____________________
6. un regard ____________________
7. un gardien ____________________
8. un passage ____________________
9. un rêve ____________________
10. une plante ____________________

D. André ou Rosalie? Relisez *Il n'est jamais trop tard!* aux pages 236–237 du livre et indiquez si chaque phrase décrit **André** ou **Rosalie.** Écrivez le nom approprié dans le blanc.

1. ____________________ est célibataire.
2. ____________________ est veuve.
3. ____________________ est tombé amoureux de ____________________ il y a très longtemps, avant la Seconde Guerre mondiale.
4. ____________________ a des enfants et des petits-enfants.
5. La première fois que ____________________ est tombée amoureuse, ça a été le coup de foudre.
6. L'amour de (d') ____________________ pour ____________________, après toutes ces années, est un exemple du grand amour.

NOM ______________________ COURS ______________________

E. Maintenant et autrefois. Voici quelques détails sur la vie actuelle *(current)* d'André et de Rosalie. Mettez les phrases suivantes à l'imparfait pour les décrire *(to describe them)* juste après la Seconde Guerre mondiale.

EXEMPLE Maintenant, André a soixante-cinq ans et il est à la retraite *(retired).*
Juste après la guerre, André avait dix-huit ans et il travaillait.

1. Maintenant, Rosalie habite à Atlanta.

____

2. Maintenant, André est amoureux de Rosalie.

____

3. Maintenant, Rosalie comprend qu'il l'aime.

____

4. Maintenant, Rosalie est veuve.

____

5. Maintenant, Rosalie va se marier *(to marry)* avec André.

____

6. Maintenant, Rosalie veut passer le reste de sa vie à Rouen.

____

F. Dans le passé. Voici des descriptions des relations amoureuses dans le monde moderne. Indiquez si vous êtes d'accord avec chaque description en traçant un cercle autour de *(circling)* **vrai** ou de **faux.** Ensuite, utilisez l'imparfait pour dire si la situation était la même il y a cinquante ans.

EXEMPLE (VRAI) FAUX Aujourd'hui, le divorce est assez commun.
Il y a cinquante ans, le divorce n'était pas très commun.

1. VRAI FAUX Les relations amoureuses sont très compliquées.

____

2. VRAI FAUX Il y a beaucoup de familles monoparentales *(single-parent).*

____

3. VRAI FAUX On rencontre rarement le vrai amour.

____

4. VRAI FAUX Les couples ont généralement un ou deux enfants.

____

5. VRAI FAUX Les jeunes cohabitent (= habitent ensemble) souvent avant le mariage.

____

G. Les petites annonces. Lisez les petites annonces suivantes et répondez à la question qui suit.

JH 23 ans, timide, aimant arts, sports, cherche JF tendre, gaie, pour amitié, sorties (cinéma, musées), relation durable, vie ensemble, peut-être mariage? Contacter: BP 09456

JF 27 ans, vive, sportive, idéaliste, indépendante, intellectuelle cherche JH 25 à 35 ans, stable, honnête, ouvert, pour relation durable. Peut-être plus? Contacter: BP 08654

Veuve, 44 ans, encore dynamique et voulant retrouver joie de vivre, cherche H, 36 à 55 ans pour sorties, conversation intelligente, bals, dîners, peut-être plus? Je suis sincère et honnête, vous devez l'être aussi.
Réponses sérieuses à: BP 067398

H mûr, 46 ans, très seul, cherche F, âge ouvert, aimant cuisine, sorties, dîners intimes, camping, vie à la maison, pour mariage/ménage durable. Répondez si vous êtes vraiment sérieuse.
Contacter: BP 076523

Qu'est-ce que les abréviations suivantes veulent dire?

1. H ______________________________ 3. F ______________________________

2. JH ______________________________ 4. JF ______________________________

SYSTÈME-D

If you have access to Système-D software, you will find the following phrases there.
PHRASES: Writing a news item; Describing people; VOCABULARY: Personality; Leisure; Sports

Journal. Vous avez un(e) ami(e) qui se sent très seul(e). Écrivez une petite annonce pour votre ami(e) en suivant les modèles précédents. Mentionnez au moins cinq ou six qualités qui sont importantes pour votre ami(e). (Vous voulez trouver quelqu'un de bien pour votre ami(e), n'est-ce pas?)

____

____

____

____

____

____

____

NOM ______________________________ COURS ______________________________

COMPÉTENCE 2 Describing your daily routine

> **D**ans le journal à la fin de cette ***Compétence,*** vous allez décrire votre routine quotidienne *(daily).*

A. Que font-ils? Expliquez ce que font les personnes suivantes dans chacune des images.

1. 

2. 

3. 

1. Marcel ____.

2. Mme Carrard ____.

3. Christine ____.

4. 

5. 

6. 

4. Lin ____.

5. Monique ____.

6. Patricia ____.

B. Et votre journée? Répondez aux questions suivantes avec une phrase complète.

1. Le matin, est-ce que vous vous réveillez facilement ou avec difficulté?

____

2. Chez vous, est-ce que tout le monde se réveille de bonne humeur généralement? Qui se réveille de mauvaise humeur?

____

3. Généralement, qui se lève en premier chez vous?

____

4. Quel jour est-ce que vous vous levez le plus tôt?

____

5. Préférez-vous prendre un bain ou une douche?

____

6. Est-ce que vous vous lavez les cheveux tous les jours?

____

7. Combien de fois par jour est-ce que vous vous brossez les dents?

____

8. Est-ce que vous vous habillez avant le petit déjeuner ou après?

____

9. Quand est-ce que vous vous amusez?

____

10. Quand est-ce que vous vous ennuyez?

____

11. Quand est-ce que vous vous reposez?

____

C. Réfléchi ou non-réfléchi? Monsieur Fétou est professeur et il est très occupé parce qu'il a trois enfants et qu'il est veuf. Voici une description de sa journée typique. Complétez chaque phrase avec la forme correcte du verbe réfléchi ou non-réfléchi, selon le contexte.

Monsieur Fétou ____________ (lever, se lever) vers six heures, il prend sa douche et il ____________ (habiller, s'habiller). Vers sept heures, il ____________ (réveiller, se réveiller) ses enfants et il ____________ (habiller, s'habiller) le plus jeune, qui a trois ans. À l'université, monsieur Fétou est le prof préféré de tous les étudiants parce qu'il ne (n') ____________ (ennuyer, s'ennuyer) jamais ses étudiants; on ____________ (amuser, s'amuser) toujours dans son cours. De retour à la maison, monsieur Fétou voudrait ____________ (reposer, se reposer) un peu, mais il n'a pas le temps. D'abord, il ____________ (préparer, se préparer) le dîner pour la famille et ensuite, vers huit heures, il ____________ (coucher, se coucher) les enfants.

NOM ____________________ COURS ____________________

Après ça, il commence à préparer ses cours pour le lendemain *(the next day)* et il ne

__________ (coucher, se coucher) jamais avant minuit. Monsieur Fétou est très occupé

mais il ne (n') __________ (ennuyer, s'ennuyer) jamais.

D. Quel verbe? Complétez les phrases suivantes avec un verbe de la liste *à l'infinitif.* Faites attention à la forme du pronom réfléchi.

se lever se raser se coucher se reposer se laver

1. Après une longue promenade, nous avons envie de __________ un peu et de boire quelque chose.
2. Si tu est fatigué(e) tu devrais *(should)* __________.
3. Mon père a une barbe parce qu'il n'aime pas __________.
4. Est-ce que vous allez __________ ou est-ce que vous allez rester au lit toute la journée?
5. J'ai besoin de __________ les mains si nous allons manger.

E. Descriptions. Composez des phrases en utilisant un élément de chaque colonne. Écrivez deux phrases pour chaque sujet dans la colonne de gauche.

		aller		se coucher tôt / tard
		aimer		se lever tôt / tard
Moi, je...		préférer		s'ennuyer en classe
Mes amis et moi, nous...	(ne)	devoir	(pas)	s'amuser le / ce week-end
Mon/Ma meilleur(e) ami(e)...		vouloir		se raser tous les jours
En général, les étudiants...		pouvoir		se maquiller
		avoir envie de		s'habiller pour sortir
		avoir besoin de		se brosser les cheveux / les dents

Moi, je ______________________________.

Moi, je ______________________________.

Mes amis et moi, nous ______________________________.

Mes amis et moi, nous ______________________________.

Mon/Ma meilleur(e) ami(e) ______________________________.

Mon/Ma meilleur(e) ami(e) ______________________________.

En général, les étudiants ______________________________.

En général, les étudiants ______________________________.

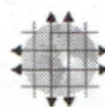

If you have access to Système-D software, you will find the following phrases there.
PHRASES: Comparing and contrasting; Making an appointment; Sequencing events
VOCABULARY: Time of day; Restaurant; Leisure; Store; Studies, courses; City

Journal. Écrivez deux paragraphes décrivant *(describing)* votre routine du lundi et du samedi. Ensuite, dans un troisième paragraphe, dites ce que vous allez faire demain.

Le lundi, ____

____

____

____

____

____

____

____.

Le samedi, ____

____

____

____

____

____

____

____.

Demain, ____

____

____

____

____

____

____

____.

NOM ______________________ COURS ______________________

COMPÉTENCE 3 Saying what you do to and for others

Dans le journal à la fin de cette ***Compétence***, vous allez raconter *(tell)* l'histoire d'un couple heureux.

A. Un couple heureux. Dites si deux personnes qui s'aiment vraiment font les choses suivantes.

EXEMPLE se respecter *Oui, ils se respectent.*

1. se parler de tout ______________________
2. se disputer souvent ______________________
3. s'embrasser souvent ______________________
4. se détester ______________________
5. se comprendre bien ______________________

B. Votre meilleur(e) ami(e) et vous. Dites si votre meilleur(e) ami(e) et vous faites les choses mentionnées dans ***A. Un couple heureux.***

EXEMPLE *Oui, nous nous respectons.*

1. ______________________
2. ______________________
3. ______________________
4. ______________________
5. ______________________

C. Une interview. Vous interviewez un couple célèbre sur leur vie ensemble. Quelles questions posez-vous pour obtenir *(to get)* les réponses données?

EXEMPLE *Où est-ce que vous vous êtes rencontrés?*
Nous nous sommes rencontrés à l'université.

1. ______________________

Nous nous sommes mariés il y a cinq ans.

2. ______________________

Nous nous disputons quand nous sommes très fatigués.

3. ____

Oui, nous nous téléphonons quelquefois pendant que *(while)* nous travaillons.

4. ____

Non, nous ne nous embrassons jamais en public!

5. ____

Nous allons souvent au cinéma pour nous amuser.

D. Ce matin. Rosalie parle de sa journée. Complétez ce paragraphe en mettant les verbes entre parenthèses au passé composé.

Je ______________________ (se réveiller) vers sept heures ce matin et Rose ______________________ (se lever) un peu plus tard. Je (J') ______________________ (faire) ma toilette et Rose ______________________ (se laver) les cheveux et ______________________ (se maquiller) avant de sortir. Nous ______________________ (aller) en ville et nous ______________________ (bien s'amuser). Nous ______________________ (faire) du shopping, puis nous ______________________ (aller) dans un café où nous ______________________ (prendre) un verre et nous ______________________ (se reposer) un peu. Après le café, nous ______________________ (se quitter). Rose et ses amis ______________________ (se retrouver) pour aller au cinéma. Moi, je ______________________ (se promener) encore un peu en ville, puis je (j') ______________________ (rentrer) à la maison.

E. Dans ma famille. Décrivez votre famille en répondant aux questions suivantes.

1. Où est-ce que vos parents se sont rencontrés?

____

2. Est-ce qu'ils se sont mariés tout de suite?

____

3. Qui dans votre famille se ressemble beaucoup?

____

4. Est-ce que vous vous disputiez souvent avec vos frères et vos sœurs quand vous étiez petit(e)?

____

5. Est-ce qu'on s'embrassait souvent dans votre famille?

____

6. De quoi *(about what)* est-ce que vous parliez généralement pendant les repas?

____

F. La rencontre. Rosalie raconte comment André et elle se sont rencontrés après toutes ces années. Que dit-elle? Écrivez un paragraphe en utilisant les verbes et expressions suivantes au passé composé.

NE PAS SE VOIR se regarder
s'embrasser SE PROMENER EN VILLE
se rencontrer par hasard se quitter

André et moi, nous nous sommes rencontrés par hasard au café aujourd'hui. Au

début *(at first)* ____

____

____

____

____

____

____.

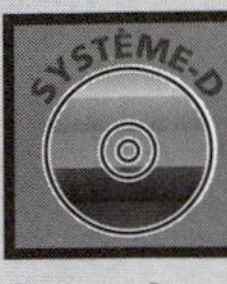

If you have access to Système-D software, you will find the following phrases there.
PHRASES: Comparing and contrasting; Describing people; Expressing an opinion
VOCABULARY: Personality

Journal. Décrivez un couple que vous connaissez qui est heureux *(happy)* ensemble. Racontez une petite histoire de leur passé et expliquez pourquoi ils continuent à bien s'entendre.

NOM ______________________ COURS ______________________

COMPÉTENCE 4 Comparing your past and present activities

Dans le journal à la fin de cette ***Compétence,*** vous allez parler de vos attitudes quand vous étiez plus jeune.

A. Une vie agréable. Décrivez-vous à l'âge de quinze ans en répondant aux questions suivantes avec des phrases complètes.

1. Est-ce que vous vous sentiez bien dans votre peau quand vous étiez étudiant(e) à l'école secondaire?

____

2. Est-ce que vous vous intéressiez aux études?

____

3. Est-ce que vous vous intéressiez plus aux sciences, aux maths, aux beaux-arts, à la littérature ou au sport?

____

4. Est-ce que vous étiez fort(e) en maths?

____

5. Est-ce que vous étiez sage ou espiègle?

____

6. Est-ce que vous vous amusiez à l'école ou est-ce que vous vous ennuyiez?

____

7. Arriviez-vous toujours à l'heure à l'école ou arriviez-vous quelquefois en retard?

____

B. Non! C'est le contraire! Exprimez le contraire des phrases suivantes en remplaçant les verbes en caractères gras *(boldfaced)* par le verbe **sortir (de)** ou **partir (de / pour).**

1. Alain et Catherine **arrivent** ici aujourd'hui.

____

2. Nous **entrons** par la porte de gauche *(left)*.

____

3. Luc **arrive de** Rouen demain.

____

4. Nous **restons à la maison** tous les soirs.

____

5. Micheline **entre dans** l'hôtel.

____

C. Le jour du départ. Voici ce que font deux touristes, Catherine et Alain, le matin de leur départ. Complétez les phases en mettant les verbes entre parenthèses au présent.

Drring! Le réveil *(alarm clock)* ____________________ (sonner *to ring*) à 6h30. Comme leur vol *(flight)* ________________ (partir) à 11h00, ils ________________ (avoir) encore du temps, alors Catherine ____________________ (dormir) encore un peu avant de se lever parce qu'elle ________________ (se sentir) un peu fatiguée. Alain ________________ (sortir) pour faire du jogging parce qu'il ________________ (vouloir) faire un peu d'exercice. Quand Alain ________________ (rentrer) du parc, il ________________ (réveiller) Catherine, puis ils ________________ (prendre) une douche et ils ________________ (s'habiller). Ensuite, ils ____________________ (prendre) le petit déjeuner et après, Alain ________________ (remarquer *to notice*) qu'il ________________ (être) déjà 10h30. Ils ____________________ (sortir) de la chambre en vitesse et l'employé à la réception ______________________________ (appeler) un taxi pour Catherine et Alain, mais ils ________________ (arriver) à l'aéroport à 11h10. Heureusement *(luckily)*, leur vol est parti avec une heure de retard.

NOM ______________________________ COURS ______________________________

D. Au passé. Récrivez le passage de l'exercice précédent au passé en mettant les verbes au passé composé ou à l'imparfait.

Drring! Le réveil a sonné à 6h30. ______________________________

____

____

____

____

____

____

____

____

____

____

____

____

____

____

____

____

E. Un dîner de fiançailles *(engagement)*. Racontez l'histoire suivante au passé en mettant les verbes entre parenthèses au passé composé ou à l'imparfait.

Rose ______________________________(décider) de faire un dîner pour Rosalie et André. Elle ______________________ (aller) au marché où elle ______________________ (acheter) tous les ingrédients pour préparer du poulet au cidre doux, une spécialité de la région. Rose ______________________(espérer) aussi trouver une bonne bouteille de champagne parce qu'elle ______________________ (vouloir) célébrer les fiançailles de sa grand-mère et de son futur grand-père. Elle ______________________ (demander) dans plusieurs magasins, mais personne n' ______________________ (avoir) de champagne. Comme c' ______________________ (être) curieux! Quand elle ______________________ (rentrer) à la maison, elle ______________________ (commencer) à tout préparer dans la cuisine. Elle ______________________ (travailler) tranquillement quand soudain Rosalie ______________________ (entrer).

— Bonjour mamie, a dit Rose, je prépare un bon dîner pour André et toi! C'est pour célébrer vos fiançailles.

— Merci Rose, c'est très gentil! Mais tu sais, il te manque *(you're missing)* une chose obligatoire pour une fête de fiançailles normande…

— Oui, je sais, mais je ______________________ (ne pas pouvoir) trouver de champagne en ville…

— Mais non! Ici en Normandie on préfère le cidre bouché, c'est une vieille tradition. Mais ne t'inquiète pas… Je (J') ______________________ (faire) des courses et j' ______________________ (acheter) deux bouteilles de cidre, alors nous en avons pour ce soir!

SYSTÈME-D

If you have access to Système-D software, you will find the following phrases there.
PHRASES: Weighing alternatives; Comparing and contrasting; Expressing an opinion
VOCABULARY: Trades, occupation; Family members; Leisure; Sickness

Journal. Décrivez deux périodes de votre vie: l'une où vous vous sentiez bien dans votre peau et l'autre où vous vous sentiez mal dans votre peau. Donnez autant de détails que possible pour décrire votre situation et pour expliquer vos sentiments.

____

____

____

____

____

____

____

____

____

NOM ______________________ COURS ______________________

CHAPITRE 8
La bonne cuisine

COMPÉTENCE 1 Ordering at a restaurant

Dans le journal à la fin de cette ***Compétence,*** vous allez écrire un paragraphe décrivant votre dernier dîner au restaurant.

A. **Un dîner.** Écrivez le nom de chaque aliment *(food)* illustré dans la liste appropriée.

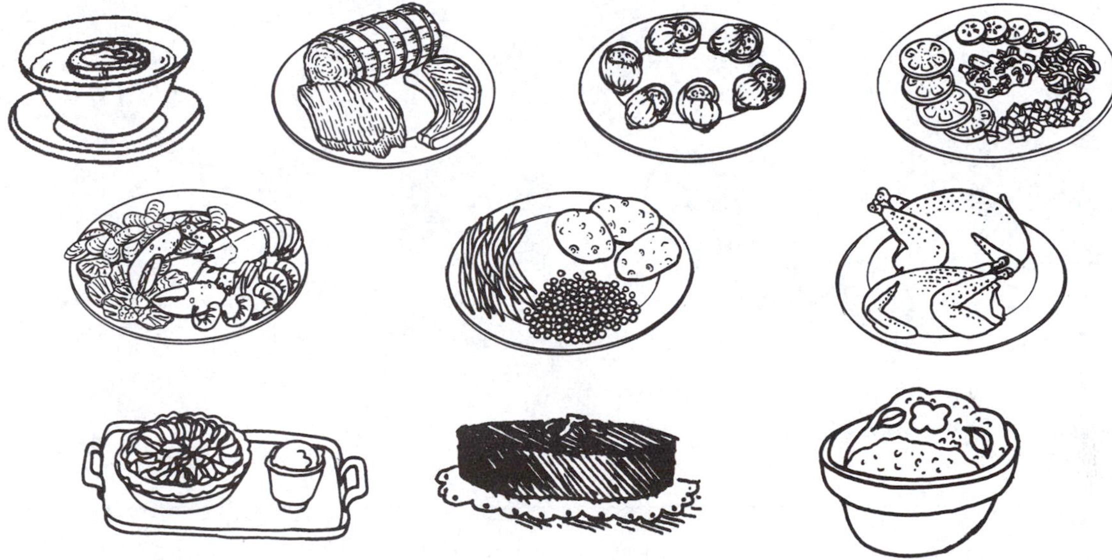

UNE ENTRÉE (UN HORS-D'ŒUVRE)	UNE VIANDE, UNE VOLAILLE OU UN FRUIT DE MER
______________________	______________________
______________________	______________________
______________________	______________________
______________________	______________________
______________________	______________________

UN LÉGUME	UN DESSERT
______________________	______________________
______________________	______________________
______________________	______________________
______________________	______________________
______________________	______________________

B. Qu'est-ce que c'est? Demandez à quelqu'un de vous passer les choses suivantes.

EXEMPLE

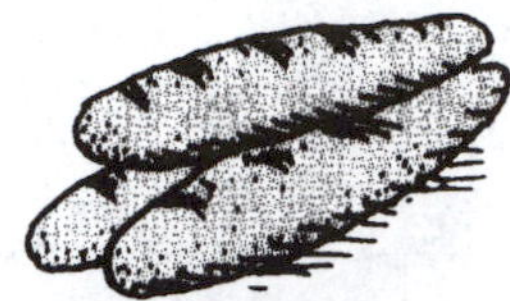

1.

2.

EXEMPLE Pouvez-vous me passer le pain, s'il vous plaît?

1. ____

2. ____

C. Au restaurant. Vous commandez les choses suivantes au restaurant. Répondez aux questions du serveur.

LE SERVEUR: Que voulez-vous comme entrée?

VOUS: ____

LE SERVEUR: Et comme plat principal?

VOUS: ____

LE SERVEUR: Et avec ça, des carottes ou du riz?

VOUS: ____

LE SERVEUR: Et comme boisson?

VOUS: ____

NOM ______________________________ COURS ______________________________

D. Explications. Au restaurant, il faut souvent demander au serveur d'expliquer le menu. Voici quelques expressions utiles:

Qu'est-ce que c'est que *la terrine de lapin?*	*What is* ***la terrine de lapin?***
Est-ce que c'est servi avec une sauce?	*Is it served with a sauce?*
C'est une sorte de tarte?	*Is it a sort of pie?*
Que veut dire *service compris?*	*What does* ***service compris*** *mean?*
C'est comme un flan?	*Is it like a flan?*

Maintenant, regardez le menu suivant du restaurant La Marine. Il y a probablement des plats que vous ne connaissez pas. Quelles questions allez-vous poser au serveur? Basez-vous sur les explications du serveur.

EXEMPLE VOUS: *Qu'est-ce que c'est que le faux-filet frites, s'il vous plaît?*
LE SERVEUR: C'est un steak avec des pommes frites.

1. VOUS: ______________________________
____
______________________________?

LE SERVEUR: C'est une assiette de légumes crus *(raw)*.

2. VOUS: ______________________________
____

LE SERVEUR: Oui, on sert les crudités avec une sauce vinaigrette.

3. VOUS: ______________________________
____
______________________________?

LE SERVEUR: Non, non, les moules marinières, ce n'est pas une sorte de pâté. Ce sont des fruits de mer.

4. VOUS: ______________________________
____
______________________________?

LE SERVEUR: Oui, c'est comme un flan, mais au caramel.

5. VOUS: ______________________________
____
______________________________?

LE SERVEUR: Cela veut dire que vous devez payer séparément vos boissons.

RESTAURANT LA MARINE

vous propose son...

Menu à 89 F — prix net — service compris

Moules marinières

Soupe de poissons

Crêpe jambon fromage

Assiette de crudités

———

6 Huîtres fines ou spéciales

Filet de poisson sauce marine

Poulet rôti frites

Faux-filet frites

———

Salade ou Fromages

———

Crème caramel

Mousse au chocolat

Glace

Coupe glacée au choix (suppl. 17 F)

Crêpe confiture, chocolat ou crème de marron

Boissons en sus

E. Préférences. Répondez aux questions suivantes avec une phrase complète.

1. Au restaurant, préférez-vous vous asseoir à l'intérieur ou sur la terrasse?

____

2. Préférez-vous être dans la section fumeur *(smoking)* ou non-fumeur?

____

3. Prenez-vous souvent un apéritif?

____

4. Préférez-vous la viande, les fruits de mer ou le poisson, ou êtes-vous végétarien(ne)?

____

5. Prenez-vous généralement un dessert?

____

6. Est-ce que vous prenez du sucre ou du lait dans votre café?

____

SYSTÈME-D

If you have access to Système-D software, you will find the following phrases there.
PHRASES: Describing objects; Expressing an opinion; Linking ideas; VOCABULARY: Restaurant; Meals; Food; Cheeses; Bread; Drinks; Fruits; Seafood; Vegetables

Journal. Écrivez un paragraphe décrivant votre dernier dîner dans un restaurant élégant. Dites...

- à quel restaurant vous êtes allé(e).
- avec qui vous avez dîné.
- quels plats et quelles boissons chacun a commandés.
- comment vous avez trouvé ce que vous avez mangé.
- comment vous avez trouvé l'ambiance *(f)*.

____

____

____

____

____

____

____

NOM ______________________ COURS ______________________

COMPÉTENCE 2 Talking about breakfast and lunch

Dans le journal à la fin de cette ***Compétence,*** vous allez décrire ce que vous mangez et buvez régulièrement.

A. Le petit déjeuner. Écrivez le nom des aliments *(foods)* et boissons qu'on prend au petit déjeuner ici ou en France.

1. ______________

2. ______________

3. ______________

4. ______________

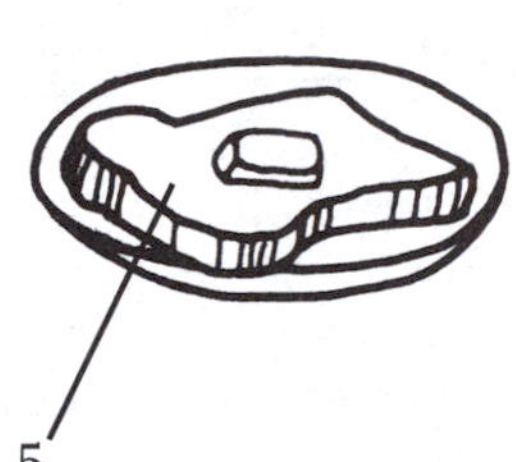

5. ______________

6. ______________

7. ______________

un petit déjeuner américain / canadien

1. ______________

2. ______________

3. ______________

4. ______________

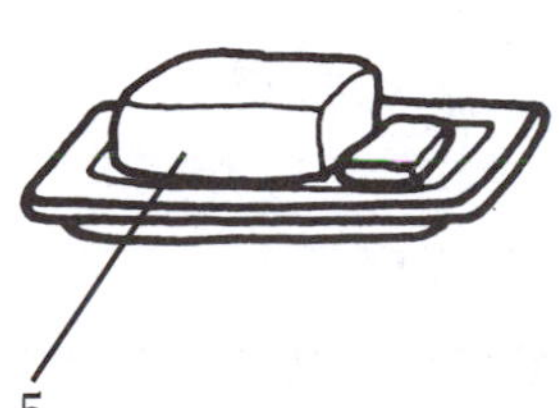

5. ______________

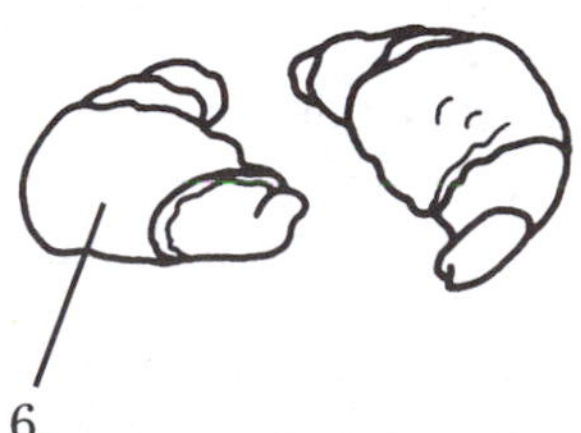

6. ______________

un petit déjeuner français

B. Des repas logiques. Nommez au moins trois choses qu'on peut prendre pour le repas nommé dans les endroits indiqués.

1. un déjeuner dans un fast-food, style américain

____

2. un dîner dans un restaurant élégant

____

C. Le partitif. André a invité des amis chez lui pour fêter ses fiançailles *(engagement).* Complétez le paragraphe suivant par **du, de la, de l', des, de** ou **d'.**

André a beaucoup ________ courses à faire avant la fête! D'abord, il doit acheter ________ boissons: ________ vin, ________ jus de fruits, ________ eau minérale et ________ bière. Ensuite, il va aller à la charcuterie pour acheter ________ pâté, ________ saucisson et ________ jambon pour les canapés. Enfin, il va passer à la boulangerie pour acheter ________ pain, ________ tartelettes et ________ croissants. Pauvre André! Combien est-ce que tout cela va coûter?

D. Qu'est-ce qu'ils boivent? Nommez une boisson que les personnes indiquées boivent probablement à l'occasion donnée. Complétez chaque phrase avec le verbe **boire** et une boisson logique.

EXEMPLE vos amis et vous, pour un pique-nique à la plage
Nous buvons du coca et des jus de fruit.

1. des amis, pour leur anniversaire de mariage

Ils ____.

2. un ami, pour une soirée de football télévisé avec des amis

Il ____.

3. vos camarades de classe et vous, après un examen difficile

Nous ____.

4. vous, pour l'anniversaire de votre petite nièce ou de votre petit neveu

Je ____.

NOM ______________________ COURS ______________________

E. Que manger et boire? Qu'est-ce que vous aimez manger ou boire dans les situations suivantes? Répondez par une phrase complète.

1. quand vous avez très soif

____

2. quand vous avez envie de quelque chose de sucré

____

3. quand vous avez envie d'un fruit

____

4. quand vous n'avez pas très faim

____

5. quand vous avez très sommeil mais que vous ne devez pas dormir

____

6. quand vous voulez célébrer la fin du semestre / trimestre

____

F. Et vous? Décrivez-vous en complétant les phrases suivantes.

1. Quelquefois, j'ai peur de (d') ______________________.
2. Demain, j'ai l'intention de (d') ______________________.
3. Cette semaine, j'ai besoin de (d') ______________________.
4. L'été prochain, j'ai envie de (d') ______________________.

G. Qu'est-ce qu'ils ont? Décrivez les personnes suivantes en utilisant une expression avec **avoir.**

EXEMPLE J'...

1. Anne...

2. Les enfants...

EXEMPLE *J'ai froid.*

1. ______________________
2. ______________________

3. Mes copains et moi...

4. Vous...?

5. Nous...

3. ____________________

4. ____________________

5. ____________________

If you have access to Système-D software, you will find the following phrases there.
PHRASES: Comparing and contrasting; Expressing an opinion; Sequencing events;
VOCABULARY: Meals; Food; Cheeses; Bread; Drinks; Fruits; Pastry; Seafood; Vegetables

Journal. Décrivez votre petit déjeuner, votre déjeuner et votre dîner pour une journée typique. Pour chaque repas, expliquez:

- où vous mangez.
- à quelle heure vous mangez.
- avec qui vous mangez.
- ce que vous mangez et ce que vous buvez.

Au petit déjeuner ____________________

____

____

____

Au déjeuner ____________________

____

____

____

Au dîner ____________________

____

____

____

____

NOM ______________________ COURS ______________________

COMPÉTENCE 3 Buying food

Dans le journal à la fin de cette ***Compétence,*** vous allez décrire comment vous faites le marché.

A. Qu'est-ce qu'on achète dans ce magasin? Nommez au moins trois choses qu'on peut acheter dans chacun des endroits suivants.

EXEMPLE

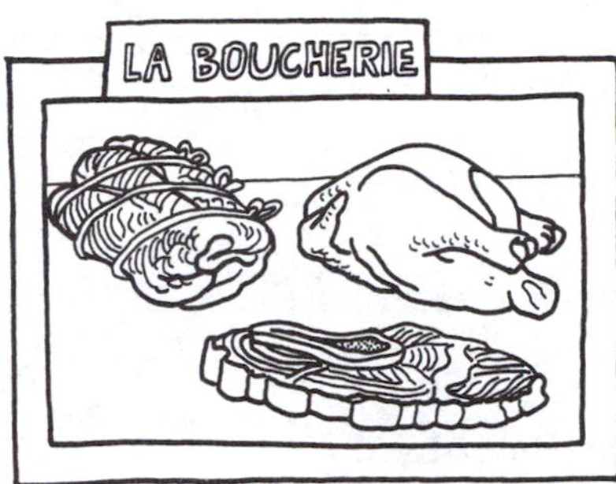

À la boucherie, on peut acheter du bœuf, du porc et du poulet.

1. 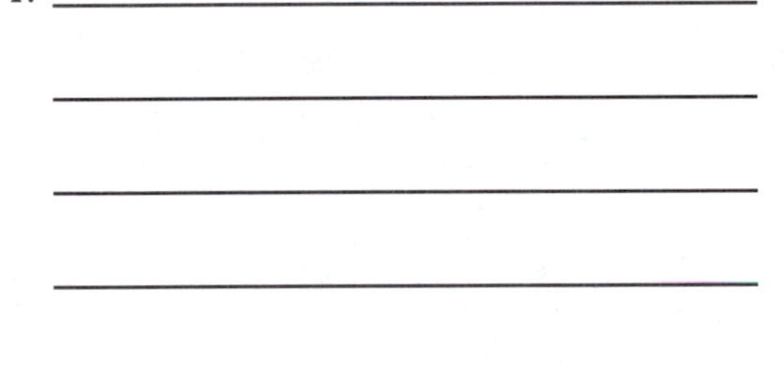

2. 

____

____

____

____

____

3. 

4.

____

____

____

B. Qu'est-ce qu'il faut? Écrivez au moins deux ingrédients nécessaires à la préparation des plats *(dishes)* suivants.

EXEMPLE un sandwich au pâté **Il faut du pain et du pâté.**

1. une omelette au jambon ______________________________
2. une salade de fruits ______________________________
3. une soupe à l'oignon ______________________________
4. une soupe de légumes ______________________________

C. Les quantités. Vous faites les courses. Complétez les phrases suivantes avec **de** ou **d'** et un nom logique pour chaque quantité.

EXEMPLE Je voudrais une bouteille ***d'eau minérale***, s'il vous plaît.

1. Il me faut une douzaine ______________________________, s'il vous plaît.
2. Donnez-moi cinq tranches ______________________________, s'il vous plaît.
3. J'ai besoin d'un kilo ______________________________, s'il vous plaît.
4. Je voudrais aussi cent grammes ______________________________, s'il vous plaît.
5. Et donnez-moi un morceau ______________________________ aussi, s'il vous plaît.
6. Et avec ça, une livre ______________________________, s'il vous plaît.

NOM ________________________________ COURS ________________________________

D. Préférences. D'abord dites si vous aimez les aliments illustrés. Ensuite, dites si vous en mangez **beaucoup, assez** ou **très peu** en utilisant le pronom **en.**

EXEMPLE  Je n'aime pas beaucoup la viande. J'en mange très peu.

1.  ____
____

2.  ____
____

3.  ____
____

4. ____
____

5.  ____
____

6. 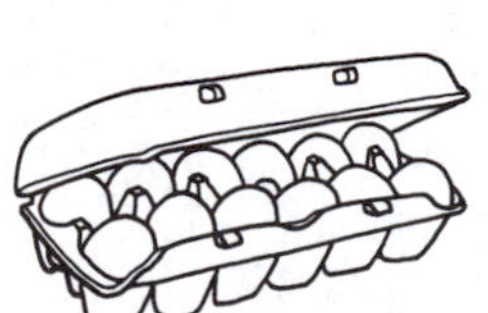 ____
____

7.  ____
____

8. 

____
____

E. Quantités. Répondez aux questions suivantes en utilisant le pronom **en** pour remplacer les mots soulignés *(underlined)*.

EXEMPLE Prenez-vous beaucoup de sucre dans votre café?
Je n'en prends pas (beaucoup) dans mon café.

1. Buvez-vous quelquefois du vin avec le dîner?

____

2. Mangez-vous souvent des hamburgers?

____

3. Buvez-vous du café le matin?

____

4. Où peut-on acheter du pain français ici?

____

5. Avez-vous mangé du fromage Neufchâtel de Normandie?

____

If you have access to Système-D software, you will find the following phrases there.
PHRASES: Linking ideas; Weighing alternatives; VOCABULARY: Fish; Flowers; Food; Bread; Cheeses; Quantity; Fruits; Vegetables; Meat; Seafood

Journal. Écrivez un paragraphe expliquant où et quand vous aimez faire vos courses. Parlez aussi de ce que vous achetez le plus souvent.

____

____

____

____

____

____

____

____

____

____

COMPÉTENCE 4 Choosing a healthy lifestyle

Dans le journal à la fin de cette ***Compétence,*** vous allez parler de ce que vous devriez faire pour améliorer votre vie.

A. La bonne santé. Parlez de votre santé en répondant aux questions suivantes avec une phrase complète.

1. Est-ce que vous faites très attention à votre santé?

____

2. Qu'est-ce que vous avez besoin de faire pour améliorer votre condition physique?

____

3. Quand vous vous sentez mal, est-ce que vous allez voir le médecin généralement?

____

4. Est-ce que vous évitez le tabac et l'alcool?

____

5. Est-ce que vous faites des haltères ou de l'aérobic?

____

6. Pour maigrir, est-ce que vous préférez manger moins ou faire de l'exercice?

____

7. Pour éviter les matières grasses, quels aliments est-ce qu'on devrait éviter?

____

8. Quels aliments sont riches en protéines?

____

B. Combien? Utilisez **plus de, moins de** et **autant de** *(as much)* pour comparer votre comportement *(behavior)* quand vous étiez au lycée à votre comportement actuel *(current).*

EXEMPLE faire de l'exercice
Je faisais plus (moins, autant) d'exercice que maintenant.

1. boire de l'eau minérale ____

2. manger de la viande ____

3. faire de l'aérobic ______________________________

4. prendre des vitamines ______________________________

5. avoir du stress ______________________________

6. boire du café ______________________________

C. Maigrir ou grossir? Dites si on fait les choses indiquées en mangeant souvent les aliments ou en buvant souvent les boissons dans les illustrations suivantes.

EXEMPLE 1. 2.

3. 4. 5.

SUCRE

LAIT

EXEMPLE maigrir *On ne maigrit pas si on mange souvent du bifteck.*

1. maigrir ______________________________

2. éviter les matières grasses ______________________________

3. rester en bonne santé ______________________________

4. grossir ______________________________

5. avoir plus d'énergie ______________________________

D. Les verbes en *-ir*. Complétez les questions suivantes avec la forme correcte du verbe logique entre parenthèses. Ensuite, répondez à chaque question par une phrase complète.

1. Quand vous allez dîner au restaurant avec votre meilleur(e) ami(e), qui ______________ (finir, choisir) le restaurant généralement?

____

2. Généralement, est-ce que vous ______________ (finir, maigrir) le repas avec un dessert?

____

3. Si vous louez une cassette vidéo, quel genre de film est-ce que vous ______________ (grossir, choisir) le plus souvent?

____

4. Est-ce que vous ______________________ (rougir, réussir) quelquefois pendant les scènes d'amour?

____

5. Est-ce que vous ______________________ (rougir, réussir) à comprendre certaines phrases quand vous regardez un film français en version originale?

____

E. Dans ces conditions. Qu'est-ce qu'on ferait dans les conditions suivantes? Complétez chaque phrase avec un verbe ou une expression dans la colonne de droite. Mettez le verbe au conditionnel.

EXEMPLE *Si nous avions faim, nous mangerions quelque chose.*

Si nous avions faim, nous…	ne pas prendre beaucoup de dessert
Si les enfants avaient sommeil, ils…	boire de l'eau
Si nous avions soif, nous…	mettre un pull ou un blouson
Si j'avais froid, je…	manger quelque chose
Si j'avais tort, je…	ne pas avoir raison
Si Rose avait envie de perdre du poid, elle…	faire la sieste *(take a nap)*
Si Rosalie et André avaient peur, ils…	ne pas se marier

1. ____

2. ____

3. ____

4. ____

5. ____

6. ____

F. Que feriez-vous? Si vous vouliez améliorer votre santé, est-ce que vous feriez les choses suivantes? Mettez les verbes au conditionnel.

EXEMPLE dormir toute la journée *Je ne dormirais pas toute la journée.*

1. faire plus d'exercice ______________________

2. éviter le stress ______________________

3. boire beaucoup d'alcool ______________________

4. aller à un club de gym ______________________

5. choisir des plats sains ______________________

6. être au régime ______________________

7. se coucher plus tôt ______________________

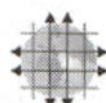

If you have access to Système-D software, you will find the following phrases there.
PHRASES: Hypothesizing; Expressing an opinion; Reassuring; VOCABULARY: Leisure; Studies, courses; University

Journal. Comment serait votre vie si tout était parfait? Écrivez un paragraphe décrivant quels changements il y aurait. Qu'est-ce qui (*what*) ne changerait pas?

NOM ______________________ COURS ______________________

CHAPITRE 9
En vacances

COMPÉTENCE 1 Talking about vacation

Dans le journal à la fin de cette ***Compétence,*** vous allez parler de vos vacances les plus agréables.

A. **Où passent-ils leurs vacances?** Regardez les illustrations suivantes et dites où les personnes indiquées ont passé leurs vacances cette année. Mentionnez aussi deux ou trois activités possibles à cet endroit.

EXEMPLE

Mes parents...

Mes parents ont passé leurs vacances à la maison. Ils n'ont pas fait grand-chose. Ils se sont reposés et ils ont travaillé dans leur jardin.

1. 

Maryse...

____

____

____

2. 

Éric et Thomas...

____

____

____

3. 

Mon frère...

____

____

____

4. 

Mon oncle et ma tante...

____

____

____

B. Que feraient-ils? Imaginez deux choses que les gens suivants feraient pendant leurs vacances dans les endroits *(places)* indiqués.

EXEMPLE Si mon meilleur ami passait ses vacances en Guadeloupe, **il irait à la plage pour faire de la planche à voile et il ferait de la plongée sous-marine aussi.**

1. Si mes amis et moi passions nos vacances à Paris, nous ______________________________

____.

2. Si mes parents passaient leurs vacances sur la Côte d'Azur, ils ______________________________

____.

3. Si je passais mes vacances à Tahiti, je ______________________________

____.

4. Si mon/ma meilleur(e) ami(e) passait ses vacances dans les Alpes près de Grenoble, il/elle

____.

5. Si ma famille et moi restions à la maison pour les vacances, nous ______________________________

____.

C. Vos vacances cette année. Vous parlez de vos vacances cette année avec un(e) ami(e). Complétez la conversation pour expliquer ce que vous comptez faire. Si vous n'avez pas encore fait de projets *(made plans)* pour vos vacances, utilisez votre imagination.

— Tu vas à la mer cette année?

— ____

— Qu'est-ce que tu as l'intention de faire?

— ____

— Combien de temps est-ce que tu penses rester?

— ____

— Quand est-ce que tu vas partir?

— ____

— Avec qui vas-tu passer les vacances?

— ____

NOM ______________________________ COURS ______________________________

D. Votre horoscope. Lisez l'horoscope et tracez un cercle autour de *(circle)* 20 verbes au futur ou au conditionnel. Aurez-vous de la chance cette semaine?

BÉLIER
DU 21 MARS AU 20 AVRIL
Mars

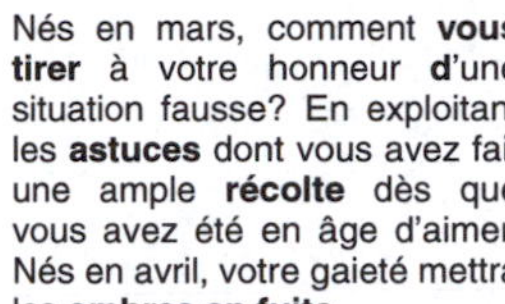

Nés en mars, comment **vous tirer** à votre honneur **d'**une situation fausse? En exploitant les **astuces** dont vous avez fait une ample **récolte** dès que vous avez été en âge d'aimer. Nés en avril, votre gaieté mettra les **ombres en fuite**.

TAUREAU
DU 21 AVRIL AU 21 MAI
Vénus

Si **maladroits** pour faire comprendre à l'être qui vous captive l'importance qu'il vient d'**acquérir** à vos yeux... Vous **échapperez** à cette gaucherie si vous êtes nés après le dix mai, mais votre sensibilité ne sera pas au rendez-vous.

GÉMEAUX
DU 22 MAI AU 21 JUIN
Mercure

Vénus vous ignore et vous lui rendez superbement **la pareille**. Les relations affectives **n'**auront **guère** d'intérêt, vous les **réduirez** au strict minimum. Bref, vous mettrez en général tous vos sentiments **en congé**.

CANCER
DU 22 JUIN AU 22 JUIL.
Lune

La présence de Vénus apportera dans votre vie privée un climat plus tendre, plus **propice** à votre **épanouissement.** Natifs de juin, ne compromettez pas vos chances de bonheur en vous montrant agressifs.

LION
DU 23 JUIL. AU 23 AOÛT
Soleil

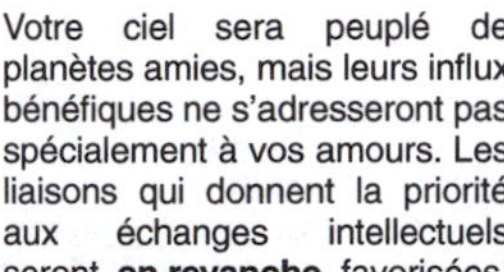

Votre ciel sera peuplé de planètes amies, mais leurs influx bénéfiques ne s'adresseront pas spécialement à vos amours. Les liaisons qui donnent la priorité aux échanges intellectuels seront, **en revanche,** favorisées.

VIERGE
DU 24 AOÛT AU 23 SEPT.
Mercure

Aucune planète ne vous sera hostile cette semaine, qu'il **s'agisse de** votre vie privée ou de votre vie professionnelle. Vous ne compterez que des amis autour de vous, sans doute parce que vous les aurez mérités.

BALANCE
DU 24 SEPT. AU 23 OCT.
Vénus

Pas toujours d'humeur ces temps-ci, **quoique** vous n'en laissez rien **transparaître**, personne ne se risquera à vous **asticoter**. Nés après le 13, vous **vous radoucirez** mais personne ne **s'en apercevra**. Repos!

SCORPION
DU 24 OCT. AU 22 NOV.
Mars et Pluton

Muets et narcissiques si vous êtes nés en octobre, vous bénificierez dans vos amours, si vous êtes nés en novembre, d'un influx vénusien qui **soufflera** sur les **cendres** de vos amours passées et en **ranimera les tisons**.

SAGITTAIRE
DU 23 NOV. AU 21 DÉC.
Jupiter

Vous ne vous sentirez pas **de taille à** vous battre tout seuls pour vos amours. Les célibataires ne prendront aucune initiative pour sortir de leur état. Les autres s'en remmettront à la providence pour consolider leurs **liens** affectifs.

CAPRICORNE
DU 22 DÉC. AU 20 JANV.
Saturne

Un gros effort serait nécessaire pour améliorer la situation présente, dans le domaine sentimental ou pour créer une relation nouvelle. Mars et Vénus ne faciliteront pas vos amours si vous êtes nés avant le 11 janvier.

VERSEAU
DU 21 JANV. AU 18 FÉV.
Uranus et Saturne

Vous ne **manquerez** pas d'enthousiasme et vous ferez volontiers l'inventaire de vos chances à venir si vous êtes célibataires, mais vous ne prendrez aucune initiative. Nés en février, vous n'aurez envie que de tranquillité.

POISSONS
DU 19 FÉV. AU 20 MARS
Neptune et Jupiter

Semaine idéale pour des vacances en amoureux, surtout si vous êtes nés avant le 11 mars. Vénus sera votre complice, elle vous rendra **séduisants** et tendres. Nés entre le 11 et le 20, c'est votre intelligence et votre esprit qui charmeront votre partenaire.

se tirer de *to get out of* **l'astuce** *(f) shrewdness* **une récolte** *harvest* **une ombre** *shadow* **en fuite** *(in flight)* **maladroit(e)** *clumsy* **acquérir** *to acquire* **échapper** *to escape* **une gaucherie** *awkardness* **la pareille** *the same* **ne... guère** *hardly* **réduire** *to reduce* **en congé** *on leave* **propice** *favorable* **un épanouissement** *blossoming* **en revanche** *on the other hand* **s'agir de** *to be a question of* **quoique** *although* **transparaître** *to show through* **asticoter** *to bug* **se radoucir** *to soften* **s'apercevoir de** *to notice* **souffler** *to blow* **une cendre** *ash* **ranimer les tisons** *to rekindle the fire* **de taille à** *up to* **les liens** *(m) ties* **manquer** *to lack* **séduisant(e)** *seductive*

E. Futur ou conditionnel? Dans le paragraphe suivant, vous dites à un ami ce que vous ferez s'il part avec vous en vacances en Guadeloupe. Plus tard vous apprenez qu'il ne peut pas vous accompagner. Récrivez le paragraphe en changeant les verbes soulignés du futur au conditionnel pour dire ce que votre ami ferait s'il pouvait partir avec vous.

Si tu vas en vacances avec nous, tu <u>verras</u> des choses incroyables. En Guadeloupe on <u>rencontrera</u> beaucoup de gens intéressants et on <u>mangera</u> de la cuisine créole. Le paysage <u>sera</u> très beau aussi. On <u>visitera</u> un volcan dormant et <u>on fera</u> de la plongée sous-marine dans l'eau claire de la mer des Antilles. Nous nous <u>amuserons</u> et tu <u>aimeras</u> beaucoup la Guadeloupe.

Si tu allais en vacances avec nous, tu verrais des choses incroyables. ______________

____

____

____

____

If you have access to Système-D software, you will find the following phrases there.
PHRASES: Describing people; Describing weather; Expressing an opinion; Sequencing events; VOCABULARY: Traveling; Geography; Countries; Leisure

Journal. Écrivez un paragraphe décrivant des vacances agréables que vous avez passées. Répondez aux questions suivantes dans votre paragraphe:

- Où êtes-vous allé(e) et avec qui?
- Combien de temps est-ce que vous êtes resté(e) dans cet endroit *(place)?*
- Quand êtes-vous parti(e) et quand êtes-vous rentré(e) chez vous?
- Quel temps faisait-il quand vous êtes arrivé(e) et quand vous êtes parti(e)?
- Comment étaient les gens que vous avez rencontrés?
- Comment était la région?
- Qu'est-ce que vous avez fait?

NOM ______________________ COURS ______________________

COMPÉTENCE 2 Making plans for a trip

Dans le journal à la fin de cette *Compétence,* vous allez parler des activités qu'on peut faire dans votre région.

A. Les continents et les pays. Indiquez où se trouvent les pays suivants en écrivant le chiffre à côté du nom.

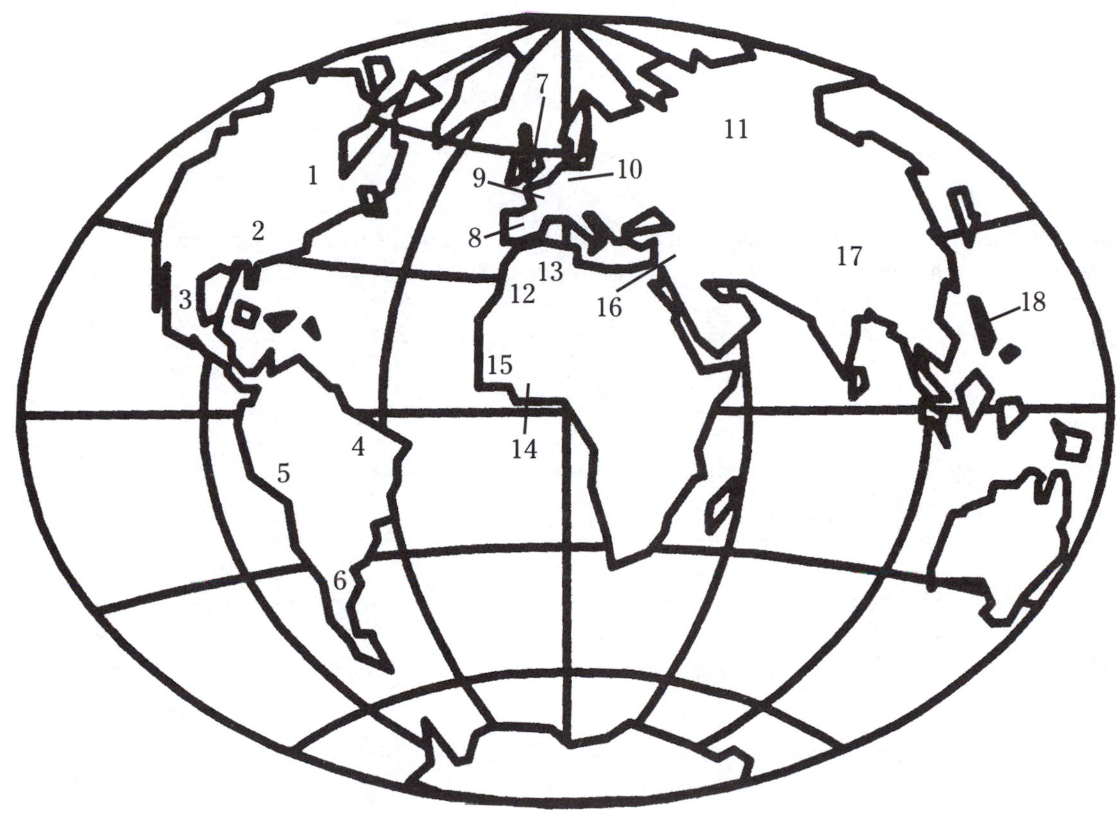

_____ l'Algérie

_____ l'Allemagne

_____ l'Argentine

_____ le Brésil

_____ le Canada

_____ la Chine

_____ la Côte-d'Ivoire

_____ les États-Unis

_____ l'Espagne

_____ la France

_____ la Grande-Bretagne

_____ Israël

_____ le Japon

_____ le Maroc

_____ le Mexique

_____ le Pérou

_____ la Russie

_____ le Sénégal

B. Dans quel pays? Répondez aux questions suivantes avec le nom des pays appropriés de *A. Les continents et les pays.* N'oubliez pas d'utiliser correctement **en, au** ou **aux** pour dire *in.*

EXEMPLE Dans quels pays est-ce qu'on parle anglais?
On parle anglais au Canada, aux États-Unis et en Grande-Bretagne.

1. Dans quels pays est-ce qu'on parle espagnol?

____

2. Dans quels pays est-ce qu'on parle français?

____

3. Dans quels pays est-ce qu'on parle arabe?

____

C. D'où viennent-ils? Vous êtes à l'aéroport. De quel pays viennent les touristes suivants? N'oubliez pas d'utiliser correctement **de, d', du** ou **des** pour dire *from.*

EXEMPLE Notre avion arrive de Moscou. Nous *venons de Russie.*

1. Mon avion arrive de Lima. Je _______________________________.
2. Leur avion arrive de Berlin. Ils _______________________________.
3. Ton avion arrive d'Abidjan? Tu _______________________________?
4. Votre avion vient de Washington? Vous _______________________________?
5. Son avion vient de Tokyo. Il _______________________________.

D. Les voyages de Christian. Voici un résumé des endroits que Christian a visités dans le monde. Complétez le paragraphe avec la préposition appropriée pour chaque ville et pays mentionnés.

Christian habite __________ États-Unis, mais il a voyagé partout! L'année dernière il est allé __________ Mexique, __________ Antilles et __________ France! Il a habité __________ Canada où il est allé à l'université de Montréal. Après, il a voyagé partout __________ Europe et il a passé quelques semaines __________ Paris où il a vu tous les monuments historiques et les musées. Ensuite, il est allé __________ Grande-Bretagne pendant une semaine, mais finalement il n'avait plus d'argent *(money)* et il a dû revenir __________ États-Unis.

E. Où sont-ils allés? Les personnes suivantes reviennent de vacances. D'où reviennent-elles? Utilisez un endroit dans la liste avec la préposition appropriée. Imaginez aussi une chose qu'elles ont fait dans cet endroit.

NOM ______________________ COURS ______________________

ÉGYPTE Antilles *Espagne* FRANCE Suisse

EXEMPLE **Mes parents reviennent d'Espagne. Ils ont visité des sites historiques et ils ont pris beaucoup de photos.**

1. Mon/Ma meilleur(e) ami(e) ______________________
____
______________________.

2. Mes cousins ______________________
____
______________________.

3. Mes amis et moi, nous ______________________
____
______________________.

4. Ma voisine ______________________
____
______________________.

F. **Chez des amis.** Vous vous occupez de la maison de vos amis pendant qu'ils sont en vacances en Afrique et vous trouvez cette note. Complétez les phrases en mettant les verbes au futur.

Nous ______________________ (arriver) en Côte-d'Ivoire à 22h00 vendredi soir. À Abidjan nous ______________________ (être) à l'hôtel International sur l'autoroute de l'Aéroport jusqu'au 20 août, quand nous ______________________ (partir) pour le Sénégal. Les enfants et Martine ______________________ (rentrer) d'Afrique le 25, mais moi, je ______________________ (faire) un voyage d'affaires. J'______________________ (aller) d'abord au Togo, ensuite je ______________________ (passer) trois jours au Congo.

G. Votre avenir. Répondez aux questions suivantes avec une phrase complète.

1. Quand est-ce que vous finirez vos études?

____

2. Quel âge aurez-vous?

____

3. Est-ce que vous ferez des études supérieures ou est-ce que vous devrez chercher du travail?

____

4. Pourrez-vous trouver facilement du travail avec votre diplôme?

____

5. Est-ce que vous habiterez dans la ville où vous habitez maintenant?

____

6. Est-ce que votre vie sera plus facile quand vous aurez votre diplôme?

____

SYSTÈME-D

If you have access to Système-D software, you will find the following phrases there.
PHRASES: Linking ideas; Sequencing events; Weighing alternatives; Giving directions;
VOCABULARY: Leisure; Store; Traveling; City; GRAMMAR: Future tense

Journal. Des amis viennent passer cinq jours dans votre région. Préparez un itinéraire expliquant ce que vous ferez ensemble chaque jour. Mettez les verbes au futur.

____

____

____

____

____

____

____

____

____

____

NOM ______________________ COURS ______________________

COMPÉTENCE 3 Discussing your trip

Dans le journal à la fin de cette ***Compétence,*** vous allez fixer un rendez-vous avec des amis.

A. L'itinéraire de Suzanne. Consultez l'itinéraire de Suzanne à la page 322 du livre et répondez aux questions suivantes avec des phrases complètes.

1. Est-ce que Suzanne a acheté un billet aller-retour ou un aller simple?

____

2. Quel jour est-ce qu'elle prendra l'avion pour aller à Abidjan?

____

3. Quel jour est-ce qu'elle retournera à Paris?

____

4. Est-ce qu'elle sera en première classe ou en classe touriste?

____

5. Est-ce qu'elle pourra fumer pendant le voyage?

____

6. À quelle heure partira-t-elle de Paris pour Abidjan?

____

7. À quelle heure arrivera-t-elle à Abidjan?

____

8. Est-ce qu'on servira un repas pendant le vol?

____

9. Est-ce que l'avion fera une escale entre Paris et Abidjan?

____

10. Combien de temps à l'avance est-ce qu'elle devrait arriver à l'aéroport?

____

11. Combien de temps à l'avance est-ce qu'elle devrait reconfirmer son retour?

____

B. Mes vacances de rêve! Imaginez que vous achetez un billet pour les vacances de vos rêves dans un autre pays. Complétez l'itinéraire suivant en utilisant l'itinéraire de Suzanne à la page 322 du livre comme exemple.

ITINÉRAIRE

À l'intention de ______________________

ALLER: ______________________

Départ de ______________________ __ h ____

______________________ __________ __________

Arrivée à ______________________ __ h ____

Un repas sera servi en vol.

RETOUR: ______________________

Départ de ______________________ __ h ____

______________________ __________ __________

Arrivée à ______________________ __ h ____

Un repas sera servi en vol.

Prix du billet aller-retour: ________ F.

Prévoyez d'arriver à l'aéroport deux heures avant l'heure de départ et n'oubliez pas de reconfirmer votre retour 72 heures avant le départ.

Maintenant, expliquez ce que vous ferez pendant ce voyage en écrivant des phrases avec les verbes suivants au futur.

EXEMPLE aller à *J'irai à Paris.*

1. aller à ______________________
2. partir de ______________________
3. (ne pas) être en première classe ______________________
4. (ne pas) pouvoir fumer pendant le vol ______________________
5. (ne pas) faire une (d') escale ______________________
6. arriver à ______________________
7. (ne pas) prendre un (de) repas pendant le vol ______________________

NOM ______________________ COURS ______________________

C. Les verbes en *–re*. Dites ce que vos amis et vous faites en conjuguant le verbe au présent. Mettez le verbe au négatif si nécessaire pour décrire correctement votre situation.

EXEMPLE Que fait votre père quand il a quelques jours de vacances?
(rendre visite à ses parents) Il **(ne) rend (pas) visite à ses parents.**

1. Que font vos amis quand vous avez rendez-vous et que vous êtes en retard?

(attendre patiemment) Ils ______________________.

(perdre patience) Ils ______________________.

2. Que faites-vous quand vous voyagez?

(descendre souvent dans un hôtel de luxe) Je ______________________

______________________.

(perdre des bagages) Je ______________________.

3. Quelle est votre relation avec vos voisins?

(s'entendre bien) Nous ______________________.

(se rendre souvent visite) Nous ______________________.

D. Qui fait ça pour vous? Dites qui fait les choses suivantes pour vous. Utilisez le pronom **me.**

EXEMPLE aider avec vos devoirs de français
Mon ami Daniel m'aide avec mes devoirs de français. /
Personne ne m'aide avec mes devoirs de français.

1. rendre souvent visite ______________________
2. inviter souvent à sortir ______________________
3. téléphoner souvent ______________________
4. attendre après les cours ______________________
5. prêter de l'argent ______________________
6. emprunter souvent quelque chose ______________________

____

E. Questions. Répondez aux questions suivantes avec une phrase complète.

1. Quand votre professeur est en retard, combien de temps est-ce que vous l'attendez?

____

2. Est-ce que vous l'avez attendu au dernier cours?

3. Est-ce que votre professeur vous pose beaucoup de questions en classe?

4. Est-ce qu'il vous explique *(explains)* la grammaire en classe?

5. Est-ce que vous l'entendez toujours bien en classe?

6. Est-ce que le professeur vous rend vos examens au début *(beginning)* ou à la fin *(end)* du cours?

7. Quand vous posez une question au professeur en anglais, est-ce qu'il vous répond en anglais ou en français?

SYSTÈME-D *If you have access to Système-D software, you will find the following phrases there.*
PHRASES: Writing a letter (informal); Asking for information; Hypothesizing; Welcoming;
VOCABULARY: Traveling; Leisure; Time of day

Journal. Des amis viennent vous rendre visite. Écrivez une lettre dans laquelle vous demandez:

- quand ils vous rendront visite.
- quel vol ils prendront.
- quand vous devriez aller les chercher à l'aéroport.
- combien de temps ils pensent rester.
- ce qu'ils voudraient faire pendant leur séjour. (Mentionnez quelques possibilités.)

NOM ______________________ COURS ______________________

COMPÉTENCE 4 Making preparations for a trip

Dans le journal à la fin de cette ***Compétence,*** vous allez expliquer pourquoi vous aimez ou pourquoi vous n'aimez pas passer du temps avec quelqu'un.

A. Préparatifs. Des amis partent en vacances. Qu'est-ce qu'ils font avant et pendant leur voyage? Racontez leur voyage en écrivant les phrases suivantes dans l'ordre logique.

PRENDRE UN TAXI POUR ALLER À L'AÉROPORT faire un itinéraire
montrer leurs passeports PARLER À L'AGENT DE VOYAGES passer à la douane
faire leurs valises emprunter de l'argent pour le voyage
écrire pour réserver une chambre d'hôtel **lire des guides touristiques**
PRENDRE L'AVION arriver en Côte-d'Ivoire **MONTER DANS L'AVION**

1. *Ils empruntent de l'argent pour le voyage.*
2. ______________________
3. ______________________
4. ______________________
5. ______________________
6. ______________________
7. ______________________
8. ______________________
9. ______________________
10. ______________________
11. ______________________
12. ______________________

B. Avant, pendant ou après? Dites si vous ferez les choses suivantes **avant de partir en voyage, pendant le voyage** ou **après le retour.** Écrivez des phrases complètes.

EXEMPLE acheter des chèques de voyage
J'achèterai des chèques de voyage avant de partir en voyage.

1. lire des guides touristiques

____

2. prendre des photos

____

3. montrer des photos du voyage à des amis

____

4. écrire des cartes postales

____

5. faire des économies

____

C. Qu'est-ce qu'ils font? Des étudiants parlent de ce qu'ils font en cours de français. Complétez ces phrases avec le verbe **dire, lire** ou **écrire.**

1. 2.  3.

1. Le professeur nous ______________ bonjour tous les jours.

2. Nous lui ______________ bonjour aussi.

3. Nous ______________ souvent au tableau.

4. 5.  6.

4. Les étudiants ______________ des questions dans le livre et ils ______________ les réponses sur une feuille de papier.

5. Je ______________ les explications de grammaire dans le livre avant le cours.

6. Nous écoutons les cassettes et nous ______________ les réponses dans le cahier. Quelquefois, je ne comprends pas bien ce qu'on ______________ sur les cassettes.

NOM ______________________ COURS ______________________

Maintenant dites si tout s'est passé de la même façon lors de *(during)* votre dernier cours de français.

1. La dernière fois, le professeur (ne) nous a (pas) dit bonjour.

2. ______________________

3. ______________________

4. ______________________

____

5. ______________________

6. ______________________

____

D. Lui ou leur? Récrivez *(Rewrite)* les phrases suivantes en utilisant le pronom **lui** ou **leur** pour remplacer les mots soulignés.

EXEMPLE Suzanne écrit une carte postale à ses amis.
Suzanne leur écrit une carte postale.

1. Suzanne téléphone à Daniel en Côte-d'Ivoire.

____

2. La Côte-d'Ivoire plaît beaucoup aux touristes français.

____

3. Daniel décrit la vie en Afrique à Suzanne.

____

4. Un guide montre le parc naturel à Daniel et Suzanne.

____

E. Et vous? Répondez aux questions suivantes en utilisant le pronom **lui** ou **leur.**

1. Est-ce que vous écrivez souvent à vos parents?

____

2. Est-ce que vous dites toujours la vérité *(truth)* à votre meilleur(e) ami(e)?

____

3. Est-ce que vous posez beaucoup de questions à votre professeur?

____

4. Est-ce que vous empruntez de l'argent à vos parents?

___

5. Est-ce que vous rendez souvent visite à vos parents?

___

6. Donnez-vous vos devoirs au professeur tous les jours?

___

F. La même chose. Vous avez passé vos vacances en Côte-d'Ivoire et vous parlez à un ami qui y a passé ses vacances l'année dernière. Chaque fois que vous dites que vous avez fait quelque chose, il dit qu'il a fait la même chose. Dans vos réponses, utilisez un pronom complément d'objet direct **(le, la, l', les)** ou indirect **(lui, leur)** ou les pronoms **y** ou **en** pour remplacer les mots soulignés.

EXEMPLE Je suis descendu à l'hôtel des Bougainvillées.
Moi aussi, j'y suis descendu.

1. J'ai rendu visite à mon frère.

___

2. J'ai lu le Guide Michelin avant de partir.

___

3. J'ai écrit une carte postale à tous nos amis.

___

4. J'ai pris beaucoup de photos.

___

SYSTÈME-D *If you have access to Système-D software, you will find the following phrases there.*
PHRASES: Describing people; Comparing and contrasting; Weighing alternatives;
VOCABULARY: Personality; GRAMMAR: Direct and indirect objects

Journal. Écrivez un paragraphe dans lequel vous décrivez votre relation avec une personne avec qui vous vous entendez bien ou avec quelqu'un avec qui vous vous entendez mal. Utilisez au moins quatre pronoms compléments d'objet direct ou indirect dans votre paragraphe.

___

___

___

___

___

NOM ______________________ COURS ______________________

CHAPITRE 10
À l'hôtel

COMPÉTENCE 1 Deciding where to stay

Dans le journal à la fin de cette *Compétence,* vous allez décrire un hôtel.

A. Comment vont-ils régler la note? Écrivez une phrase qui explique comment les personnes suivantes vont régler la note à l'hôtel.

EXEMPLE Patricia Elle va régler la note en espèces.

1. M. et Mme Duménage ______________________

2. M. et Mme Lefric ______________________

3. vos amis et vous ______________________

???

B. Quel hôtel? Relisez les descriptions du *Guide Michelin* pour *l'Hôtel Floride Étoile* et *l'Hôtel Concorde La Fayette* aux pages 350 et 351 du livre. Ensuite, lisez ci-dessous les publicités pour ces hôtels, prises *(taken)* des pages jaunes de l'annuaire de téléphone de Paris. Imaginez qu'un(e) camarade et vous travaillez à la réception de ces deux hôtels pendant l'été. Répondez aux questions suivantes avec des phrases complètes.

L'HÔTEL FLORIDE ÉTOILE

1. Où se trouve l'hôtel?

____

____

2. Avez-vous 40 chambres pour un groupe?

____

3. Acceptez-vous les cartes de crédit American Express?

____

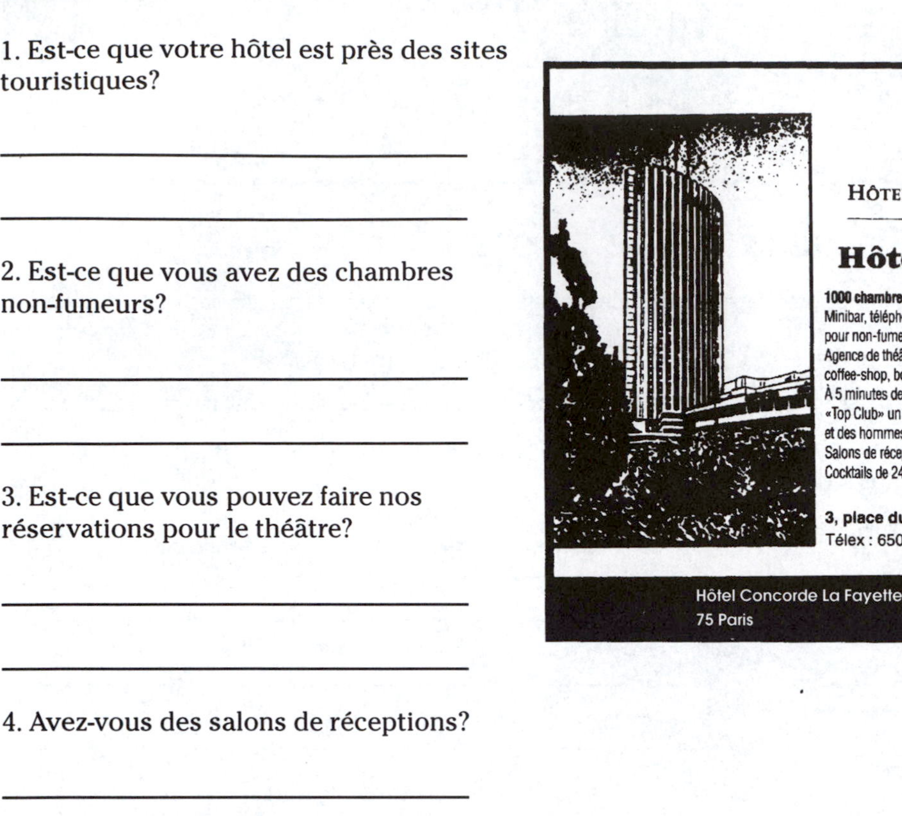

L'HÔTEL CONCORDE LA FAYETTE

1. Est-ce que votre hôtel est près des sites touristiques?

____

____

2. Est-ce que vous avez des chambres non-fumeurs?

____

____

3. Est-ce que vous pouvez faire nos réservations pour le théâtre?

____

____

4. Avez-vous des salons de réceptions?

____

____

C. À la réception. Vous êtes à la réception d'un hôtel. Complétez votre conversation avec l'hôtelier. Posez des questions logiques qui correspondent aux réponses données.

VOUS: ______________________________?

L'HÔTELIER: Oui. J'ai une chambre avec un grand lit.

VOUS: ______________________________?

L'HÔTELIER: C'est 295 F la nuit.

NOM ______________________________ COURS ______________________________

VOUS: ____?

L'HÔTELIER: Oui. J'ai une autre chambre à 180 F la nuit mais elle est petite.

VOUS: ____?

L'HÔTELIER: Non, il y a un supplément de 25 F par personne.

VOUS: ____?

L'HÔTELIER: Non, mais il y a un très bon restaurant qui est tout près.

D. Dans un hôtel. Décrivez votre dernier séjour *(stay)* dans un hôtel en répondant aux questions suivantes avec une phrase complète.

1. Dans quel hôtel êtes-vous descendu(e)?

____

2. Aviez-vous des réservations quand vous êtes arrivé(e)?

____

3. Est-ce que votre chambre était agréable?

____

4. Est-ce qu'il y avait un grand lit ou deux lits?

____

5. À quel étage était votre chambre?

____

6. Est-ce qu'il y avait un ascenseur à l'hôtel?

____

7. Y avait-il une piscine?

____

8. Est-ce que vous avez pris le petit déjeuner dans votre chambre?

____

9. Est-ce qu'il avait un restaurant à l'hôtel?

____

10. Qu'est-ce que vous pouviez voir de la fenêtre de votre chambre?

____

11. Quel était le prix de votre chambre?

____

12. Comment est-ce que vous avez réglé la note?

____

SYSTÈME-D *If you have access to Système-D software, you will find the following phrases there.*
PHRASES: Describing objects; Encouraging; Inviting; Persuading; Welcoming;
VOCABULARY: Bedroom; City; Direction and distance; Furniture

Journal. Vous travaillez dans le meilleur hôtel de votre ville. Écrivez une description de l'hôtel pour des touristes francophones. Donnez autant de détails que possible.

NOM ______________________ COURS ______________________

COMPÉTENCE 2 Giving directions

> **D**ans le journal à la fin de cette ***Compétence,*** vous allez expliquer comment aller chez vous en partant de votre université.

A. En ville. Consultez l'illustration et complétez les phrases suivantes logiquement.

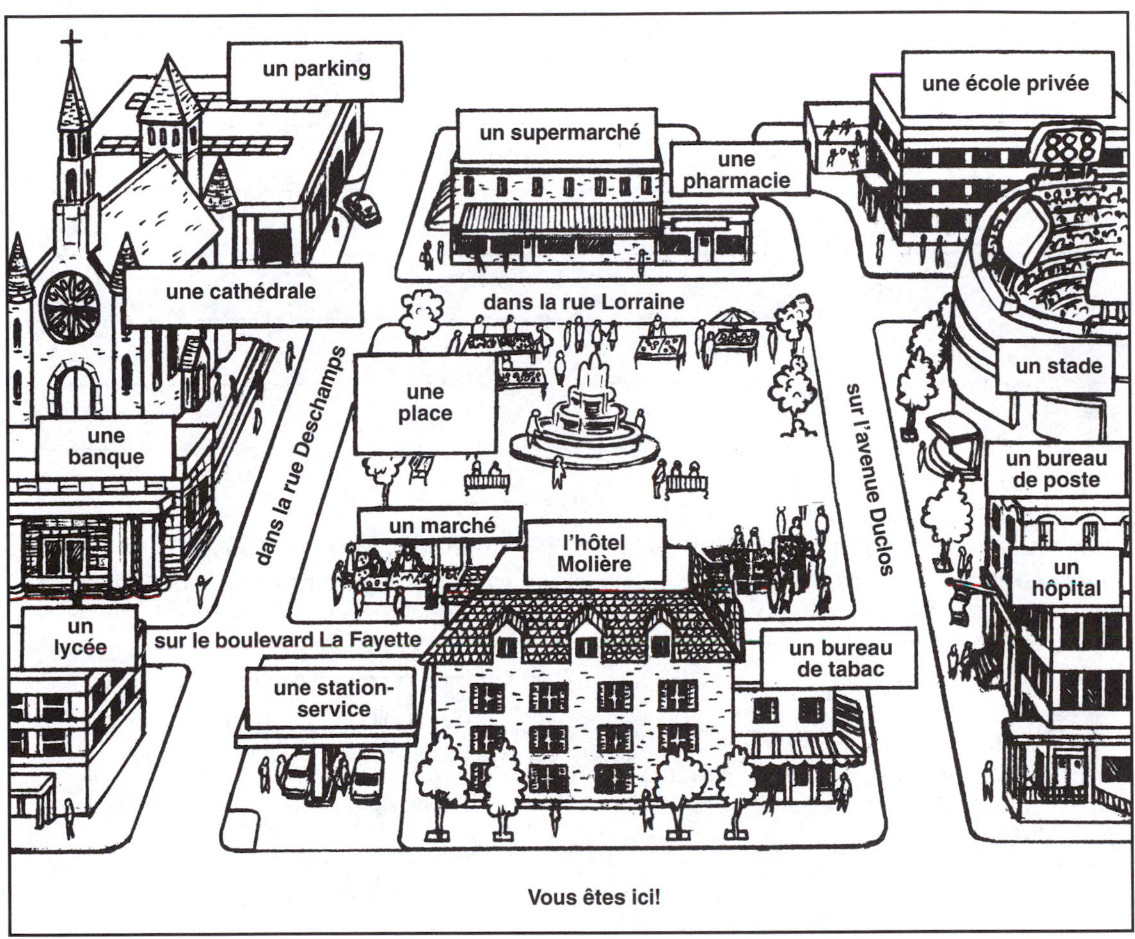

1. La station-service est ______________________ l'hôtel Molière et le bureau de tabac est ______________________ l'hôtel.

2. Il y a un bureau de poste ______________________ l'hôpital.

3. Le stade est de ______________________ côté du bureau de poste.

4. Il y a une banque ______________________ du boulevard La Fayette et de la rue Deschamps.

5. ______________________ du parking, de l'autre ______________________ de la rue Deschamps, il y a un supermarché.

6. Au ______________________ de l'avenue Duclos, il y a une école privée.

B. Pour aller à... Vous êtes en face de l'hôtel Molière. Indiquez comment aller aux endroits suivants sur l'illustration de ***A. En ville.***

EXEMPLE le parking *Pour aller au parking, tournez à droite dans la rue Deschamps et continuez tout droit jusqu'au bout de la rue. Le parking est au coin de la rue Lorraine et de la rue Deschamps.*

1. le supermarché ______________________________

____

____

2. le marché ______________________________

____

____

3. la pharmacie ______________________________

____

____

C. Comment sortir de l'hôtel? Il y a une panne d'électricité *(electric failure)* dans l'hôtel où vous travaillez et on ne voit plus rien. Expliquez à quelqu'un dans la chambre 1 comment sortir de l'hôtel. Mettez les phrases suivantes dans l'ordre logique avec le verbe à l'impératif. Utilisez des mots comme **d'abord, et, là** et **enfin** dans votre paragraphe.

continuer tout droit jusqu'à l'escalier
sortir de la chambre
descendre l'escalier jusqu'au rez-de-chaussée
tourner à gauche dans le couloir *(corridor)*
sortir de l'hôtel
traverser le hall *(lobby).*

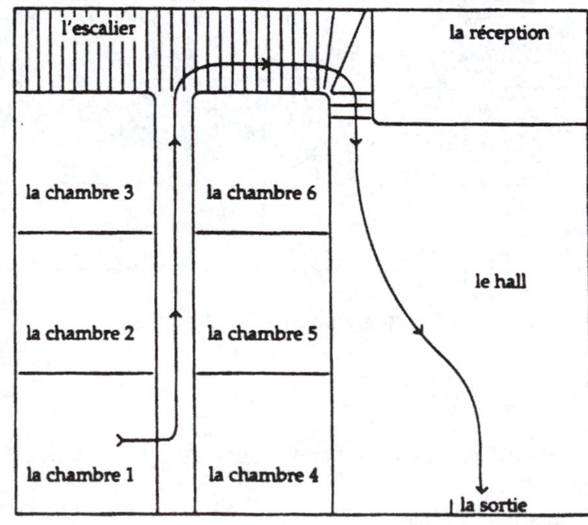

____

____

____

____

____

____

____

____

____

NOM ______________________ COURS ______________________

D. Sur le campus. Un nouvel étudiant français veut savoir où se trouvent certaines choses sur votre campus. Répondez à ses questions en étant aussi précis(e) que possible.

EXEMPLE Est-ce qu'on peut manger sur le campus?
Oui, le restaurant universitaire se trouve à côté de la bibliothèque dans la rue Alta Vista. / Non, il n'y a pas de restaurant universitaire sur le campus, mais il y a des fast-foods tout près d'ici, au bout de la rue Riverside.

1. Où se trouve la bibliothèque? ______________________

____

____

2. Où est-ce qu'il y a une librairie? ______________________

____

____

E. Faisons-le ensemble! Vous dites à votre camarade de chambre de faire les choses suivantes, mais il/elle n'a pas envie de les faire, alors vous lui suggérez de les faire ensemble. Dans les deux dernières phrases, remplacez les mots soulignés par un pronom complément d'objet direct **(le, la, l', les)** ou par un pronom complément d'objet indirect **(lui, leur).**

EXEMPLE préparer le dîner
— Prépare le dîner!
— Je n'ai pas envie de le préparer.
— Alors, préparons-le ensemble!

1. faire la lessive

— ______________________

— ______________________

— ______________________

2. téléphoner à l'agent de voyages

— ______________________

— ______________________

— ______________________

F. Et moi? Un ami part en vacances. Dites-lui de faire ou de ne pas faire les choses suivantes.

EXEMPLE vous écrire — Écris-moi!
s'ennuyer — Ne t'ennuie pas!

1. s'amuser ______________________________

2. vous montrer ses photos après ______________________________

3. vous demander de l'argent pour le voyage ______________________________

4. se perdre ______________________________

G. *Voir* ou *croire?* Complétez chaque question avec le verbe **voir** ou **croire.** Ensuite, répondez aux questions.

1. Où dans notre pays est-ce qu'on ______________ beaucoup de touristes étrangers?

____

2. ______________ -vous que plus de vacanciers *(vacationers)* vont à la plage ou à la montagne chaque année?

____

3. ______________ -vous souvent des touristes étrangers dans votre ville?

____

SYSTÈME-D *If you have access to Système-D software, you will find the following phrases there.* PHRASES: Inviting; Giving directions; VOCABULARY: Direction and distance; Geography; Means of transportation

Journal. Vous invitez des amis de la classe de français chez vous ce week-end. Écrivez cinq ou six phrases pour expliquer comment aller chez vous en partant de votre classe de français.

____

____

____

____

____

____

____

NOM ____________________ COURS ____________________

COMPÉTENCE 3 Giving advice

Dans le journal à la fin de cette *Compétence,* vous allez donner des conseils à des amis sur leurs vacances.

A. On fait du camping. Vous allez faire du camping. En vous servant du vocabulaire à la page 360, dites ce qu'on utilise pour faire les choses suivantes.

Qu'est-ce qu'on utilise…

1. pour se laver les mains? ____________________
2. pour porter ses affaires quand on fait une randonnée? ____________________
3. pour se protéger contre les insectes? ____________________
4. pour se protéger du soleil? ____________________
5. pour voir clair quand il fait nuit? ____________________
6. pour dormir sous une tente? ____________________

B. Qu'est-ce qu'il faut faire? Vous allez faire du camping avec des enfants. Dites-leur s'il faut ou s'il ne faut pas faire les choses suivantes.

EXEMPLES suivre vos conseils — *Il faut suivre mes conseils.*
aller nager seuls — *Il ne faut pas aller nager seuls.*

1. avoir de la patience ____________________
2. se coucher trop tard ____________________
3. oublier d'apporter un sac de couchage ____________________
4. mettre de la crème solaire ____________________
5. se protéger du soleil ____________________

C. Baby-sitting. Vous faites du baby-sitting. Dites aux enfants de faire chacune des choses indiquées. Ils répondent qu'ils ne veulent pas la faire.

EXEMPLE

1.

2.

3.

EXEMPLE

— *Je veux que vous vous leviez tout de suite.*

— *Mais, nous ne voulons pas nous lever.*

1. — ____

— ____

2. — ____

— ____

3. — ____

— ____

D. Une vieille dame. Lisez la lettre suivante qu'un lecteur a envoyée à la revue ***Jeune Afrique.*** Ensuite, complétez les phrases qui suivent.

«C'est l'histoire d'une vieille dame...»
«Le beau et le bon unissent les hommes, le mal et le laid les divisent.» (Tolstoï)

C'est l'histoire d'une vieille dame tunisienne qui a désiré rendre visite à son fils et à ses petits-enfants qui sont français et qui résident à Paris. Après avoir attendu le certificat d'**hébergement,** que son fils n'a réussi à obtenir qu'après avoir présenté toute une série de garanties qui prouvent qu'il est bon citoyen et qu'il a payé ses **droits fiscaux,** la pauvre dame est obligée de **faire la queue** devant le consulat de France à Tunis.

En arrivant, on l'informe qu'un certificat médical payant lui est indispensable pour l'**octroi** du visa, qui est lui aussi payant, évidemment; et comme elle est vieille, un taxi lui est d'ailleurs aussi indispensable pour ses déplacements. Après tous ces va-et-vient, le dossier est enfin en règle. Mais il faudra repasser le lendemain pour retirer le passeport; et **rebelote,** se lever tôt, faire la queue, attendre...

Avec le billet d'avion, l'allocation touristique, le timbre à l'aéroport, ce voyage qui devrait être un plaisir se transforme en un marathon infernal, **épuisant** à la fois pour le moral, la santé et le **porte-monnaie.** Pour voir ses petits-enfants avant de mourir, la vieille dame **a failli** mourir avant même de quitter l'aéroport.

Nos vieux parents ont dépassé l'âge d'être candidats à l'émigration clandestine et n'ont plus la force physique ni les moyens matériels pour supporter les charges des voyages. On ne doit pas les **enterrer** vivants. On vient d'abolir l'apartheid, on a détruit le mur de Berlin, et au moment où on fête le cinquième centenaire de la rencontre de deux mondes, nous sommes en train de **creuser** un **fossé** entre deux autres mondes.

---

l'hébergement *(m) lodging* **les droits fiscaux** *(m) taxes* **faire la queue** *to stand in line* **l'octroi** *(m) granting* **rebelote** *all over again* **épuisant(e)** *exhausting* **le porte-monnaie** *pocketbook* **avoir faillir** (+ infinitive) *to almost* (+ past participle) **enterrer** *to bury* **creuser** *to dig* **un fossé** *ditch, gulf*

Maintenant, complétez les phrases suivantes d'après la lettre. Mettez le verbe entre parenthèses au subjonctif.

1. D'abord, il a fallu que son fils ________________ (attendre) le certificat d'hébergement.

2. Pour obtenir ce certificat, il a fallu qu'il ________________ (présenter) des garanties qu'il est bon citoyen.

3. Plus d'une fois, il a fallu que la vieille dame ________________ (se lever) tôt, qu'elle ________________ (faire) la queue et qu'elle ________________ (attendre) longtemps devant le consulat pour obtenir son passeport.

4. Il ne faut pas qu'un voyage pour le plaisir ________________ (devenir) un marathon infernal.

5. Il ne faut pas que nous ________________ (enterrer) nos vieux parents vivants.

E. Qu'est-ce qu'elle a dit? Vous prenez l'avion avec deux amis qui ne font jamais attention à ce qu'on leur dit. Expliquez-leur ce que les membres de l'équipage *(crew members)* veulent qu'ils fassent.

EXEMPLE — Ne vous levez pas, s'il vous plaît!
— Qu'est-ce qu'elle a dit?
— Elle ne veut pas que vous vous leviez.

1. — Faites attention à la marche *(step)!*

— Qu'est-ce qu'elle a dit?

— ____

2. — Donnez-moi votre bagage à main, s'il vous plaît!

— Qu'est-ce qu'elle a dit?

— ____

3. — Montrez-moi votre carte d'embarquement *(boarding pass),* s'il vous plaît!

— Qu'est-ce qu'elle a dit?

— ____

4. — N'ayez pas peur!

— Qu'est-ce qu'elle a dit?

— ____

5. — Soyez calmes!

— Qu'est-ce qu'elle a dit?

— ____

F. Réactions. Comment répondriez-vous si une amie vous disait les choses suivantes? Commencez chaque phrase avec une expression qui exprime une émotion.

EXEMPLE Je me sens mal.
Je suis désolé(e) que tu te sentes mal.

1. J'ai mal au ventre *(a stomach ache).*

____

2. Je suis enceinte *(pregnant)*.

____

3. Je ne bois plus d'alcool.

____

4. Je grossis beaucoup.

____

G. Sentiments. Exprimez un désir, une préférence ou une émotion en complétant les phrases suivantes.

1. Je préfère que mes amis ____.

2. Je voudrais que mon/ma meilleur(e) ami(e) ____.

3. C'est dommage que mon/ma meilleur(e) ami(e) ____.

4. Mes amis sont toujours étonnés que je ____.

H. À l'université. Quels conseils donneriez-vous à un(e) nouvel(le) étudiant(e)? Complétez les phrases suivantes.

1. Il faut que tu ____.

2. Il vaut mieux que tu ____.

3. Il ne faut pas que tu ____.

4. Il est très important que tu ____.

SYSTÈME-D *If you have access to Système-D software, you will find the following phrases there.* PHRASES: Hypothesizing; Advising; Encouraging; Persuading; VOCABULARY: Leisure; Sport; Traveling

Journal. Des amis vont passer leur vacances dans le même endroit *(place)* où vous avez passé vos vacances récemment. D'abord nommez l'endroit et décrivez-le. Ensuite, faites-leur des suggestions en utilisant des expressions comme **il faut que..., il ne faut pas que..., il vaut mieux que...** ou **je recommande que...**

____

____

____

____

____

NOM ______________________ COURS ______________________

COMPÉTENCE 4 Finding out about jobs abroad

Dans le journal à la fin de cette ***Compétence,*** vous allez faire des suggestions aux auteurs de votre livre de français.

A. Quelle est sa profession? Nommez un(e) ami(e), un(e) parent(e) ou une personne célèbre qui a la même profession que les personnes sur ces dessins.

EXEMPLE *Ma cousine est infirmière.*

1. 
2. 
3. 
4. 

1. ______________________
2. ______________________
3. ______________________
4. ______________________

B. Quelle profession? Donnez la profession des personnes suivantes.

EXEMPLE Matlock représente les accusés au tribunal.
Il *est avocat.*

1. Laverne travaille avec un médecin.

____

2. M. Homais travaille dans une école avec des enfants.

____

3. Rebecca Milfeld joue dans un orchestre.

____

4. Céline Dion chante à la télévision.

____

5. Kevin Costner et Clint Eastwood jouent dans un nouveau film.

____

C. L'avenir professionnel. Lisez l'article suivant de la revue pour femmes, *Amina,* publiée au Sénégal. Dans cet article, on explique comment être promu(e) *(promoted)* dans son travail.

APPRENEZ À ÉVALUER VOS CAPACITÉS PROFESSIONNELLES

Avez-vous déjà eu l'impression que malgré tous vos efforts, personne n'apprécie votre travail? Peut-être que vous ne donnez à personne une raison de le faire. Il est important que vous sachiez évaluer vos capacités professionnelles vous-mêmes.

Voici quelques conseils qui vous aideront à mieux évaluer vos capacités professionnelles vous-mêmes.

- Faites régulièrement connaître vos divers projets à vos supérieurs au moyen de notes.
- Faites-leur également parvenir des rapports de toutes les réunions.
- De temps à autre, parlez de vos projets à d'autres personnes travaillant dans la même société que vous en espérant qu'elles en parleront à leurs supérieurs. Cela vous fera connaître et peut-être estimer.
- Faites une liste de vos divers projets et distribuez des photocopies lors des réunions afin de pouvoir mieux en parler.

Même les chefs de service ont un supérieur hiérarchique. Si vous souhaitez avoir un poste dans un autre service, il vaut mieux avoir de bonnes relations avec votre chef de service. Pour cela vous devez faire les choses suivantes:

- Soyez ouverte au dialogue. Mettez-le (Mettez-la) au courant de tout. Ne gardez pas d'informations secrètes: vous donnerez l'impression de «faire bande à part».
- Admettez toujours vos erreurs. N'ayez pas peur de vous impliquer et ne vous excusez pas si vous vous êtes trompée à propos de quelque chose.
- Soyez «fidèle». Même si vous n'appréciez pas toutes les décisions prises par votre supérieur(e), vous devez en tant que membre de son groupe de travail lui apporter votre soutien. Vous devez savoir que lorsqu'une décision est prise, même si ce n'est pas celle que vous auriez prise, vous devez l'accepter.
- Faites votre travail rapidement, avec bonne humeur et du mieux que vous pouvez.

QUE FAIRE POUR ÊTRE PROMUE?

Voici la marche à suivre :

- Sachez quelles sont vos forces et vos faiblesses et exploitez vos forces au maximum.
- Acceptez toutes les tâches qui vous sont confiées avec le sourire, même si certaines sont ennuyeuses.
- Écoutez tout ce que l'on vous rapporte mais ne faites pas de commentaire. Souvenez-vous que «la parole est d'argent mais le silence est d'or». Si vous ne voulez pas d'ennuis, soyez discrète.
- Travaillez beaucoup. Peu importe si vous travaillez plus d'heures que vous ne devriez, si vous fournissez un travail de qualité.
- Ne dites jamais de mal, même par sous-entendu, de vos supérieurs.
- Acceptez les remarques si elles sont valables.

Maintenant, en consultant l'article précédent, dites à un(e) ami(e) cinq choses qu'il faut qu'il/elle fasse pour améliorer sa situation professionnelle et deux choses qu'il ne faut pas qu'il/elle fasse.

Il faut que tu ______________________________

____

____

______________________________.

Il ne faut pas que tu ______________________________

____

____

______________________________.

D. *Savoir* ou *connaître?* Complétez le passage suivant avec la forme appropriée de **savoir** ou **connaître.**

La famille Étourdie a beaucoup de problèmes avec les choses ordinaires de la vie. Le matin, M. Étourdie ne ______________ jamais où il a laissé ses lunettes, mais heureusement, Mme Étourdie ______________ très bien son mari et elle les trouve pour lui. Leurs enfants Georges et Cécile ______________ bien qu'ils doivent se préparer pour aller à l'école, mais comme ils ______________ leur mère, ils ______________ qu'ils peuvent jouer à des jeux vidéo jusqu'au moment de partir. Pauvre Mme Étourdie! Comment est-ce qu'elle trouve cette énergie? C'est simple, elle ______________ bien son mari et ses enfants et elle ______________ organiser leur routine. Et elle ______________ aussi que c'est elle la plus intelligente!

E. Quel verbe? Complétez chaque question avec la forme correcte de **savoir** ou de **connaître.** Ensuite répondez aux questions.

1. Est-ce que vous ______________ bien la géographie de l'Afrique?

____

2. Est-ce que vous ______________ quels pays africains sont francophones?

____

3. Est-ce que vous ______________ la date de la fête nationale en Côte-d'Ivoire?

____

4. Est-ce que vous ______________ quelqu'un d'Afrique?

____

F. Pronoms relatifs. Complétez les questions suivantes avec le pronom relatif **qui** ou **que.** Ensuite, répondez à chaque question.

1. Trouve-t-on facilement du travail dans la profession ________ vous avez choisie?

____

2. Quelles sont les professions ________ vous intéressent?

____

3. Quelles sont les professions __________ vous trouvez ennuyeuses?

____

4. Aimeriez-vous travailler avec une compagnie __________ a des succursales *(branch offices)* à l'étranger?

____

If you have access to Système-D software, you will find the following phrases there.
PHRASES: Advising; Expressing an opinion; Agreeing and disagreeing;
GRAMMAR: Subjunctive

Journal. Maintenant que vous finissez vos études de français avec *Horizons,* vous avez sans doute des opinions sur ce qui est important dans un livre de français. Voici l'occasion de partager vos opinions dans une lettre aux auteurs. Avant d'écrire votre lettre, complétez les phrases suivantes pour vous organiser. N'oubliez pas d'utiliser le subjonctif.

Il est très important qu'un livre de français ______________________________ .

Il n'est pas nécessaire qu'un livre de français ______________________________ .

Dans *Horizons,* ça m'a plu que ______________________________ .

Je préférerais que ce livre ______________________________ .

Dans la prochaine édition, il vaudrait mieux que ______________________________ .

Maintenant, écrivez votre lettre aux auteurs.

Messieurs et Mesdames,

Je m'appelle ______________________________

et j'étudie le français à ______________________________

où nous utilisons *Horizons.*

____

____

____

____

____

J'espère que ces commentaires et suggestions vous seront utiles à l'avenir.

Veuillez accepter, Mesdames et Messieurs, l'expression de mes sentiments distingués.

____

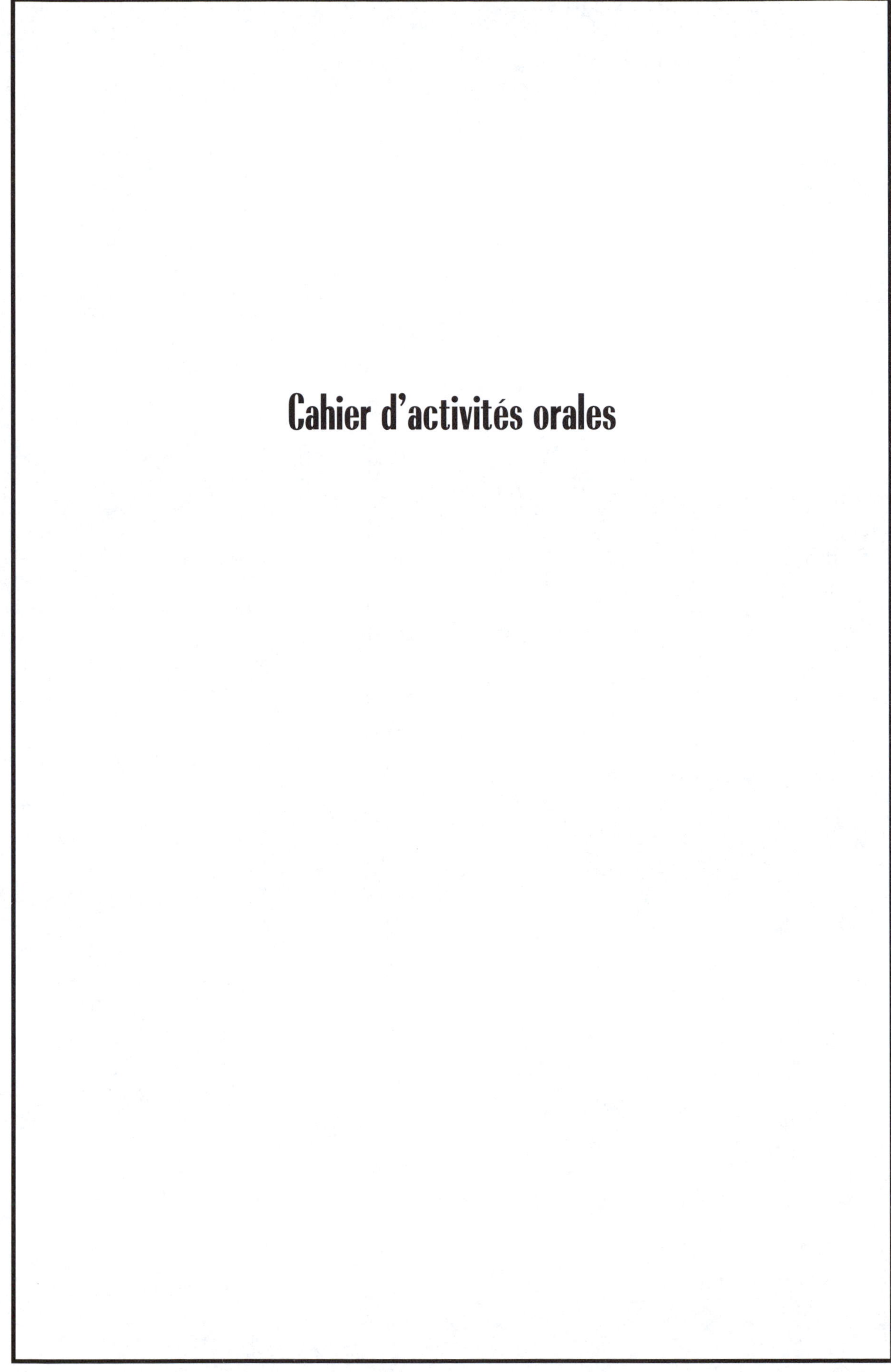

Cahier d'activités orales

NOM ______________________________ COURS ______________________________

CHAPITRE PRÉLIMINAIRE
On commence!

COMPÉTENCE 1 Greeting people

A. Les voyelles de base. Correct pronunciation of the basic vowels is essential to developing speaking and listening skills. Listen and repeat each of these words after the speaker. Notice that the final consonant at the end of many words in French is silent. Rewind and repeat this exercise if needed.

EXEMPLE YOU SEE AND HEAR: la
YOU REPEAT: **la**

[a]	la	ma	sa	ta
[ə]	le	me	se	te
[i]	lit	mis	si	ti
[o]	lot	mot	sot	tôt
[y]	lu	mû	su	tu

Now you will hear two of the words from each vertical row in the exercise. Circle the words you hear. Rewind and listen again as needed.

B. Salutations. You will hear three short conversations in which people greet each other. Write the number of each conversation below the picture it matches.

____

____

____

C. Prononciation: Les consonnes muettes et la liaison. Stop the tape and review the ***Prononciation*** section on page 7 of the textbook. Then read the following list of words and indicate whether the final consonant of each word is pronounced or silent by underlining those that should be pronounced and crossing out those that should be silent. (Remember the mnemonic device CaReFuL!) Turn on the tape and listen and repeat as you hear each word pronounced, checking your pronunciation and your decision about the final consonant. Rewind and repeat this exercise if needed.

EXEMPLES YOU SEE: parc — YOU SEE: pas
YOU MARK: par<u>c</u> — YOU MARK: pa~~s~~
YOU HEAR AND REPEAT: par<u>c</u> — YOU HEAR AND REPEAT: pa~~s~~

1. Marc
2. salut
3. très
4. assez
5. mal
6. bonjour
7. actif
8. Luc

Stop the tape and read the following sentences. Indicate where liaison occurs by drawing a link between the appropriate words. Turn on the tape and listen and repeat as you hear each sentence pronounced, checking your pronunciation and your decision about the liaison.

EXEMPLE YOU SEE: Comment vous appelez-vous?
YOU MARK: **Comment vous‿appelez-vous?**
YOU HEAR AND REPEAT: **Comment vous‿appelez-vous?**

1. Comment t'appelles-tu?
2. Comment allez-vous?
3. Je suis en classe.
4. Comment dit-on… ?
5. Comment ça va?
6. À tout à l'heure!

Now repeat each line of these conversations after the speakers during the pause provided. Pay attention to the final consonants. Stop the tape if you need additional time to respond.

CONVERSATION 1

— Bonjour, monsieur.
— Bonjour, mademoiselle.
— Comment allez-vous?
— Je vais très bien, merci. Et vous?
— Oh, pas très bien.

CONVERSATION 2

— Bonsoir, monsieur. Je suis Louise Roudesli. Et vous? Comment vous appelez-vous?
— Je m'appelle Antoine Amini.

CONVERSATION 3

— Salut, je m'appelle Anne. Et toi, tu t'appelles comment?
— Moi, je m'appelle Pascal.
— Comment ça va?
— Assez bien. Et toi?
— Moi, ça va.
— Et bien, au revoir! À bientôt!
— Oui, à demain!

D. Dictée. You will hear a series of questions or statements. Write each one down. Stop the tape during the pauses to have sufficient time to write. When you are done, rewind and listen again to correct your work.

1. ______________________________
2. ______________________________
3. ______________________________
4. ______________________________
5. ______________________________

Now you will hear more questions or remarks. Respond appropriately in French. Stop the tape during the pauses to have sufficient time to write.

1. ______________________________
2. ______________________________
3. ______________________________
4. ______________________________

NOM ______________________ COURS ______________________

COMPÉTENCE 2 Spelling and counting

A. L'alphabet. Say each letter of the alphabet after the speaker. Repeat this exercise until you feel comfortable reciting the alphabet by yourself.

a b c d e f g h i j k l m n o p q r s t u v w x y z

As you hear the names of these courses of study, spell each one out. You do not need to spell out the short words **le, la, l',** or **les.** After a pause for you to respond, you will hear the correct answer. Verify your response.

le français	l'anglais	la littérature	la biologie
la zoologie	la comptabilité	les mathématiques	les sciences sociales
la psychologie	la chimie	le droit	l'histoire

B. Ça s'écrit comment? You will hear some introductions in which the last name of the person introduced will be spelled out. Listen and write the names in the appropriate blank. Stop the tape between items to allow enough time to respond. Rewind and listen again as needed.

1. Je m'appelle Gilbert ______________________.

2. Nous nous appelons Jean et Marie ______________________.

3. Mon ami s'appelle Georges ______________________.

4. Les enfants s'appellent François et Hélène ______________________.

C. Comptez de un à trente! Repeat each number after the speaker. Notice that the final consonants of some numbers are pronounced, while others are silent. Some consonants in the middle of the word are also silent. Repeat this exercise until you feel comfortable counting from 1 to 30 by yourself.

1 un	**6** six	**11** onze	**16** seize	**21** vingt et un	**26** vingt-six
2 deux	**7** sept	**12** douze	**17** dix-sept	**22** vingt-deux	**27** vingt-sept
3 trois	**8** huit	**13** treize	**18** dix-huit	**23** vingt-trois	**28** vingt-huit
4 quatre	**9** neuf	**14** quatorze	**19** dix-neuf	**24** vingt-quatre	**29** vingt-neuf
5 cinq	**10** dix	**15** quinze	**20** vingt	**25** vingt-cinq	**30** trente

D. Quels chiffres? You will hear eight numbers said in random order. As you hear each one, circle it in the list of numbers in ***C. Comptez de un à trente!***

E. Calculs. You will hear some simple math problems. Stop the tape after each one in order to write the numbers and solve the problem. All the problems and answers will be repeated at the end. Listen and verify your responses.

EXEMPLE	YOU HEAR:	Deux et deux font…
	YOU WRITE:	2 + 2 = 4
	AT THE END, YOU HEAR:	Deux et deux font quatre.

1. _____ + _____ = _____
3. _____ + _____ = _____
5. _____ + _____ = _____
2. _____ + _____ = _____
4. _____ + _____ = _____
6. _____ + _____ = _____

F. Prononciation: Les voyelles nasales. Stop the tape and review the ***Prononciation*** section on page 12 of the textbook. Then turn on the tape and repeat these nasal sounds and the model words that contain them after the speaker.

[ɛ̃] un / um / in / im / ain / aim	un	cinq	quinze	vingt
[ɑ̃] en / em / an / am	trente	Henri	Jean	comment
[ɔ̃] on / om	bonjour	onze	bonsoir	

Now repeat these pairs of words after the speaker.

1. un on
2. vent vingt
3. bon banc
4. main mon
5. sent sain
6. train trente

Now you will hear the speaker say one word from each of the preceding pairs. Circle the one you hear.

G. Messages urgents. You will hear three short telephone messages. Listen to the example, then stop the tape and read the information in it. Then listen to the other two messages. After each one, stop the tape and fill in the appropriate information. Rewind and listen again as needed.

EXEMPLE

MESSAGE URGENT

Pour: Madame Dufour

De la part de: Monsieur Dufour

Rendez-vous: À l'hôtel Biarritz

Numéro de téléphone: 01. 13. 25. 11. 09

1.

MESSAGE URGENT

Pour: ____________________

De la part de: ____________________

Rendez-vous: Au cinéma

Numéro de téléphone: ____________________

2.

MESSAGE URGENT

Pour: ____________________

De la part de: ____________________

Rendez-vous: Au café

Numéro de téléphone: ____________________

NOM ______________________ COURS ______________________

COMPÉTENCE 3 Talking about your schedule

A. Quelle heure est-il? You will be asked what time it is for each of the following clocks. After a pause for you to respond, you will hear the correct answer. Verify your response and your pronunciation.

EXEMPLE VOUS VOYEZ *(YOU SEE)*:

VOUS ENTENDEZ *(YOU HEAR)*:	Quelle heure est-il?
VOUS DITES *(YOU SAY)*:	**Il est une heure.**
VOUS ENTENDEZ *(YOU HEAR)*:	Il est une heure.

1. 
2. 
3. 
4. 
5. 
6. 
7. 
8. 

B. Les jours de la semaine. Listen and repeat the names of the days of the week. Rewind and listen again until you feel comfortable saying them.

lundi mardi mercredi jeudi vendredi samedi dimanche

C. C'est quel jour? Your friend is always one day behind. When he asks, tell him that it's the next day. After a pause for you to respond, you will hear the correct answer. Verify your response and your pronunciation.

EXEMPLE	VOUS ENTENDEZ:	— Aujourd'hui, c'est lundi?
	VOUS DITES:	**— Non, aujourd'hui, c'est mardi.**
	VOUS ENTENDEZ:	— Non, aujourd'hui, c'est mardi.

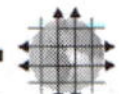

D. À la télévision. You will hear announcements for several television programs. Listen for the day and time that each will be shown and write the information in the appropriate blanks. Stop the tape after each announcement to allow enough time to respond. Rewind and listen again as needed.

EXEMPLE	VOUS ENTENDEZ:	Mesdames, mesdemoiselles, messieurs, bonjour! Voici les émissions de la semaine: d'abord, un film d'aventures, *Tarzan: La malédiction de Muguma* lundi de neuf heures à onze heures…
	VOUS ÉCRIVEZ *(YOU WRITE)*:	*Tarzan: La malédiction de Muguma:* **lundi** de **neuf heures** à **onze heures**

1. *Les Simpson:* ________________ de ________________________________

à ________________________________

2. *Des chiffres et des lettres:* ________________ de ________________________________

à ________________________________

3. *Le mystère Picasso:* ________________ de ________________________________

à ________________________________

4. *Robocop II:* ________________ de ________________________________

à ________________________________

5. *Studio Gabriel:* ________________ de ________________________________

à ________________________________

E. Mon emploi du temps. Listen as a student describes her usual schedule. After listening to what she says, stop the tape and complete these sentences as she would. Rewind and listen again as needed.

1. Je suis à l'université *(at the university)* le lundi, ________________________________

et ________________________________.

2. Le matin, je suis en classe de huit heures et demie à ________________________________.

3. L'après-midi, je suis en classe de ________________________ à

________________________________ .

4. Le soir, je travaille de ________________________________ à

________________________________.

NOM ______________________ COURS ______________________

COMPÉTENCE 4 Getting acquainted in class

A. La salle de classe. Listen and repeat as you hear the names of the objects and people in this classroom.

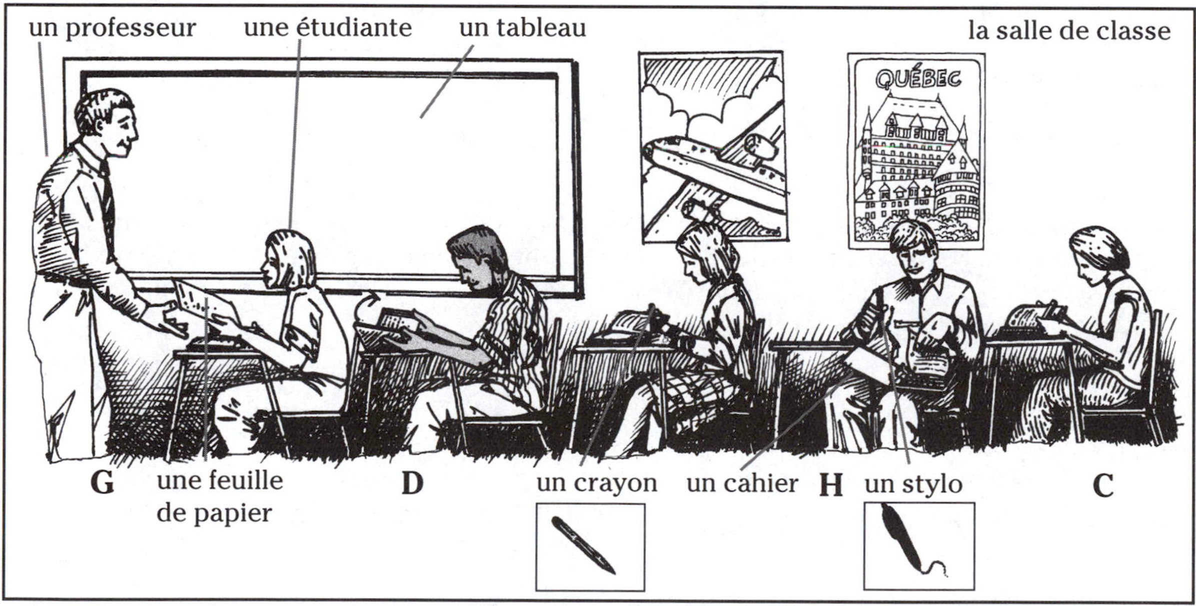

Now you will hear the names of only some of the objects or peoples. On the pictures, circle those you hear.

B. Qu'est-ce qu'ils font? You will hear a series of classroom commands. Look at the pictures in ***A. La salle de classe*** again. Next to the number of the command you hear, write the letter of the action that corresponds to it. The first one has been done as an example. Stop the tape between commands to allow enough time to respond.

1. B 2. _____ 3. _____ 4. _____ 5. _____ 6. _____ 7. _____ 8. _____

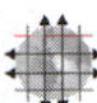

Now rewind the tape and listen to the classroom commands again. As you hear each one, draw a line connecting the first part of the command in the left column with its ending in the right column. The first one has been done as an example. Stop the tape between items to allow enough time to respond.

Écoutez	votre livre à la page 23.
Ouvrez	la réponse au tableau en phrases complètes.
Répondez	à la question 2 de l'exercice C.
Prenez	au tableau.
Écrivez	la question.
Fermez	votre livre.
Donnez-moi	votre feuille de papier.
Allez	une feuille de papier et un stylo.

C. En classe. Stop the tape and read these sentences and phrases. Turn on the tape and listen to a conversation between a professor and some students. Mark an **X** next to the phrase each time you hear it.

_____ Comment? Répétez, s'il vous plaît.

_____ Comment dit-on… ?

_____ Qu'est-ce que ça veut dire… ?

______Oui, je comprends.

______ Non, je ne comprends pas.

______ Je ne sais pas.

D. Masculin et féminin. When the masculine form of an adjective ends in a consonant other than **c, r, f,** or **l,** the final consonant is usually silent. Since the feminine form of an adjective usually ends in **-e,** this consonant is no longer final and is pronounced. You will hear several pairs of adjectives. Repeat each pair after the speaker.

1. américain — américaine
2. français — française
3. intéressant — intéressante
4. anglais — anglaise
5. canadien — canadienne

Now you will hear one of the adjectives from each pair. Listen and circle the form you hear.

E. Autoportraits. You will hear two people give a short description of themselves. Listen to each one, then stop the tape and finish the statements as each person would.

1. Je m'appelle ______________________________.

Je suis ______________________________.

J'habite à ______________________________.

Je parle ______________________________

______________________________.

1. Je m'appelle ______________________________.

Je suis ______________________________.

J'habite à ______________________________.

Je suis ______________________________

______________________________.

NOM ______________________ COURS ______________________

CHAPITRE 1
À l'université

COMPÉTENCE 1 Identifying people

A. Écoutez et répétez. You will hear sentences about a male, a female, and a group. Listen and repeat after the speaker, paying careful attention to your pronunciation. Rewind and repeat until you feel comfortable saying the phrases.

C'est Jean-Marc.
Il n'est pas américain.
Il est français.
Il est grand et beau.
Il est sportif.

C'est Sophie.
Elle n'est pas américaine.
Elle est française.
Elle est petite et belle.
Elle est sportive.

Ce sont mes amis.
Ils ne sont pas américains.
Ils sont français et canadiens.
Ils sont jeunes et sympathiques.

B. Jean-Marc. You will hear pairs of sentences. Repeat the sentence from each pair that correctly describes the photo of Jean-Marc in ***A. Écoutez et répétez.*** After a pause for you to respond, you will hear the correct answer. Verify your response and your pronunciation.

EXEMPLE	VOUS ENTENDEZ:	C'est un jeune homme. / C'est une jeune femme.
	VOUS DITES:	**C'est un jeune homme.**
	VOUS ENTENDEZ:	C'est un jeune homme.

C. Première rencontre. Listen as two people meet for the first time. Then stop the tape and complete the statements about them by circling the appropriate words in italics. Rewind and listen again as needed.

1. Le jeune homme s'appelle *Alex / Daniel / Jean-Luc / Alain.*
2. La jeune femme s'appelle *Marie / Sophie / Alice / Catherine.*
3. Ils sont dans le même cours *de français / d'anglais / d'espagnol.*
4. Elle est de *Paris / Montréal / Nice / Marseille.*
5. Il est de *Paris / Montréal / Nice / Marseille.*
6. Elle est à Nice pour *étudier / voir la France.*

D. Présentations. Listen as David introduces his friends Bruno and Martine to Annette. The first time, simply listen to the conversation at normal speed. It will then be repeated at a slower speed with pauses for you to write in the missing words in the sentences. You will need to stop the tape during the pauses to have sufficient time to respond. When you are done, rewind and listen again to correct your work.

Annette, c'est mon ____________ Bruno. ____________ de Marseille et il

étudie à l'________________ de Nice. Nous sommes dans le même

________________ d'espagnol. Il parle espagnol ________________ .

Annette, ____________ mon amie Martine. ____________ de

Montréal. Elle est ________________ .

E. Lecture: *Qui est-ce?* Stop the tape and reread the story ***Qui est-ce?*** on pages 30–31 of the textbook. Then turn on the tape. You will hear three excerpts based on the encounter between Yvette and David. Listen to each one and decide which illustration depicts what is happening. Write the number of the excerpt in the blank below the appropriate picture. Stop the tape between items to allow enough time to respond.

____

____

____

NOM ______________________ COURS ______________________

COMPÉTENCE 2 Describing people

A. Prononciation: *Il est* + adjectif / *Elle est* + adjectif. Stop the tape and review the ***Prononciation*** section on pages 34–35 of the textbook. Then turn on the tape, listen, and repeat. Be careful to pronounce the vowels in **il/ils** and **elle/elles** distinctly and to differentiate between the masculine and feminine forms of the adjectives when appropriate.

Il est français. / Elle est française.
Il est petit. / Elle est petite.
Il est sportif. / Elle est sportive.
Il est célibataire. / Elle est célibataire.

Ils sont américains. / Elles sont américaines.
Ils sont grands. / Elles sont grandes.
Ils sont paresseux. / Elles sont paresseuses.
Ils sont mariés. / Elles sont mariées.

B. On parle de qui? You will hear a series of sentences. For each one, decide who is being described: **David, Annette, Annette et Yvette,** or **tous les trois** *(all three).* Put a check mark in the appropriate column.

EXEMPLE VOUS ENTENDEZ: Il est français.
VOUS ÉCRIVEZ:

	DAVID	ANNETTE	ANNETTE ET YVETTE	TOUS LES TROIS
EXEMPLE	✓			
1.				
2.				
3.				
4.				
5.				
6.				

C. Jean-Marc et Sophie. You will hear several sentences describing Jean-Marc. After each sentence, say that the same is true for Sophie, changing the form of the adjective as needed. After a pause for you to respond, you will hear the correct answer. Verify your response and your pronunciation.

EXEMPLE VOUS ENTENDEZ: Jean-Marc? Il est assez sportif. Et Sophie?
VOUS DITES: **Elle est assez sportive aussi.**
VOUS ENTENDEZ: Elle est assez sportive aussi.

D. Prononciation: Les pronoms sujets et le verbe *être*. Listen and repeat the subject pronouns and the verb **être,** paying particular attention to the pronunciation.

ÊTRE			
je	suis	nous	sommes
tu	es	vous	êtes
il	est	ils	sont
elle	est	elles	sont

Now stop the tape and complete the sentences you see with the correct form of the verb **être.** Then turn on the tape and verify your answers, repeating each sentence after the speaker.

1. Moi, je ________________ David Cauvin.
2. Bruno, c'________________ mon ami.
3. Il ________________ de Marseille.
4. Bruno et Martine ________________ très sympathiques.
5. Nous ________________________ dans le même cours d'espagnol.
6. Et toi, tu ________________ étudiante aussi?
7. Yvette et toi, vous ________________ américaines, n'est-ce pas?

E. Les pronoms sujets. Bruno is speaking to Annette, but his remarks are incomplete. Write the number of the sentence you hear next to its logical completion. The first one is done as an example. Stop the tape between items to allow enough time to respond.

__________ Je suis étudiant à l'université de Nice.

____1____ Ils sont sympathiques.

__________ Il est étudiant aussi.

__________ Vous êtes sportives?

__________ elle est plutôt sportive.

__________ Tu es étudiante?

__________ Nous sommes assez sportifs.

Now listen to Bruno's complete remarks and check your work.

F. Encore des questions. You will hear questions about you and your university life. Answer each one with a complete sentence. Stop the tape between items to allow enough time to respond.

1. ____
2. ____
3. ____
4. ____
5. ____
6. ____

NOM ______________________ COURS ______________________

COMPÉTENCE 3 Talking about the university

A. Les cours. Practice pronouncing the names of courses by repeating each one after the speaker.

LES LANGUES

l'allemand

l'anglais

l'espagnol

le français

LES SCIENCES HUMAINES

l'histoire

la psychologie

les sciences politiques

LES BEAUX-ARTS

les cours de théâtre

la musique

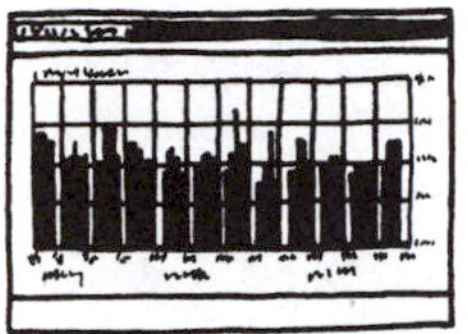

LES COURS DE COMMERCE

la comptabilité

le marketing

LES COURS TECHNIQUES

l'informatique

les mathématiques

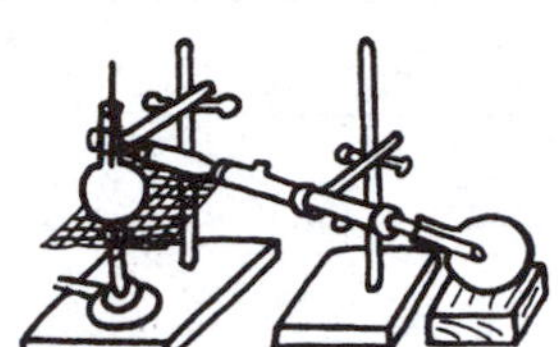

LES SCIENCES

la biologie

la chimie

la physique

B. Quels cours? Listen as two students talk about their classes. Circle all the courses you hear mentioned in the lists of courses in ***A. Les cours.***

Now rewind the tape and listen to the conversation again. Then complete the following statements according to the conversation. Rewind and listen again as needed.

1. Le cours d'informatique de la jeune femme est à ______________ heures de l'après-midi.
2. Elle pense que le cours d'informatique est un peu ______________________ .
3. Le prof de théâtre du jeune homme est très ______________________ .
4. La sœur du jeune homme étudie la ______________________ .

C. Prononciation: L'article défini. Stop the tape and review the ***Prononciation*** section on page 40 of the textbook. Then turn on the tape and practice pronouncing the forms of the definite article by repeating these words after the speaker.

le campus   la bibliothèque   l'université   les cours   les activités

D. Préférences. You will hear the names of activities common to university life. As you hear each one, decide how much you like it and write it under the appropriate column.

EXEMPLE VOUS ENTENDEZ: les boums
VOUS ÉCRIVEZ:

J'AIME BEAUCOUP...	J'AIME ASSEZ...	JE N'AIME PAS BEAUCOUP...	JE N'AIME PAS DU TOUT...
les boums			

E. Chacun ses goûts. Listen as a student expresses his opinions about his university and write the form of the definite article **(le, la, l', les)** that you hear in each sentence. Stop the tape between items to allow enough time to respond.

1. ________ 2. ________ 3. ________ 4. ________ 5. ________ 6. ________

Now rewind the tape, listen again, and list what this student does and does not like. Stop the tape between items to allow enough time to respond. The first one has been done as an example.

♥ l'université, ______________________________

Ⓥ ______________________________

F. Toujours des questions. Questions can be asked in several ways. Questions that can be answered with *yes* or *no* are asked with rising intonation. You will hear a series of questions. Repeat each one after the speaker, imitating the intonation.

Now rewind the tape and listen to the questions again. This time, answer them. Stop the tape after each question to allow enough time to respond.

1. ______________________________
2. ______________________________
3. ______________________________
4. ______________________________
5. ______________________________
6. ______________________________

COMPÉTENCE 4 Saying what's in the neighborhood

A. Identification. Identify these places, as in the example. After a pause for you to respond, you will hear the correct answer. Verify your response and your pronunciation.

EXEMPLE	VOUS ENTENDEZ:	C'est un théâtre ou un cinéma?
	VOUS DITES:	**C'est un cinéma.**
	VOUS ENTENDEZ:	C'est un cinéma.

EXEMPLE
un théâtre / un cinéma

1. **un café / un restaurant**

2. **un court de tennis / un club de gym**

3. **un laboratoire de langues / une bibliothèque**

4. **une boîte de nuit / une bibliothèque**

Now look the illustrations again as you hear each of the places named. Say whether each of the places pictured is found near your university. After a pause for you to respond, you will hear a model response. Verify your response and your pronunciation.

EXEMPLE	VOUS ENTENDEZ:	un cinéma
	VOUS DITES:	**Il y a un cinéma dans le quartier universitaire. / Il n'y a pas de cinéma dans le quartier universitaire.**
	VOUS ENTENDEZ:	Il y a un cinéma dans le quartier universitaire. / Il n'y a pas de cinéma dans le quartier universitaire.

B. Prononciation: L'article indéfini. Stop the tape and review the ***Prononciation*** section on page 46 of the textbook. Then turn on the tape and practice pronouncing the forms of the indefinite article by repeating these words after the speaker.

un cours	une classe
un concert	une boum
un film	une langue
un ami	une amie
un exercice	une activité

C. Quelle forme? You will hear a series of questions about your university. Circle the form of the indefinite article you hear in each one.

1. un	une	des	3. un	une	des	5. un	une	des
2. un	une	des	4. un	une	des	6. un	une	des

Now rewind the tape and listen to the questions about your university again. This time, write appropriate answers. Stop the tape between items to allow enough time to respond. Rewind and listen again as needed.

1. ____________________
2. ____________________
3. ____________________
4. ____________________
5. ____________________
6. ____________________

D. L'université. Listen as two students talk about one of their courses. Then stop the tape and circle the words in italics that correctly complete each sentence. In some cases, you may need to circle more than one. Rewind and listen again as needed.

1. Les étudiants sont dans le même cours *d'anglais / d'espagnol / de français.*
2. Le professeur est *sympathique / intellectuel / bête.*
3. Ils sont en classe *le lundi / le mardi / le mercredi / le jeudi / le vendredi* à *12h / 1h / 1h30.*
4. La salle de classe est *agréable / désagréable / vieille / moderne.*

E. Camarades de chambre. The following people are looking for housemates. Listen to each description. Then stop the tape and circle the names of two students who, in your opinion, would make good housemates. Finally, explain your choice in English.

Daniel Ahmad Philippe Pierre Annette Hyemi

____

____

Now rewind the tape and listen again. Then complete the statement in French explaining which person you prefer to live with and why.

Je préfère habiter avec ____________ parce que ____________

____________________.

NOM ______________________ COURS ______________________

CHAPITRE 2
Après les cours

COMPÉTENCE 1 Talking about your free time

A. Loisirs. You will hear each of these leisure activities named. Sometimes more than one phrase describes a particular scene. Repeat each phrase after the speaker.

B. Qu'est-ce qu'ils font? Listen as the Dufours discuss what they and their older children, Henriette, Thierry, and Yves, are doing this evening. Circle the picture of each activity you hear mentioned in ***A. Loisirs.***

Now rewind the tape and listen to the Dufours' conversation again. Then stop the tape and complete these sentences.

1. Thierry voudrait ______________________________.

2. Henriette voudrait ______________________________.

3. Yves voudrait ______________________________.

4. Mme Dufour voudrait ______________________________.

C. Les loisirs. You will hear a short dialogue in which two students, Alain and Francine, discuss what they like to do as leisure activities. Listen to what they say. Then stop the tape and list as many activities as you can for each student.

ALAIN: Après les cours, j'aime ______________________________

______________________________.

Le week-end, j'aime ______________________________

______________________________.

FRANCINE: Je suis plutôt sportive et j'aime ______________________________

______________________________.

J'aime aussi ______________________________

______________________________.

D. Stratégie: *Listening for specific information.* Listen as David, Annette, and Yvette discuss what they would like to do tomorrow. Afterward, stop the tape and complete these statements to say what each of them likes to do.

DAVID: J'aime ______________________________.

YVETTE: Je préfère ______________________________.

ANNETTE: Mais moi, je préfère ______________________________.

Now rewind the tape and listen to the conversation again. Then stop the tape and complete the statements by circling one of the choices given in italics.

1. Demain c'est *vendredi / samedi / dimanche / lundi.*
2. David et Yvette vont jouer au tennis *demain matin / demain après-midi / demain soir.*
3. Ils décident d'aller voir un film *français / américain.*
4. Ils décident d'aller voir un film *avec Gérard Depardieu / de Steven Spielberg.*

NOM ______________________ COURS ______________________

COMPÉTENCE 2 Telling what you and others do

A. Prononciation: La consonne *r* et l'infinitif. Stop the tape and review the ***Prononciation*** section on page 66 of the textbook. Then turn on the tape and repeat these infinitives after the speaker.

sortir	jouer	faire	prendre
dormir	inviter	lire	être
	chanter		
	manger		

B. Le week-end. Listen as David and Gisèle say what they like to do. Then stop the tape and complete the sentences with an appropriate expression.

1. Le week-end, Gisèle aime ______________________.
2. David préfère ______________________.
3. Gisèle aime aussi ______________________.
4. David n'aime pas ______________________.
5. Gisèle aime beaucoup ______________________.
6. David préfère ______________________.

C. Prononciation: Les verbes en *-er*. Stop the tape and review the ***Prononciation*** section on page 69 of the textbook. Then read the following sentences and cross out the verb endings that are silent. Finally, turn on the tape and repeat the sentences after the speaker, checking your work.

1. David et Bruno jouent assez bien au tennis.
2. Tu aimes aller au cinéma le week-end?
3. J'étudie beaucoup.
4. Est-ce que vous dansez bien?
5. Nous regardons souvent des cassettes vidéo.
6. Annette travaille souvent sur l'ordinateur.

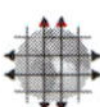

D. La partie de tennis. David and Annette are watching Bruno and Yvette play tennis. First, listen as the passage is read at normal speed. Then, listen as it is repeated in short phrases at a slower speed, with pauses for you to fill in the missing words. Stop the tape between items to allow enough time to respond. Rewind the tape and listen again to check your work.

Samedi, David et Annette ____________________ Bruno et Yvette jouer au tennis. Bruno ____________________, mais Yvette joue encore mieux et elle gagne *(wins)* la partie en deux sets, 6–4 et 6–3. Après la partie de tennis, le perdant *(the loser),* Bruno, ____________________ ses amis à aller au restaurant.

BRUNO: Je vous invite ____________________. Qu'est-ce que vous ____________________ ? Est-ce que vous ____________________ la cuisine italienne?

YVETTE: Oh oui, j'aime ____________________ les spaghetti.

ANNETTE: Moi aussi, mais je ne ____________________ pas libre cet après-midi.

E. Ça y est! C'est à vous! Answer the questions you hear about your activities with complete sentences. When appropriate, use an adverb like **beaucoup, peu, bien, mal, souvent, rarement, quelquefois,** or **ne... jamais.** Stop the tape between items to allow enough time to respond.

1. ____________________
2. ____________________
3. ____________________
4. ____________________
5. ____________________
6. ____________________
7. ____________________
8. ____________________
9. ____________________
10. ____________________

COMPÉTENCE 3 Talking about your day

A. Prononciation: Les lettres *qu*. Stop the tape and review the ***Prononciation*** section on page 76 of the textbook. Then turn on the tape and repeat these questions after the speaker. When you have finished, turn off the tape and match the questions to their logical responses by writing the number of the question in the blank next to the corresponding answer.

1. Est-ce que tu travailles?	________ À l'université.
2. Où est-ce que tu travailles?	________ Avec Ali.
3. Quels jours est-ce que tu travailles?	________ Parce que j'aime le sport.
4. De quelle heure à quelle heure?	________ J'aime bien faire du jogging.
5. Avec qui est-ce que tu travailles?	________ Tous les jours sauf le week-end.
6. Qu'est-ce que tu aimes faire le week-end?	________ De midi à quatre heures.
7. Pourquoi?	________ Oui, je travaille beaucoup.

B. C'est logique? You will hear a series of questions. Circle the most logical response to each one. Stop the tape between items to allow enough time to respond.

1.	tous les jours	le dimanche soir
2.	toute la journée	à midi et demi
3.	avec une amie	au restaurant
4.	un sandwich	au restaurant
5.	à la maison	au cinéma

C. Prononciation: Les verbes à changements orthographiques. Stop the tape and review the ***Prononciation*** section on page 74 of the textbook. Then turn on the tape and repeat these words after the speaker.

je préfère   nous préférons   tu répètes   vous répétez

Stop the tape, look at the following words, and decide how the **c** or **g** is pronounced. Where **c** is pronounced like **s,** write an **s** in the blank. Where **g** is pronounced like **j,** write **j.** If the indicated **c** or **g** has a hard sound, leave the blank empty. Finally, turn on the tape and check your work, repeating each word after the speaker.

___ café   ___ célèbre   ___ ici   ___ cocorico   ___ culture   ___ créole   ___ commençons

___ gare   ___ général   ___ gitane   ___ gosse   ___ guitare   ___ gré   ___ voyageons

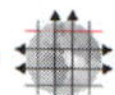

D. Questions. Bruno and Annette are talking. You will hear their conversation twice. The first time, just listen to it at normal speed. Then listen as it is repeated in short phrases at a slower speed, with pauses for you to fill in the missing words. Stop the tape between items to allow enough time to respond. When you are done, rewind and listen again to correct your work.

BRUNO: ______________________ est-ce que tu es à l'université?

ANNETTE: ______________________________ sauf le week-end, bien entendu.

BRUNO: Alors, ______________________________ tes cours?

ANNETTE: ______________________... et le week-end, bien sûr.

BRUNO: ______________________________ préparer les cours?

ANNETTE: ______________________________... et quelquefois à la bibliothèque avec des amis.

E. Quelle est la question? You are eavesdropping on your friend Jean-Luc, who is talking on the phone about plans for this weekend. You cannot hear the questions of the person on the other end of the line, but you can figure them out by Jean-Luc's answers. After each sentence, circle the question word that was used to elicit the answer you heard.

EXEMPLE VOUS ENTENDEZ: Je voudrais aller danser.
VOUS VOYEZ: que à quelle heure
VOUS RÉPONDEZ: (que)

1. quand où
2. avec qui à quelle heure
3. avec qui quand
4. comment pourquoi
5. quand à quelle heure

Now rewind the tape. After each statement is read, stop the tape and write a complete question using **est-ce que** and the question words you circled in the first part of this activity.

EXEMPLE VOUS ENTENDEZ: Je voudrais aller danser samedi soir.
VOUS ÉCRIVEZ: ***Qu'est-ce que tu voudrais faire samedi soir?***

1. ______________________________
2. ______________________________
3. ______________________________
4. ______________________________
5. ______________________________

NOM ______________________ COURS ______________________

COMPÉTENCE 4 Ordering at the café

A. Au café. Order each of these items by repeating the order after the speaker.

B. Je voudrais... You will hear a conversation in which a family is ordering at a café. Listen to their orders and circle the illustrations in ***A. Au café.***

C. Comptons! Listen to the numbers until you are ready to say them. Then rewind the tape and say them along with the speaker. Repeat this exercise until you feel comfortable counting from 30 to 100 by yourself.

30... 40... 50... 60... 70... 80... 90... 100

D. Prononciation: Les chiffres. Stop the tape and review the ***Prononciation*** section on page 80 of the textbook. Decide whether the final consonants of these numbers should be pronounced. Cross out those that are silent and mark those that are pronounced in liaison with a link mark (‿). Then play the tape and repeat after the speaker, checking your answers.

deux étudiants / deux livres   six étudiants / six livres   huit étudiants / huit livres

E. Ça fait combien? Answer the question **C'est combien?** with the prices given. After a pause for you to respond, you will hear the correct answer. Verify your response and your pronunciation.

1. 67 F
2. 74 F
3. 76 F
4. 99 F
5. 16 F 25
6. 38 F 50
7. 44 F 90
8. 84 F 50
9. 100 F 20

F. Les numéros de téléphone. You will hear the phone numbers for several business advertisements. Complete each ad by writing the number in the space provided.

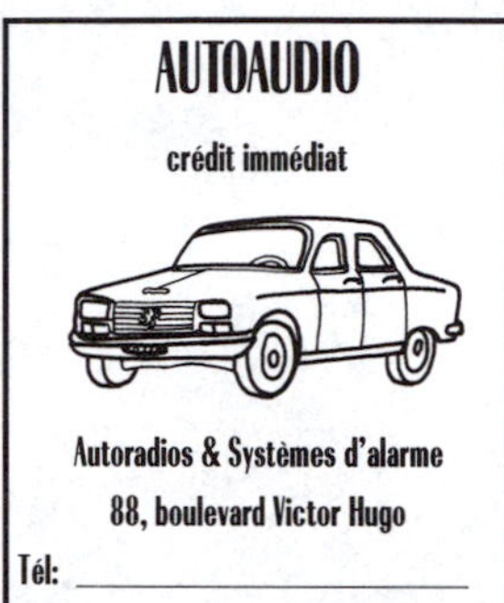

G. Prononciation: L'inversion et la liaison. Stop the tape and review the ***Prononciation*** section on page 82 of the textbook. Decide whether the final consonants of the verbs should be pronounced. Cross out those that are silent and mark those that are pronounced in liaison with a link mark (‿). Turn on the tape and repeat the sentences after the speaker, verifying your pronunciation.

1. Aimes-tu aller au café?
2. Yvette et Annette sont-elles au café?
3. David voudrait-il aller au café aussi?
4. Voudrais-tu aller prendre un verre?

H. On dîne ensemble? Two friends are talking. You will hear their conversation twice. The first time, just listen to it at normal speed. Then listen as it is repeated in short phrases at a slower speed, with pauses for you to fill in the missing words.

— Où sont Annette et Yvette ce soir? ______________ à l'université?

— Non, elles sont au café.

— David, ______________ avec elles?

— Non, il n'aime pas aller au café le soir.

— Que ______________ faire?

______________ à la maison?

— Non, il dîne souvent au restaurant.

— ______________ un bon restaurant dans ce quartier?

— Il y a un très bon restaurant italien tout près. ______________ la cuisine

italienne? ______________ venir manger avec moi?

NOM ______________________ COURS ______________________

CHAPITRE 3
Un nouvel appartement

COMPÉTENCE 1 Telling where you live

A. Qu'est-ce que c'est? Identify the places and things in this apartment as in the example. After a pause for you to respond, you will hear the correct answer. Verify your response and your pronunciation.

EXEMPLE	VOUS ENTENDEZ:	C'est la chambre ou la salle de bains?
	VOUS DITES:	**C'est la chambre.**
	VOUS ENTENDEZ:	C'est la chambre.

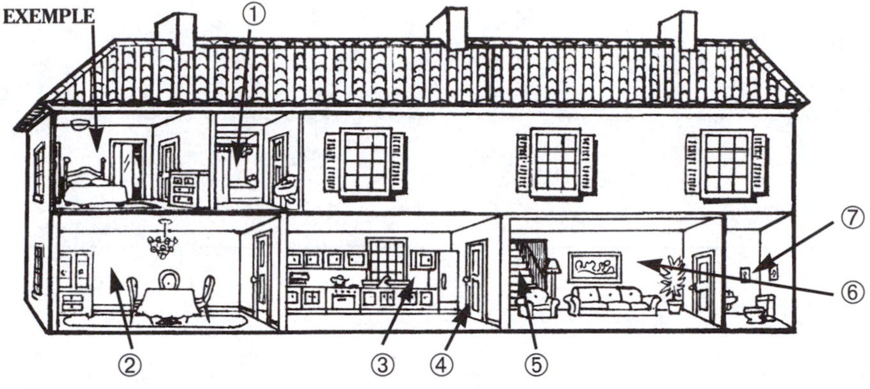

B. Et vous? Answer the questions you hear using the vocabulary on pages 96–97 of the textbook. Stop the tape between questions to allow enough time to respond.

1. ______________________
2. ______________________
3. ______________________
4. ______________________
5. ______________________

C. Où habitent-ils? Didier, Sophie, and Caroline are talking about their living arrangements. Listen carefully, then stop the tape and write the name of each person under the place where he or she lives.

dans un immeuble en ville

____

dans une maison à la campagne

____

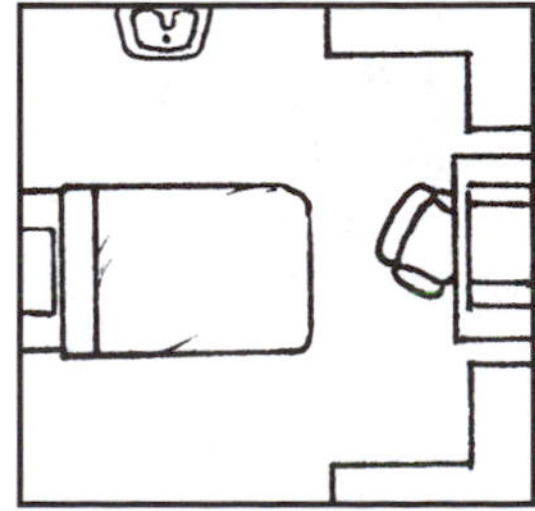

à la résidence universitaire

____

Now rewind the tape, listen again, and answer these questions with complete sentences.

1. Qui habite dans un appartement?

____

2. À quel étage se trouve l'appartement?

____

3. Est-ce que l'immeuble est près de l'université?

____

4. Qui habite à la campagne?

____

5. Est-ce que cette *(this)* étudiante habite seule?

____

6. Comment est la maison?

____

7. Qui habite à la résidence universitaire?

____

8. Comment sont les chambres à la résidence?

____

9. Pourquoi est-ce que la résidence est pratique *(practical)?*

____

D. Robert cherche un taxi. Robert is looking for a taxi to take him to Thomas's apartment. Listen to the conversation and indicate whether these statements are **vrai** or **faux.**

1. Le premier taxi est libre.	vrai	faux
2. Robert pose une question à un homme dans la rue.	vrai	faux
3. La station de taxi est dans la deuxième rue.	vrai	faux
4. La rue Dauphine est loin de la station de taxi.	vrai	faux
5. Le chauffeur de taxi dit: «C'est cinquante cents la minute.»	vrai	faux
6. Robert décide d'aller à la rue Dauphine en autobus.	vrai	faux

NOM ______________________ COURS ______________________

COMPÉTENCE 2 Talking about your possessions

A. C'est à moi! A friend is asking if these items are yours. Identify them as yours, as in the example. After a pause for you to respond, you will hear the correct answer. Verify your response and your pronunciation.

EXEMPLE

VOUS ENTENDEZ:	C'est ton chien?
VOUS DITES:	**Oui, c'est mon chien.**
VOUS ENTENDEZ:	Oui, c'est mon chien.

B. Où? Familiarize yourself with these locations by repeating them after the speaker.

C. Vrai ou faux? Look at the picture of the room in ***B. Où?*** and indicate if what you hear said is **vrai** or **faux.**

1. vrai faux	3. vrai faux	5. vrai faux	7. vrai faux
2. vrai faux	4. vrai faux	6. vrai faux	8. vrai faux

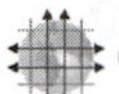

D. Prononciation: *avoir* et *être*. Stop the tape and review the ***Prononciation*** section on page 102 of the textbook. Then turn on the tape, listen, and repeat.

AVOIR			
j'	ai	nous z avons	
tu	as	vous z avez	
il	a	ils z ont	
elle	a	elles z ont	

ÊTRE		AVOIR	
tu	es	tu	as
il	est	il	a
elle	est	elle	a
ils	sont	ils z	ont
elles	sont	elles z	ont

As you hear these questions, write the form of the verb you hear in the appropriate column.

	AVOIR	ÊTRE
1.	________________	________________
2.	________________	________________
3.	________________	________________
4.	________________	________________

Now rewind the tape. Imagine that a friend is asking you these same questions and answer them.

1. ____
2. ____
3. ____
4. ____

E. Une conversation au café. Listen as Robert talks with a friend. The first time, simply listen to the conversation at normal speed. It will then be repeated at a slower speed with pauses for you to write in the missing words in the sentences.

DIDIER: Alors, Robert, tu ____________________ l'appartement de Thomas?

ROBERT: Oui, ________________ un appartement de trois ____________________. Ma chambre ____________ très grande, mais ____________________ grand-chose: un bureau, une chaise, un ordinateur...

DIDIER: Je voudrais bien habiter dans un appartement. ____________________ de la chance *(luck)!* Tu peux *(can)* inviter tes amis, même le soir, ou fumer, ou faire une boum.

NOM ______________________ COURS ______________________

COMPÉTENCE 3 Describing your house

A. Ça se trouve... As you hear items named, say in which room they are located according to the illustration. After a pause for you to respond, you will hear the correct answer. Verify your response and your pronunciation.

EXEMPLE	VOUS ENTENDEZ:	Où sont la table et les chaises?
	VOUS DITES:	**La table et les chaises sont dans la salle à manger.**
	VOUS ENTENDEZ:	La table et les chaises sont dans la salle à manger.

B. Prononciation: *De, du, des.* Listen as Robert talks about his new apartment and roommates. Fill in the blanks with **de, de la, de l', du,** or **des** and the noun that follows.

EXEMPLE VOUS ENTENDEZ ET VOUS COMPLÉTEZ: Les fenêtres *du salon* sont petites.

1. Le placard ______________________ est petit.
2. La porte ______________________ ne ferme pas bien.
3. Les murs ______________________ sont blancs.
4. La place préférée ______________________ de Claude, c'est mon fauteuil.
5. La vue de la fenêtre ______________________ est jolie.

C. Chez Thomas. Thomas tends to exaggerate everything. How does he answer a friend's questions? Be sure to use the appropriate possessive adjective **(mon, ma, mes, ton, ta, tes, son, sa, ses, notre, nos, votre, vos, leur, leurs)** in the response.

EXEMPLES VOUS ENTENDEZ: — Votre appartement est grand?
VOUS ÉCRIVEZ: — Oui, *notre appartement* est assez grand.

VOUS ENTENDEZ: — La chambre de Claude est agréable?
VOUS ÉCRIVEZ: — Oui, *sa chambre* est très agréable.

1. — Oui, ______________________ est très cher.

2. — Oui, ______________________ sont très spacieuses *(spacious).*

3. — Oui, ______________________ est très moderne.

4. — Oui, ______________________ est très agréable.

5. — Oui, ______________________ est très confortable.

6. — Oui, ______________________ sont très sympas.

7. — Oui, ______________________ sont intéressants.

8. — Oui, ______________________ est très agréable.

9. — Oui, ______________________ est très beau.

10. — Oui, ______________________ sont quelquefois très embêtants.

D. On sort? Didier and Robert are going out to dinner, and Didier has arranged to pick Robert up at his apartment. Listen to their conversation, stop the tape, and answer the questions in English. You may need to rewind the tape and listen more than once.

1. Name two things Didier particularly admires about Robert's apartment.

______________________ ______________________

2. What is one of the things Didier likes about where he lives?

____

3. What are two inconveniences he mentions about where he lives?

______________________ ______________________

4. Why does Thomas decline Didier's invitation to the restaurant?

____

5. What is the name of the restaurant?

____

NOM ______________________ COURS ______________________

COMPÉTENCE 4 Giving your address and phone number

A. L'inscription à l'université. You are enrolling at a Canadian university. Provide the information requested in each question.

1. ______________________
2. ______________________
3. ______________________
4. ______________________
5. ______________________

B. Prononciation: La voyelle *e* de *ce, cet, cette, ces.* Stop the tape and review the ***Prononciation*** section on page 114 of the textbook. Then turn on the tape, listen, and repeat these words.

ce	de	je	ne	que	le	me
ces	des	mes	tes	les	aller	danser
cet	cette	quel	elle	cher	frère	mère

C. Mes préférences. A friend is asking about your preferences. Listen to his questions and circle the form of **quel** that would be used in each one, based on the gender and number of the noun that follows.

EXEMPLE VOUS ENTENDEZ: Quel est ton restaurant préféré?
VOUS ÉCRIVEZ: (quel) quels quelle quelles

1. quel quels quelle quelles
2. quel quels quelle quelles
3. quel quels quelle quelles
4. quel quels quelle quelles

Now rewind the tape and listen to your friend's questions again. This time, answer his questions. Stop the tape to allow enough time to respond.

EXEMPLE VOUS ENTENDEZ: Quel est ton restaurant préféré?
VOUS ÉCRIVEZ: Mon restaurant préféré, c'est Pizza Nizza.

1. ______________________
2. ______________________
3. ______________________
4. ______________________

D. Les chiffres et les mois de l'année. Listen and repeat after the speaker, paying careful attention to your pronunciation. Rewind and repeat until you feel comfortable saying the numbers and the months.

100	700	1 000 000	janvier	juillet
220	800	1 304 570	février	août
310	999	1 800 000	mars	septembre
454	1 000		avril	octobre
500	2 150		mai	novembre
670	5 322		juin	décembre

E. Dates. Say these dates in French. After a pause for you to respond, you will hear the correct answer. Verify your response and your pronunciation.

EXEMPLE VOUS VOYEZ: le 15 mars 1951
VOUS ENTENDEZ: Quelle est la date?
VOUS DITES: **C'est le quinze mars mille neuf cent cinquante et un.**
VOUS ENTENDEZ: C'est le quinze mars mille neuf cent cinquante et un.

1. le 17 septembre 1949
2. le 4 juillet 1776
3. le 7 décembre 1945
4. le 1er juillet 1867
5. le 14 juillet 1789
6. le 1er janvier 2001

F. C'est combien? You will hear commercials for several household items. Write down the price **(le prix)** and the order number **(le numéro de commande)** of each item in numerals. You may need to rewind and listen several times. The first one has been done as an example.

	PRIX	NUMÉRO DE COMMANDE
1. la chaise dactylo *(typing chair)*	285 F	653.06.33
2. le porte-plantes *(plant stand)*	________	________
3. la mini-chaîne stéréo	________	________
4. le magnétoscope Tokai	________	________
5. la lampe Python	________	________

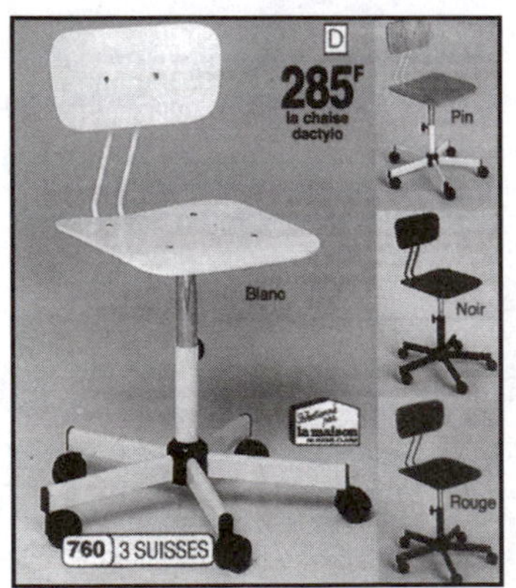

NOM ______________________ COURS ______________________

CHAPITRE 4
En famille

COMPÉTENCE 1 Talking about your family

A. Qui est-ce? Listen as Thomas explains his relationship to various family members. Fill in the missing words in the sentences. Stop the tape between items to allow enough time to respond.

EXEMPLE VOUS ENTENDEZ: C'est le père de mon père.
VOUS ÉCRIVEZ: C'est **le père** de mon père.

1. C'est ______________________ de mon père.
2. C'est ______________________ de ma tante.
3. C'est ______________________ de ma tante et de mon oncle.
4. C'est ______________________ de ma tante et de mon oncle.
5. C'est ______________________ de mon père.

Now rewind the tape and listen again. Write the number of each description in the corresponding blank in the illustration.

EXEMPLE VOUS ENTENDEZ: C'est le père de mon père.
VOUS ÉCRIVEZ:

Exemple

B. Je vous présente... You will hear the first part of some introductions. For each one, repeat what you hear and complete the sentence with the corresponding female family member as in the example. After a pause for you to respond, you will hear the correct answer. Verify your response.

EXEMPLE VOUS ENTENDEZ: Voici mon père et...
VOUS DITES: **Voici mon père et ma mère.**
VOUS ENTENDEZ: Voici mon père et ma mère.

C. Des photos. Thomas is showing photos of his family to Robert. The first time, simply listen to what Thomas says at normal speed. It will then be repeated with pauses for you to fill in the missing information in the sentences. Rewind the tape and listen again to correct your work.

Voilà les photos de ______________________. Philippe, c'est ______________________. Ça, c'est Sylvie, ______________________. Et là, c'est une photo de Yannick, ______________________. Ça, c'est une photo de

________________, Danielle et de ________________, Hugues. Ils ont

________________: ________________, Guillaume

et ________________, Marie. Cette dernière *(last)* photo, c'est

une photo de ________________. ________________

maintenant.

D. Et vous? Answer the questions you hear about your family in French. Stop the tape between items to allow enough time to respond.

1. ________________
2. ________________
3. ________________
4. ________________
5. ________________
6. ________________

E. La famille de Thomas. You will hear Thomas talk about his family. After you listen, stop the tape and answer the questions in complete sentences in French.

1. Combien de frères et sœurs a Thomas?

____

2. Qui est divorcé?

____

3. Combien de frères et sœurs a le père de Thomas?

____

4. Est-ce que les trois frères de son père sont mariés?

____

5. Est-ce que les parents de la mère ou du père de Thomas habitent avec sa famille?

____

COMPÉTENCE 2 Describing people and things

A. Couleurs. What's your favorite color? Repeat the words for the colors after the speaker. Then turn off the tape and write your favorite color in the blank. Afterward, turn the tape back on.

bleu vert rose jaune noir blanc gris beige marron rouge violet orange

Ma couleur préférée, c'est le ______________________.

What color are your hair and eyes? Repeat the options after the speaker. Then, turn off the tape and write what is true for you. Notice that there is liaison with **les yeux** and that **cheveux** and **yeux** both rhyme with **deux.**

J'ai les cheveux... bruns / noirs / gris / blonds / blancs / roux / châtains.

J'ai les‿yeux... noirs / verts / bleus / marron / gris / couleur noisette *(hazel).*

Moi, j'ai les cheveux ________________ et les yeux ______________________________.

B. Les parents de Gisèle. You will hear Gisèle describe her parents. Repeat each sentence after she says it.

_____ Mon père s'appelle Christian.
_____ Il a cinquante-huit ans.
_____ Il a l'air sportif.
_____ Il est de taille moyenne.
_____ Il a les cheveux courts et noirs.
_____ Il a une moustache et une barbe.
_____ Il porte un pantalon et une chemise.

_____ Ma mère s'appelle Diane.
_____ Elle a trente-deux ans.
_____ Elle a l'air intellectuelle.
_____ Elle est assez grande.
_____ Elle a les cheveux longs et noirs.
_____ Elle porte des lunettes.
_____ Elle porte une robe.

Now stop the tape and look at the picture of Gisèle's parents. Decide whether each sentence you heard is **vrai** or **faux** and write **V** or **F** in the blank next to it.

Paul, 48 ans Diane, 42 ans

C. Prononciation: La lettre *l*. Stop the tape and review the ***Prononciation*** section on page 134 of the textbook. Read the following sentences and circle the words where **ll** preceded by **i** is pronounced as in the word **famille.** Then, turn on the tape and repeat each sentence. Pay special attention to the pronunciation of the letter **l** and check your work.

_____ 1. Ma famille habite dans une petite ville tranquille.

_____ 2. Plus d'un million de personnes habitent dans notre ville.

_____ 3. J'aime les vieilles maisons et les belles voitures.

Now stop the tape, reread each sentence aloud, and indicate whether it is **vrai** or **faux** for you by writing **V** or **F** in the blank next to it.

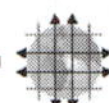

D. Adjectifs. Stop the tape and review the irregular adjectives on page 134 of the textbook. Turn on the tape and listen to Thomas describe his family, friends, and possessions. Complete the second part of each statement with the corresponding feminine form of the adjective given in the first part, as in the model. After a pause for you to respond, you will hear the correct answer. Verify your response and your pronunciation.

EXEMPLE	VOUS ENTENDEZ:	Mon cousin est beau. Ma cousine…
	VOUS DITES:	**Ma cousine est belle aussi.**
	VOUS ENTENDEZ:	Ma cousine est belle aussi.

E. Descriptions. You will hear several people describe their cars. Listen carefully to the descriptions and write down the three adjectives used to describe each one. Stop the tape between items to allow enough time to respond.

EXEMPLE	VOUS ENTENDEZ:	J'ai une petite voiture jaune. C'est une voiture japonaise.
	VOUS ÉCRIVEZ:	petite, jaune, japonaise

1. ______________________________

2. ______________________________

3. ______________________________

4. ______________________________

F. Chacun ses goûts. You will hear Thomas and Robert talk about cars. The first time, just listen as you hear their conversation at normal speed. It will then be repeated with pauses for you to fill in the missing words.

— Regarde ______________________ dans le garage.

C'est la voiture de mon père. Il adore ______________________.

— ______________________ voiture!

— Moi, je ______________________ voiture de ma mère.

Elle a acheté une Mercedes d'occasion *(used)*. ______________________

voiture aussi mais elle est moins ______________ et plus facile à

conduire *(to drive)*.

— Une Mercedes? ______________________!

Moi, je ______________________ voiture mais presque tous mes amis ont

ou une voiture ou une moto.

NOM ______________________ COURS ______________________

COMPÉTENCE 3 Saying where you go in your free time

A. Où sont-ils? For each picture, you will hear two places named. Identify the place that corresponds to the picture. After a pause for you to respond, you will hear the correct answer. Verify your response and your pronunciation.

EXEMPLE	VOUS ENTENDEZ:	Où sont-ils? Ils sont dans les petits magasins ou au bar?
	VOUS RÉPONDEZ:	**Ils sont dans les petits magasins.**
	VOUS ENTENDEZ:	Ils sont dans les petits magasins.

EXEMPLE

1. 

2. 

3. 

4. 

5. 

6. 

7. 

8. 

9. 

10. 

11. 

B. Où est-ce qu'on va? You will hear a list of activities. Look back at the pictures from ***A. Où sont-ils?*** and say where one goes to do the activity named. After a pause for you to respond, you will hear the correct answer. Verify your response and your pronunciation.

EXEMPLE	VOUS ENTENDEZ:	Pour aller nager, on va...
	VOUS DITES:	**Pour aller nager, on va à la piscine ou à la plage.**
	VOUS ENTENDEZ:	Pour aller nager, on va à la piscine ou à la plage.

C. Le verbe *aller.* Pay careful attention to the pronunciation of the verb **aller.** Repeat the conjugation and sample sentences after the speaker.

	ALLER			
je	vais	nous ‿z‿	allons	Où est-ce que tu vas?
tu	vas	vous ‿z‿	allez	Vous allez en cours?
il	va	ils	vont	Je vais à l'université.
elle	va	elles	vont	Ils vont à un concert.
on	va			

D. Prononciation: Les lettres *a, au* et *ai.* Stop the tape and review the ***Prononciation*** section on page 140 of the textbook. Then, turn on the tape and repeat the following sentences, making sure to distinguish between the vowel sounds **a, au,** and **ai.**

__________ Aujourd'hui, mes camarades de classe et moi allons au café après les cours.

__________ Mes amis dînent rarement au restaurant.

__________ Je vais souvent à la plage avec des amis en mars ou en avril.

__________ Je voudrais avoir une longue barbe blanche à l'âge de cent ans.

Now stop the tape, reread each sentence aloud, and indicate whether it is true or false for you by writing **V** or **F** in the blank.

E. Souvent, quelquefois, rarement ou jamais? Answer the questions you hear, indicating how often you go to the places mentioned. Stop the tape between items to allow enough time to respond.

1. ______________________________
2. ______________________________
3. ______________________________
4. ______________________________

F. Invitations. Suggest a logical place to do whatever your friend wants to do. Choose from the boxed list. First make a suggestion using **on,** then say *Let's,* using the **nous** form of the verb. After a pause for you to respond, you will hear the correct answers. Verify your response.

AU MUSÉE au centre commercial *à la bibliothèque*
AU CAFÉ **à la librairie** à la piscine **au parc**

EXEMPLE VOUS ENTENDEZ: Je voudrais aller voir une exposition.
VOUS DITES: **On va au musée?**
Allons au musée!
VOUS ENTENDEZ: On va au musée?
Allons au musée!

COMPÉTENCE 4 Telling what you are going to do

A. Ce week-end. Look at the pictures illustrating what various friends are or are not going to do this weekend. What does each one say? Follow the model.

EXEMPLE VOUS ENTENDEZ: quitter l'appartement tôt
VOUS DITES: **Je ne vais pas quitter l'appartement tôt.**
VOUS ENTENDEZ: Je ne vais pas quitter l'appartement tôt.

EXEMPLE

1.

2.

3.

4.

5.

6.

7.

8.

B. Les expressions qui indiquent le futur. You will hear several pairs of expressions of time. Repeat the one that is the most distant in the future. After a pause for you to answer, you will hear the correct reponse. Verify your answer and pronunciation.

EXEMPLE	VOUS ENTENDEZ:	demain matin / demain soir
	VOUS RÉPÉTEZ:	**demain soir**
	VOUS ENTENDEZ:	demain soir

C. Qu'est-ce que vous allez faire? Answer the questions you hear, telling what you plan to do at the indicated times. Write the time expression in your answer. Stop the tape between items to allow enough time to respond.

EXEMPLE	VOUS ENTENDEZ:	Qu'est-ce que vous allez faire ce soir?
	VOUS ÉCRIVEZ:	*Je vais préparer mes cours ce soir.*

1. ______________________________

2. ______________________________

3. ______________________________

4. ______________________________

5. ______________________________

D. Qu'est-ce qu'on fait? Listen as Robert and Thomas discuss their plans for this evening. Then stop the tape and select the correct answer based on what you heard. Rewind and listen again as needed.

1. Ce soir, Robert et Thomas vont…

   a. regarder la télé   **b.** voir une cassette vidéo   **c.** aller au cinéma

2. Ils vont voir…

   a. un film français   **b.** un film italien   **c.** un film américain

3. C'est un…

   a. très bon film   **b.** film amusant   **c.** film triste

4. C'est l'histoire *(story)*…

   a. d'un couple   **b.** d'une petite fille   **c.** d'un jeune garçon

5. Le film est…

   a. en français   **b.** en italien   **c.** en anglais

NOM ______________________ COURS ______________________

CHAPITRE 5
Les projets

COMPÉTENCE 1 Buying clothes

A. Les vêtements. Practice pronouncing the names of clothing and accessories by repeating the names of the pictured items after the speaker.

B. Quels vêtements? You will hear several short conversations. In the illustrations in ***A. Les vêtements,*** circle all the items you hear mentioned.

C. Une cliente exigeante. You will hear a scene in which a young woman is shopping. Listen to the conversation, then stop the tape and complete these statements.

1. La jeune femme cherche ______________________________.

2. Comme taille, elle fait du ______________________________.

3. Elle ne prend pas le premier article suggéré par la vendeuse parce qu'elle n'aime pas le ______

______________________________.

4. Elle n'aime pas le deuxième non plus parce qu'elle cherche quelque chose en ______________

______________________________.

5. Elle ne veut pas le troisième non plus parce qu'il est trop ______________________________.

6. Le quatrième bikini vient *(comes)* en bleu et il est aussi en ______________________________.

D. Et vous? Answer the questions you hear in complete sentences in French.

1. ____

2. ____

3. ____

4. ____

5. ____

E. C'est possible? You will hear some statements about Alice's activities that contain the preposition **pour** *(in order to)* or **sans** *(without)*. Indicate whether what is said is *possible* or *not possible* by circling **possible** or **pas possible.**

1.	possible	pas possible	3.	possible	pas possible	5.	possible	pas possible
2.	possible	pas possible	4.	possible	pas possible	6.	possible	pas possible

F. Dans l'ordre logique. You will hear about some of Vincent's activities today. Listen to the first part of what he does and use the logical order of events to decide what he probably does *immediately* after. Circle your response.

1. **a.** il prend l'enveloppe.
   b. il remet l'enveloppe sur la table.
2. **a.** il lit la lettre.
   b. il repose l'enveloppe sur la table.
3. **a.** il boit son café.
   b. il descend l'escalier.
4. **a.** il entre dans le café.
   b. il quitte le café.
5. **a.** il descend de l'autobus.
   b. il attend l'autobus.
6. **a.** il descend et entre dans le cinéma.
   b. il sort du cinéma.

NOM ____________________ COURS ____________________

COMPÉTENCE 2 Deciding what to do

A. Quel temps fait-il? For each illustration, you will be asked what the weather is like. After a pause for you to respond, you will hear the correct answer. Verify your response and pronunciation.

EXEMPLE	VOUS ENTENDEZ:	Quel temps fait-il?
	VOUS DITES:	**Il fait chaud.**
	VOUS ENTENDEZ:	Il fait chaud.

EXEMPLE

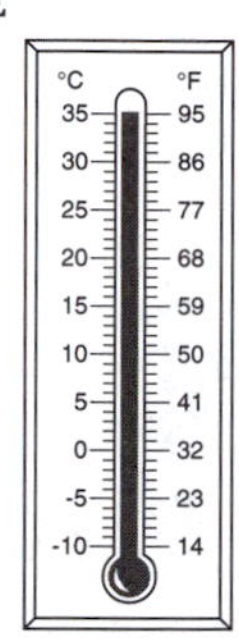

1.

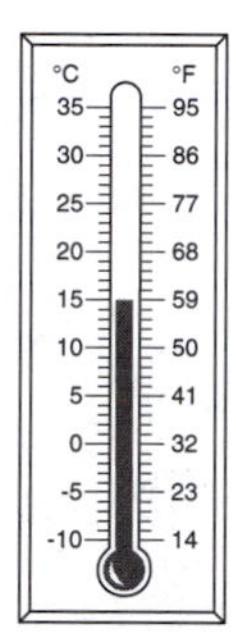

2.

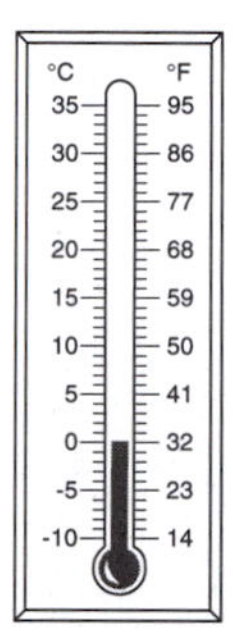

3.

4.

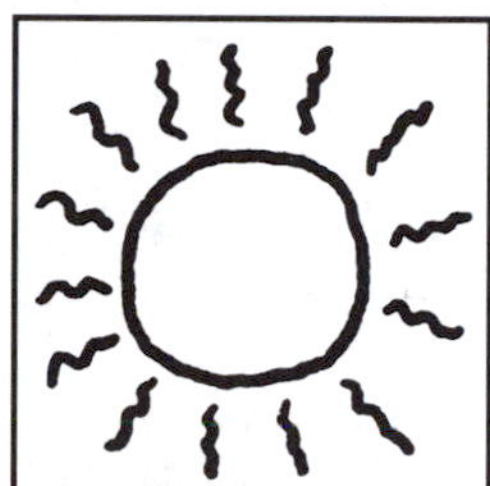

5.

6.

B. La météo. You will hear a weather report for France. Afterward stop the tape and note as many details as you can *in English* about the weather in the indicated places. Rewind and listen again as needed.

1. sur l'ensemble du pays ____________________

2. en Normandie ____________________

3. les températures dans le nord *(north)* du pays et à Paris ____________________

4. les températures dans le sud *(south)* ____________________

5. en montagne *(mountains)* ____________________

C. Le verbe *faire* et les expressions avec *faire*. Repeat the forms of the verb **faire** and the sample sentences after the speaker.

FAIRE				
je	fais	nous	faisons	Je ne fais rien ce soir.
tu	fais	vous	faites	Qu'est-ce que tu fais?
il	fait	ils	font	On fait quelque chose ensemble?
elle	fait	elles	font	Nous faisons toujours le ménage.
on	fait			Vous faites souvent du camping?
				Ils font la cuisine.

D. Avoir besoin ou avoir envie? Based on what these people say they are going to do, say if they probably *need to* or *feel like* doing the activity they name, using either **avoir besoin de** or **avoir envie de**. After a pause for you to respond, you will hear the appropriate answer. Verify your response and pronunciation.

EXEMPLES VOUS ENTENDEZ: J'ai l'intention de faire mes devoirs ce week-end.
VOUS DITES: **Il a besoin de faire ses devoirs.**
VOUS ENTENDEZ: Il a besoin de faire ses devoirs.

VOUS ENTENDEZ: J'ai l'intention de faire du ski ce week-end.
VOUS DITES: **Elle a envie de faire du ski.**
VOUS ENTENDEZ: Elle a envie de faire du ski.

E. Suggestions. You will hear some friends telling how they feel. Stop the tape after each one and make a logical suggestion using one of the expressions given in the **impératif.**

MANGER QUELQUE CHOSE aller au café *faire du jogging*
LOUER UNE CASSETTE VIDÉO **aller au centre commercial**

EXEMPLE VOUS ENTENDEZ: J'ai envie de manger.
VOUS ÉCRIVEZ: Mange quelque chose!

1. ______________________________

2. ______________________________

3. ______________________________

4. ______________________________

F. Et vous? Answer the questions you hear in complete sentences in French.

1. ______________________________

2. ______________________________

3. ______________________________

4. ______________________________

NOM ______________________ COURS ______________________

COMPÉTENCE 3 Saying what you did

A. Une journée chargée. You will hear Alice say some of the things she did yesterday. Write the number of the sentence below the picture it matches. Not all the activities pictured will be mentioned.

______

______

______

______

______

______

______

______

______

B. Et vous? Look at the pictures in ***A. Une journée chargée.*** You will be asked if you did each of the activities depicted yesterday. After a pause for you to respond, you will hear the appropriate answer. Verify your response and pronunciation.

EXEMPLE	VOUS ENTENDEZ:	Est-ce que vous avez dormi jusqu'à dix heures du matin hier?
	VOUS DITES:	**Oui, j'ai dormi jusqu'à dix heures du matin hier. / Non, je n'ai pas dormi jusqu'à dix heures du matin hier.**
	VOUS ENTENDEZ:	Oui, j'ai dormi jusqu'à dix heures du matin hier. / Non, je n'ai pas dormi jusqu'à dix heures du matin hier.

C. Les expressions qui désignent le passé. Stop the tape and draw a line to match the phrases expressing present time in the left column with a parallel expression of past time from the right column. The first one has been done as an example. When you have finished, turn on the tape and correct your work. Repeat each of the time expressions after the speaker to work on pronunciation.

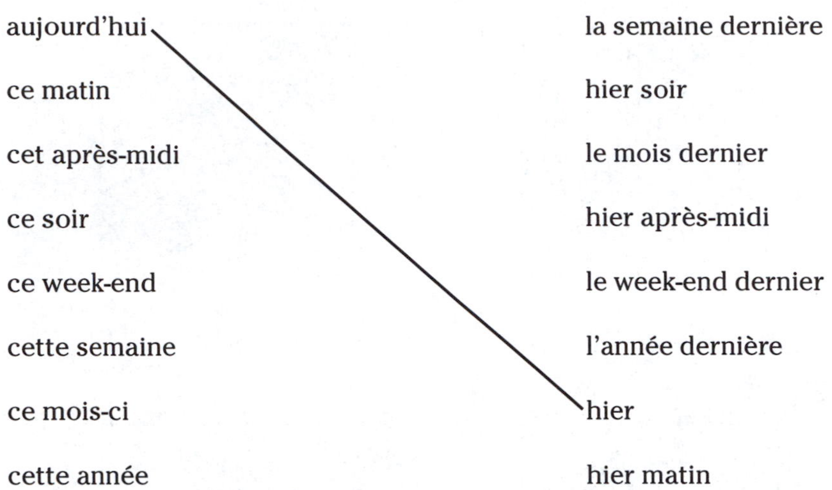

aujourd'hui	la semaine dernière
ce matin	hier soir
cet après-midi	le mois dernier
ce soir	hier après-midi
ce week-end	le week-end dernier
cette semaine	l'année dernière
ce mois-ci	hier
cette année	hier matin

D. Le week-end dernier. In French, answer the questions you hear about what you did last week-end.

1. ______________________________
2. ______________________________
3. ______________________________
4. ______________________________
5. ______________________________
6. ______________________________
7. ______________________________
8. ______________________________

NOM ______________________ COURS ______________________

COMPÉTENCE 4 Telling where you went

A. Alice a fait un voyage. Listen as Alice talks about a weekend trip she took. Then stop the tape and complete these statements based on what she says. When you have finished, turn on the tape and check your work. Repeat the sentences after the speaker to correct your pronunciation.

Elle est allée à Deauville. Elle n'y est pas allée en train, elle y est allée en ______________

______________________.

Elle est partie le samedi matin et elle est arrivée vers ______________ heure.

Elle est descendue dans un charmant ______________________.

Dimanche, elle est allée à la ______________.

Elle est rentrée tard le ______________ soir.

B. La journée d'Alice. Look at the illustration of what Alice did today and listen as she talks about her activities. Then stop the tape and answer these questions in complete sentences.

1. Vers quelle heure est-ce qu'Alice a quitté son appartement?

____

2. Où est-ce qu'elle est montée dans l'autobus?

____

3. Où est-ce qu'Alice est descendue de l'autobus?

____

4. À quelle heure est-ce qu'elle est rentrée chez elle?

____

C. Prononciation: Les auxiliaires *avoir* et *être*. Stop the tape and review the ***Prononciation*** section on page 184 of the textbook. Then start the tape and repeat the following forms of the verbs **avoir** and **être** after the speaker, being careful to pronounce them distinctly.

1.	tu as	tu es	3.	elle a	elle est
2.	ils ont	ils sont	4.	il a	il est

Now you will hear a friend's questions in the **passé composé** with either **avoir** or **être** as the auxiliary. Circle the auxiliary that you hear in the lists above.

Now rewind the tape and listen to the questions again. Answer them with complete sentences. Stop the tape between items to allow enough time to respond.

1. ______________________________

2. ______________________________

3. ______________________________

4. ______________________________

D. Claire décrit son week-end. Claire has spent a weekend in Deauville. Listen as she describes her weekend to Alice. The first time, simply listen to the conversation at normal speed. It will then be repeated at a slower speed with pauses for you to write in the missing words in the sentences. You will need to stop the tape during the pauses to have sufficient time to respond. When you are done, rewind and listen again to correct your work.

ALICE: Alors, Claire, raconte-moi ton week-end à Deauville!

CLAIRE: D'abord, nous ______________ le train et nous ______________ dans un charmant petit hôtel. Le premier soir, nous ______________ dans un très bon restaurant où nous avons goûté *(tasted)* des spécialités de la région. C'était très bon!

Dimanche, nous ______________ la journée à la plage.

ALICE: Est-ce que tu ______________ au casino?

CLAIRE: Oui, dimanche soir, mais nous ______________.

Mon mari n'aime pas jouer pour de l'argent *(money)*. Après, nous ______________ à un concert de jazz au centre culturel. J' ______________ la musique. Nous ______________ à l'hôtel à trois heures du matin!

NOM ______________________ COURS ______________________

CHAPITRE 6
Les invitations

COMPÉTENCE 1 Talking about movies

A. Quel genre de film? You will be asked to identify the genre of the films depicted. After a pause for you to respond, you will hear the correct answer. Verify your response and your pronunciation.

EXEMPLE	VOUS ENTENDEZ:	C'est quel genre de film, une comédie ou un film policier?
	VOUS DITES:	**C'est une comédie.**
	VOUS ENTENDEZ:	C'est une comédie.

EXEMPLE

____

1.

____

2.

____

3.

____

4.

____

5.

____

6.

____

7.

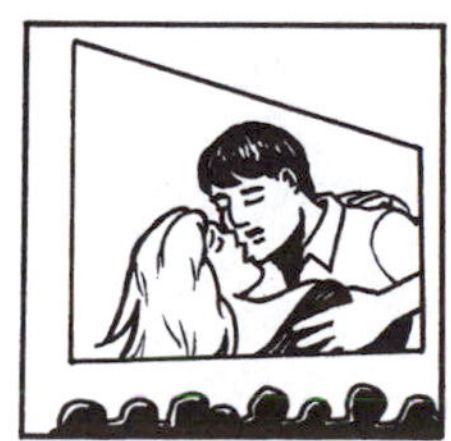

____

8.

____

B. Les préférences. You will hear several people express their wishes about seeing a particular kind of film. Listen to each statement, stop the tape, and write the number of the statement in the blank below the corresponding illustration in ***A. Quel genre de film?***

C. Le répondeur automatique. It's Monday afternoon and Alice is listening to messages on her answering machine. After each message, stop the tape and write the requested information in the chart.

	Qui parle?	Quelle est l'activité proposée?	Quel jour?	À quelle heure?
MESSAGE 1				
MESSAGE 2				
MESSAGE 3				
MESSAGE 4				

D. Au cinéma. Alice and Vincent have just arrived at the cinema. Listen to their conversation. Then stop the tape and indicate if these statements are true or false by circling **vrai** or **faux.**

1. Alice n'a jamais vu *Les Quatre Cents Coups.* VRAI FAUX
2. Vincent a envie de voir un autre film. VRAI FAUX
3. Les séances des deux films sont à des heures différentes. VRAI FAUX
4. Alice n'a pas aimé le film qu'elle a vu. VRAI FAUX

Now rewind the tape and listen to the conversation again. Answer these questions in French.

1. Combien de fois est-ce que Vincent a déjà vu le film qu'Alice voudrait aller voir?

____

2. Pourquoi est-ce qu'Alice a aimé le film? Donnez une des raisons.

____

3. Quel genre de film est-ce que Vincent est allé voir?

____

4. Qu'est-ce qu'Alice suggère de faire après le film?

____

NOM ______________________ COURS ______________________

COMPÉTENCE 2 Planning an outing

A. Tu veux bien...? Michèle loves to go out with friends, but is not at all athletic. You will hear friends invite her to do various things. In each case, decide how she would respond. Circle your answer.

1. Avec plaisir! — Je regrette, mais je dois partir maintenant.
2. Oui, je veux bien! — Je regrette, mais je ne suis pas libre.
3. Avec plaisir! — Malheureusement, je suis occupée.
4. D'accord! — Je voudrais bien, mais je dois travailler.
5. Quelle bonne idée! — Je regrette, mais je ne peux pas.

B. Prononciation: Les verbes *vouloir, pouvoir* et *devoir*. Repeat the phrases after the speaker, paying attention to the pronunciation of the forms of **vouloir, pouvoir,** and **devoir.**

Je veux aller au cinéma, mais je ne peux pas. Je dois travailler.
Tu veux sortir ce soir, mais tu ne peux pas. Tu dois préparer tes cours.
Éric veut aller au musée, mais il ne peut pas. Il doit rester avec son petit frère.
Nous voulons partir en week-end, mais nous ne pouvons pas. Nous devons travailler.
Vous voulez aller à la plage, mais vous ne pouvez pas. Vous devez faire le ménage.
Ils veulent aller au café, mais ils ne peuvent pas. Ils doivent aller en classe.

Notice the difference between the pronunciation of the third-person singular and plural forms of these verbs. Listen and repeat.

Elle veut aller au cinéma, mais elle ne peut pas. Elle doit rester à la maison.
Elles veulent aller au cinéma, mais elles ne peuvent pas. Elles doivent rester à la maison.

Now listen to Alice talk about Vincent and Éric. In each statement, decide whether she is just talking about Vincent or whether she is talking about both Vincent and Éric. Circle your answer.

1. singulier pluriel	3. singulier pluriel	5. singulier pluriel
2. singulier pluriel	4. singulier pluriel	6. singulier pluriel

Now rewind the tape, listen again, and write in the missing words. Stop the tape as needed.

1. ______________________________ cet après-midi.
2. ______________________________ avec moi ce soir.
3. ______________________________ parce qu'__________ ______________________________.
4. ______________________________ à Deauville ce week-end.
5. ______________________________ ce week-end.
6. ______________________________ à la maison aujourd'hui.

C. Prononciation: Le verbe *prendre*. Stop the tape and review the ***Prononciation*** section on page 204 of the textbook. Then turn on the tape. Listen and repeat.

PRENDRE			
je	prends	nous	prenons
tu	prends	vous	prenez
il	prend	ils	prennent
elle	prend	elles	prennent
on	prend		

Je prends quelquefois l'autobus mais je préfère y aller à pied.
Tu prends souvent le train?
On prend le métro?
Nous prenons l'autobus.
Vous prenez souvent l'autobus?
Les Parisiens prennent souvent le métro.

D. À quel musée vont-ils? Listen as Éric and Michèle discuss which museum they would like to visit. Then stop the tape and indicate whether these statements are accurate by circling **oui** or **non.**

1. Ils ont le choix *(choice)* entre trois musées. OUI NON
2. Éric est un peu impatient. OUI NON
3. Éric veut voir l'exposition de tableaux impressionnistes. OUI NON
4. Ils vont aller voir l'exposition de dinosaures aussi. OUI NON
5. Ils vont au musée en autobus. OUI NON

Rewind the tape and listen again to the conversation between Éric and Michèle. Then stop the tape and answer these questions.

1. Qu'est-ce que Michèle veut voir au musée de Sciences Naturelles?

____

2. Pourquoi est-ce qu'Éric pense qu'ils ne peuvent pas voir les deux musées?

____

3. Comment vont-ils aller au musée?

____

4. Est-ce qu'Éric aime vraiment les sciences naturelles?

____

COMPÉTENCE 3 Describing childhood memories

A. Les fêtes. What holidays do these pictures represent? After a pause for you to respond, you will hear the correct answer. Verify your response and your pronunciation.

EXEMPLE	VOUS ENTENDEZ:	C'est quelle fête, Noël ou Pâques?
	VOUS DITES:	**C'est Pâques.**
	VOUS ENTENDEZ:	C'est Pâques.

EXEMPLE

1.

2.

3.

4.

B. La fête de Michèle. Listen as Éric, Michèle, and Éric's Algerian neighbor Karima discuss an upcoming party. Then, stop the tape and indicate whether these sentences are true or false by circling **vrai** or **faux.**

1. Éric et Michèle font une boum pour l'anniversaire d'Éric. VRAI FAUX
2. En France, on célèbre sa fête *(Saint's Day)* et son anniversaire. VRAI FAUX
3. En Algérie, on ne célèbre pas la fête de Noël. VRAI FAUX
4. Karima trouve que c'est une bonne idée de faire une boum pour célébrer sa fête. VRAI FAUX

C. En famille. You will hear speakers say how they used to celebrate various holidays when they were young. After each statement, stop the tape and write down whether your family used to celebrate in a similar way. Use the **imparfait.** If you did not celebrate a particular holiday, say **On ne célébrait pas...**

EXEMPLE	VOUS ENTENDEZ:	À Noël, on ouvrait des cadeaux.
	VOUS ÉCRIVEZ:	*Nous aussi, on ouvrait des cadeaux. / Nous, on n'ouvrait pas de cadeaux à Noël. / Nous, on ne célébrait pas Noël.*

1. ____
2. ____
3. ____
4. ____

D. Prononciation: Les terminaisons de l'imparfait. Stop the tape and review the ***Prononciation*** section on page 208 of the textbook. Then turn on the tape. Listen and repeat to practice the pronunciation of the endings of the imperfect tense.

Quand j'étais jeune, j'habitais avec ma famille.
Quand tu étais jeune, où habitais-tu?
Nous habitions à la campagne. Nous allions souvent en ville.
Vous habitiez en ville? Vous aviez une jolie maison?
Il y avait beaucoup de jeunes dans le village. On prenait l'autocar pour aller en ville.
Mes amis aimaient sortir. Ils allaient souvent au cinéma.

E. Maintenant ou avant? Listen to questions about this semester (or trimester) and last semester (or trimester). Listen carefully for the verb tense and circle **ce semestre / trimestre** if you hear a present tense verb or **le semestre / trimestre dernier** if the verb is in the imperfect.

1. ce semestre / trimestre — le semestre / trimestre dernier
2. ce semestre / trimestre — le semestre / trimestre dernier
3. ce semestre / trimestre — le semestre / trimestre dernier
4. ce semestre / trimestre — le semestre / trimestre dernier
5. ce semestre / trimestre — le semestre / trimestre dernier
6. ce semestre / trimestre — le semestre / trimestre dernier

Now rewind the tape and answer each of the questions. Begin each answer with either **Ce semestre / trimestre** or **Le semestre / trimestre dernier.** Stop the tape between items to allow enough time to respond.

1. ______________________________
2. ______________________________
3. ______________________________
4. ______________________________
5. ______________________________
6. ______________________________

F. La jeunesse de Michèle. Michèle's life has changed very little from when she was young. Listen to statements about her present situation and say that they also used to be true when she was young. Use the **imparfait.** After a pause for you to respond, you will hear the correct answer. Verify your response and your pronunciation.

EXEMPLE	VOUS ENTENDEZ:	Ses parents travaillent beaucoup.
	VOUS DITES:	**Ses parents travaillaient beaucoup quand elle était jeune.**
	VOUS ENTENDEZ:	Ses parents travaillaient beaucoup quand elle était jeune.

NOM ______________________ COURS ______________________

COMPÉTENCE 4 Narrating what happened

A. Prononciation: Le passé composé et l'imparfait. Stop the tape and review the ***Prononciation*** section on page 215 of the textbook. Then turn on the tape. Listen and repeat to practice distinguishing the **imparfait,** the **présent,** and the **passé composé.**

je parlais / j'ai parlé

tu regardais / tu as regardé

elle travaillait / elle a travaillé

il est allé / il allait

nous partons / nous partions

vous mangez / vous mangiez

B. Passé composé ou imparfait? Listen to a series of questions about your childhood and decide if you are being asked about a single event that happened **(passé composé)** or about how things used to be in general **(imparfait)**. Circle your answers.

1. passé composé imparfait
2. passé composé imparfait
3. passé composé imparfait
4. passé composé imparfait
5. passé composé imparfait
6. passé composé imparfait

Now rewind the tape and answer the questions about your childhood, using complete sentences. Stop the tape to allow enough time to respond.

1. ______________________________
2. ______________________________
3. ______________________________
4. ______________________________
5. ______________________________
6. ______________________________

C. La journée d'Alice. Listen as Alice describes her day. Each sentence has two verbs, one in the **imparfait** to describe background information, and the other in the **passé composé** to describe what happened. Stop the tape after each sentence and write the two verbs and their subjects under the appropriate column.

EXEMPLE VOUS ENTENDEZ: Il faisait beau quand je suis sortie de la maison.

	BACKGROUND INFORMATION	WHAT HAPPENED
EXEMPLE	il faisait (beau)	je suis sortie
1.	_____	_____
2.	_____	_____
3.	_____	_____
4.	_____	_____
5.	_____	_____
6.	_____	_____

D. Une sortie. Listen as Alice talks about the last time she and Vincent went to a restaurant. The first time, simply listen to the conversation at normal speed. It will then be repeated at a slower speed with pauses for you to write in the missing words. Stop the tape during the pauses to have sufficient time to respond. Rewind and listen again to correct your work.

On _____ ensemble au restaurant samedi soir. On _____ la maison vers sept heures. Comme *(Since)* il _____ beau, on _____ au restaurant à pied. Il _____ environ sept heures et demie quand on _____. Je _____ très faim et on _____ tout de suite. On _____ un verre de vin avant. Le repas _____ délicieux et j' _____. Après, nous _____ trop fatigués, alors nous _____ une promenade. Il _____ environ dix heures quand nous _____ et nous _____ directement au lit. Le lendemain, c' _____ dimanche et j' _____ jusqu'à onze heures.

NOM ______________________________ COURS ______________________________

CHAPITRE 7

La vie quotidienne

COMPÉTENCE 1 Talking about relationships

A. Un sondage. You are going to hear someone being interviewed about her ideas on relationships. First review the relevant vocabulary by repeating these phrases after the speaker. Underline the italicized choice that best describes you.

Je suis *célibataire / fiancé(e) / marié(e) / séparé(e) / divorcé(e) / veuf (veuve).*

Je tombe *souvent / rarement* amoureux (amoureuse).

Je crois / Je ne crois pas au grand amour et au coup de foudre.

Le côté sentimental de la vie est *très / assez / peu* important pour moi en ce moment.

Je ne veux pas avoir d'enfants. / Un jour, j'espère avoir des enfants. / J'ai des enfants.

Now turn on the tape and listen to the interview. Then stop the tape and complete the statements as the person interviewed would. Also indicate if you agree by circling **Je suis d'accord** or **Je ne suis pas d'accord.**

1. Pour moi, l'amour rime *(rhymes)* avec ______________________________ .

   Je suis d'accord. Je ne suis pas d'accord.

2. Le ______________________________ ? Pour moi, c'est juste de l'attraction physique.

   Je suis d'accord. Je ne suis pas d'accord.

3. Avoir une bonne relation, c'est du ______________________________ .

   Je suis d'accord. Je ne suis pas d'accord.

4. Dans un couple, on doit ______________________________ beaucoup de choses, mais pas tout.

   Je suis d'accord. Je ne suis pas d'accord.

B. Révisons un peu. You are going to hear about how Rosalie first met her husband. First review how the endings of the **imparfait** sound by repeating these sentences after the speaker.

__________ C'était la fin de la guerre.

__________ J'avais dix-huit ans.

__________ Il ne parlait pas très bien français.

__________ Nous habitions à Rouen.

__________ Mon oncle et ma tante étaient dans la Résistance.

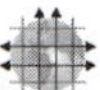

Now rewind the tape and listen to the sentences again. The verb endings in all of these sentences sound alike except for one. Place an **X** in the blank next to that sentence.

Now stop the tape, read the sentences again, and write in English what you think each one means.

1. ______________________________
2. ______________________________
3. ______________________________
4. ______________________________
5. ______________________________

C. Une histoire d'amour. Listen as Rosalie tells Rose about how she first fell in love when she was young. Then stop the tape and indicate whether these statements are true or false by circling **vrai** or **faux.**

1. Ça a été le coup de foudre entre Rosalie et le soldat américain.

   VRAI FAUX

2. Le soldat américain parlait bien français.

   VRAI FAUX

3. Ils se sont mariés aux États-Unis.

   VRAI FAUX

Rewind and listen to Rosalie and Rose again. Then answer these questions with short answers in French.

1. En quelle année est-ce que Rosalie a rencontré *(met)* le soldat américain?

   ____

2. Quel âge avait-elle?

   ____

3. Est-ce que Rosalie parlait anglais?

   ____

NOM ______________________________ COURS ______________________________

COMPÉTENCE 2 Describing your daily routine

A. D'abord… You will hear two statements. Repeat the action that would logically come first. After a pause for you to respond, you will hear the correct answer. Verify your response and your pronunciation.

EXEMPLE	VOUS ENTENDEZ:	Je fais ma toilette. / Je quitte la maison.
	VOUS DITES:	**Je fais ma toilette.**
	VOUS ENTENDEZ:	Je fais ma toilette.

B. Chez Henri et Patricia. You will hear several statements about the daily lives of Patricia and Henri. Write the number of each statement next to the drawing depicting it. Stop the tape between items to allow enough time to respond.

a.

____

b.

____

c.

____

d.

____

e.

____

f.

____

C. Que vont-ils faire? Stop the tape and look at the illustrations in ***B. Chez Henri et Patricia*** again. Imagine that these are the activities that Henri and Patricia are going to do tomorrow. Then turn on the tape and answer each question you hear according to what is depicted. Stop the tape between items to allow enough time to respond.

1. ____
2. ____
3. ____
4. ____
5. ____
6. ____

D. Ça s'écrit comment? Stop the tape and review the section on spelling change verbs on page 241 of the textbook. Then turn on the tape, listen to the questions, and write the missing words. Stop the tape between items to allow enough time to respond.

1. À quelle heure est-ce que ____ en général?

2. Est-ce que ____ te lever tôt ou tard?

3. Comment _______________________________________ ton professeur de français?

4. Est-ce que ____ dans son cours?

5. Est-ce que ____________________________ obtenir *(to get)* un A dans son cours?

6. Est-ce que _________________________________ toujours de parler français avec un bon accent?

Now rewind the tape and listen to the questions again. This time, imagine that a friend is asking you these questions. Stop the tape after each one and answer it about yourself.

1. ____

2. ____

3. ____

4. ____

5. ____

6. ____

E. Et vous? Answer the questions you hear in complete sentences in French.

1. ____

2. ____

3. ____

4. ____

5. ____

6. ____

7. ____

8. ____

COMPÉTENCE 3 Saying what you do to and for others

A. La rencontre. Listen as Rosalie describes her first meeting with André since they were young. Write the number of each sentence you hear next to the illustration depicting it.

a.

____

b.

____

c.

____

d.

____

e.

____

Now rewind the tape and listen to all of the sentences again. Then stop the tape and answer these questions.

1. Est-ce qu'André et Rosalie se sont vus tout de suite au café?

____

2. Qu'est-ce qu'ils ont fait quand ils se sont vus?

____

3. Après le déjeuner, qu'est-ce qu'ils ont fait?

____

4. Vers quelle heure est-ce qu'André et Rosalie se sont quittés?

____

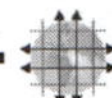

B. Des actions réciproques. You will hear a series of statements about Rosalie's and André's interactions. Transform each statement using the appropriate reciprocal form of the verb as in the example. After a pause for you to respond, you will hear the correct answer. Verify your response and your pronunciation.

EXEMPLE	VOUS ENTENDEZ:	André téléphone à Rosalie et Rosalie téléphone à André.
	VOUS DITES:	**Ils se téléphonent.**
	VOUS ENTENDEZ:	Ils se téléphonent.

C. La grande nouvelle! Listen as Rosalie makes an important announcement to Rose. Then stop the tape and write sentences explaining how often Rosalie and André do these things, according to what is said in the conversation.

TOUS LES JOURS toujours *souvent*
QUELQUEFOIS rarement jamais

1. se quitter ______________________________
2. se disputer ______________________________
3. s'entendre bien ______________________________

Now rewind the tape, listen to the conversation again, and indicate whether these statements are true or false by circling **vrai** or **faux.**

1. Rosalie ne s'est jamais sentie si heureuse, sauf avec son mari.	VRAI	FAUX
2. Rose se demande *(wonders)* si sa grand-mère ne s'est pas décidée un peu rapidement.	VRAI	FAUX
3. Rosalie et André se sont retrouvés il y a déjà un an.	VRAI	FAUX
4. André est tombé amoureux de Rosalie quand elle avait 18 ans.	VRAI	FAUX

D. Et vous? Answer the questions you hear with complete sentences in French. Stop the tape between items to allow enough time to respond.

1. ______________________________
2. ______________________________
3. ______________________________
4. ______________________________
5. ______________________________
6. ______________________________
7. ______________________________

NOM ______________________ COURS ______________________

COMPÉTENCE 4 Comparing your past and present activities

A. Prononcez bien! Repeat these expressions after the speaker, paying careful attention to the difference in pronunciation between the present and imperfect verb endings.

MAINTENANT	QUAND J'ÉTAIS AU LYCÉE
Je me sens bien dans ma peau.	Je me sentais un peu malheureux (malheureuse).
J'arrive en classe à l'heure.	J'arrivais en classe en retard.
Je m'intéresse aux études.	Je m'intéressais au sport.
J'aime sortir avec des copains.	J'aimais partir en week-end avec ma famille.
Je suis plutôt gentil(le) la plupart du temps.	Quelquefois, j'étais raisonnable, mais d'autres fois, j'étais insupportable.

Now listen to a series of questions and decide if you are being asked about now (present tense) or when you were in high school (imperfect). Circle your response.

1. MAINTENANT AU LYCÉE
2. MAINTENANT AU LYCÉE
3. MAINTENANT AU LYCÉE
4. MAINTENANT AU LYCÉE
5. MAINTENANT AU LYCÉE
6. MAINTENANT AU LYCÉE

Now rewind and listen to the questions again. Stop the tape after each one and write your answer.

1. ____
2. ____
3. ____
4. ____
5. ____
6. ____

B. Présent, imparfait ou passé composé? Rosalie is talking to Rose. Listen to what she says and indicate the tense of the verb by circling **présent, imparfait,** or **passé composé.**

1. PRÉSENT IMPARFAIT PASSÉ COMPOSÉ
2. PRÉSENT IMPARFAIT PASSÉ COMPOSÉ
3. PRÉSENT IMPARFAIT PASSÉ COMPOSÉ
4. PRÉSENT IMPARFAIT PASSÉ COMPOSÉ

C. Prononciation: Les verbes comme *dormir* et *sortir*. Stop the tape and review the ***Prononciation*** section on page 254 of the textbook. Then turn on the tape and repeat these verb forms after the speaker.

DORMIR		PARTIR		SORTIR		SE SENTIR	
je	dors	je	pars	je	sors	je	me sens
tu	dors	tu	pars	tu	sors	tu	te sens
il	dort	il	part	il	sort	il	se sent
elle	dort	elle	part	elle	sort	elle	se sent
on	dort	on	part	on	sort	on	se sent
nous	dormons	nous	partons	nous	sortons	nous	nous sentons
vous	dormez	vous	partez	vous	sortez	vous	vous sentez
ils	dorment	ils	partent	ils	sortent	ils	se sentent
elles	dorment	elles	partent	elles	sortent	elles	se sentent

Now you will hear a verb form from the lists above without the subject pronoun. Circle all of the verb forms that are prononced that way. In some cases, there may be several possibilities.

D. À chacun ses goûts! Listen as Henri talks about going out of town for the weekend. The first time, simply listen to his conversation at normal speed. It will then be repeated at a slower speed with pauses for you to write in the missing words in the sentences. You will need to stop the tape during the pauses to have sufficient time to respond. When you are done, rewind and listen again to correct your work.

Patricia adore ______________________________ en week-end, mais moi, je ______________________________ tout à fait bien dans ma peau dans une ville inconnue *(unknown)*. Patricia et les enfants ______________________________ bien partout. En plus, je dois ______________________________ très tôt parce que nous ______________________________ toujours vers six ou sept heures du matin. Patricia et les enfants ______________________________ tôt aussi, mais ils ______________________________ souvent dans la voiture. Moi, je ne ______________________________ bien que dans mon lit. Patricia ne comprend pas parce qu'elle ______________________________ toujours bien. Moi, j'aime mieux passer le week-end ici chez nous. On ______________________________ le soir avec des amis et on ______________ jusqu'à 10 heures le lendemain matin. Ça, c'est un week-end agréable!

NOM ______________________ COURS ______________________

CHAPITRE 8
La bonne cuisine

COMPÉTENCE 1 Ordering at a restaurant

A. Bon appétit! Stop the tape and look at the lists of foods by category. For each category, draw a line through any item that is not appropriate. Then turn on the tape and verify your answers by repeating the items that are not crossed out after the speaker.

UNE ENTRÉE OU UN HORS-D'ŒUVRE:

des escargots   de la soupe   un bifteck   de la salade de tomates   du pâté
des œufs durs   des crudités   de la glace

UN PLAT PRINCIPAL:

de la viande:
des crevettes   du rosbif   du bifteck   des haricots verts   une côte de porc

de la volaille:
du canard   du gâteau   du poulet   des crudités

du poisson:
du fromage   du saumon   du pain   du thon

des fruits de mer:
des moules   des crevettes   des huîtres   du homard   du poivre

UN LÉGUME:

des haricots verts   des pommes   des pommes de terre   des petits pois

POUR FINIR LE REPAS:

un dessert   du sel et du poivre   du café   du fromage   de la tarte
de la glace   du gâteau

B. Prononciation: Le *h* aspiré. Stop the tape and review the ***Prononciation*** section on page 269 of the textbook. Then turn on the tape. Listen and repeat the examples of non-aspirate and aspirate **h.**

H NON-ASPIRÉ:	les huîtres	des huîtres	beaucoup d'huîtres
H ASPIRÉ:	les hors-d'œuvre	des hors-d'œuvre	beaucoup de hors-d'œuvre
H NON-ASPIRÉ:	l'huile *(oil)*	de l'huile	pas d'huile
H ASPIRÉ:	le homard	du homard	pas de homard

C. Au restaurant. Stop the tape and look over this menu. Then turn on the tape and listen to a scene at a restaurant. List what the woman and the man order from the menu.

LA FEMME

Entrée: ____________________

Plat principal: ____________________

Dessert: ____________________

L'HOMME

Entrée: ____________________

Plat principal: ____________________

Dessert: ____________________

Le Bistrot - 87 F.

Service 15% Compris

Adrian vous propose son petit Menu Bistrot composé uniquement de produits frais de saison.

Première Assiette

9 Huîtres "Fines de claires no3" Sur lit de glace
Assiette de Coquillages farcis à l'ail
Cocotte de moules marinières
Salade aux lardons, Oeuf poché
Terrine de canard maison, au poivre vert
Plateau de fruits de mer "l'écailler" +50 Frs

Deuxième Assiette

Brochette de poissons, beurre blanc
Moules de pays, frites
Sardines grillées aux herbes
Langue de boeuf, sauce piquante
Poêlée de Rognon de boeuf, flambée au cognac
Bavette poêlée à la fondue d'oignons

Troisième Assiette

Crème Caramel
Fraises au vin ou fraises au sucre
Feuillantine aux pommes
Glace et sorbet artisanaux
Ile flottante
Coupe normande

Arrivage Journalier de Poissons, d'Huîtres et de Fruits de Mer

NOM ______________________ COURS ______________________

COMPÉTENCE 2 Talking about breakfast

A. Au petit déjeuner. When asked, say that you would like *some* of each of the items pictured. Be sure to use the correct form of the partitive **du, de la, de l', or des.** After a pause for you to respond, you will hear the correct answer. Verify your response and your pronunciation.

EXEMPLE	VOUS ENTENDEZ:	Qu'est-ce que vous voulez?
	VOUS DITES:	**Je voudrais du café au lait.**
	VOUS ENTENDEZ:	Je voudrais du café au lait.

1. 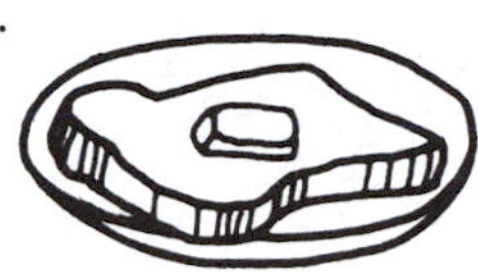

2. 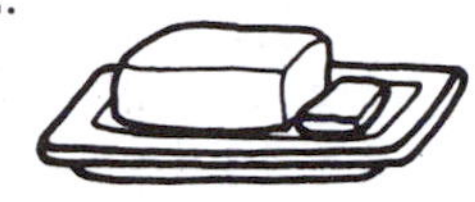

3. 

4. 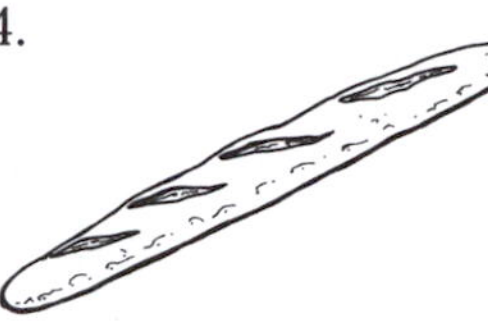

5. 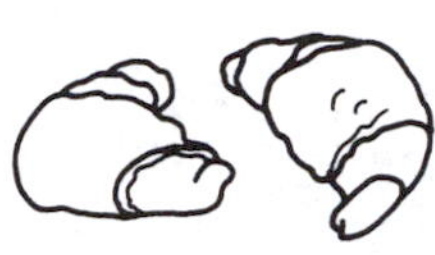

6. 

7. 

8. 

Now listen to a conversation about French eating habits. Circle the pictures of all the items you hear mentioned.

B. Prononciation: Le verbe *boire*. Listen to a short passage comparing the types of drinks popular with Americans to those popular with the French. Then stop the tape. Imagine that a French person is speaking. Complete each question or statement logically, by circling the appropriate choice in italics. Then turn on the tape and verify your responses by repeating each sentence after the speaker. Pay particular attention to the pronunciation of the verb **boire.**

Le matin, je bois *du vin / du café.*

Est-ce que tu bois *du vin / du lait* le matin?

En France, on ne boit jamais *d'eau minérale / de lait* avec les repas.

Nous buvons souvent *du coca / du vin* avec un bon repas.

Vous buvez aussi *du vin / du coca* avec vos repas?

Les Français boivent quelquefois un café *avant / après* le dîner.

C. Qu'est-ce qu'ils ont? Talk about the people in the pictures by selecting one of the options given. After a pause for you to respond, you will hear the correct answer. Verify your response and your pronunciation.

EXEMPLE VOUS ENTENDEZ: Est-ce qu'elle a faim ou soif?
VOUS DITES: **Elle a faim.**
VOUS ENTENDEZ: Elle a faim.

1. 
2. 
3. 
4. 
5. 
6. 

D. On prend quelque chose? Listen to the conversation between Rose and Angèle as they decide where to go eat. Then, stop the tape and indicate whether these statements are true or false by circling **vrai** or **faux.**

1. Angèle voudrait aller boire quelque chose. VRAI FAUX
2. Rose suggère un café du quartier. VRAI FAUX
3. Angèle n'aime pas les restaurants fast-foods. VRAI FAUX
4. Angèle décide d'essayer un fast-food. VRAI FAUX

Rewind the tape and listen to the conversation again. Then stop the tape and give in English one advantage and one disadvantage of fast-food restaurants mentioned by Rose and Angèle.

AVANTAGE

____

DÉSAVANTAGE

____

NOM ______________________ COURS ______________________

COMPÉTENCE 3 Buying food

A. Fruits et légumes. As you hear an item named, identify it as a fruit or a vegetable. After a pause for you to respond, you will hear the correct answer. Verify your response and your pronunciation.

EXEMPLE	VOUS ENTENDEZ:	Une carotte, c'est un fruit ou un légume?
	VOUS DITES:	**Une carotte, c'est un légume.**
	VOUS ENTENDEZ:	Une carotte, c'est un légume.

B. Qu'est-ce qu'on peut acheter? Stop the tape and read the items listed under the name of each shop. Circle the items you could buy in each shop. Then start the tape and verify your answers by repeating the correct items after the speaker.

À la boulangerie-pâtisserie, on peut acheter…

des tartelettes   du poulet   un pain complet   une baguette

À la boucherie, on achète de la viande et de la volaille…

du bœuf   des moules   du porc   du poulet

À la charcuterie, on achète…

des tartelettes   des plats préparés   du saucisson   des saucisses

À l'épicerie, on achète…

des fruits   des légumes   des moules   des produits surgelés

C. Quantités. Stop the tape and indicate the logical quantity to buy of each item. Circle the correct choice in italics. Then start the tape and verify your answers by repeating each item after the speaker.

Je voudrais *un litre / une douzaine* de lait.

Je voudrais *une bouteille / un paquet* de vin.

Je voudrais *une tranche / un pot* de jambon.

Je voudrais *un kilo / un gramme* de pommes de terre.

Je voudrais *une boîte / un pot* de confiture.

Je voudrais *un paquet / un verre* de sucre.

Je voudrais *une livre / une douzaine* d'œufs.

Je voudrais *un morceau / une carafe* de fromage.

D. Et vous? Listen to the questions and answer with complete sentences, using the pronoun **en** to replace the items mentioned. Stop the tape between questions to allow enough time to respond.

1. ____

2. ____

3. ____

4. ____

E. Où sont-ils? You will hear four conversations in which people are buying food items in small shops. Write the number of each conversation in the blank next to the store where it takes place.

a. __________ 

b. __________

c. __________ 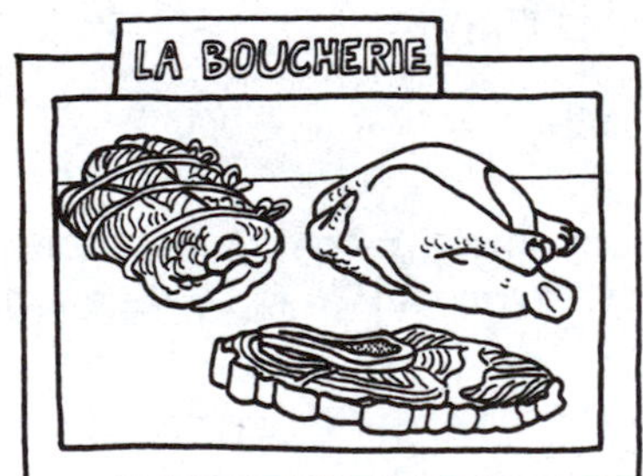

d. __________

Now rewind the tape and listen to the conversations again. Stop the tape and circle the items in the drawings that each customer buys. Then write the price in the blanks.

1. __________ 2. __________ 3. __________ 4. __________

NOM ________________________ COURS ________________________

COMPÉTENCE 4 Choosing a healthy lifestyle

A. Que veulent-ils faire? Listen to what changes these people are making in their lifestyle and fill in the missing words. Then indicate what each wants to do: *lose weight* **(maigrir),** *gain weight* **(grossir),** *become stronger* **(devenir plus fort[e]),** or *improve his/her health* **(améliorer sa santé).** Circle your answer. You may choose more than one response in some cases. Stop the tape between items to allow enough time to respond.

1. Henri essaie d'éviter l' ____________________, le ________________________

et le ____________________________ .

Il voudrait: maigrir grossir devenir plus fort améliorer sa santé

2. Yannick fait des ____________________________ et prend des

____________________________.

Il voudrait: maigrir grossir devenir plus fort améliorer sa santé

3. Rosalie mange moins de ____________________________________ et plus de

____.

Elle voudrait: maigrir grossir devenir plus forte améliorer sa santé

4. Rose est ____________________ et elle fait ________________________.

Elle voudrait: maigrir grossir devenir plus forte améliorer sa santé

5. André fait ______________________________ tous les jours.

Il voudrait: maigrir grossir devenir plus fort améliorer sa santé

B. Prononciation: Le conditionnel. Stop the tape and decide whether people who want to improve their health would do these things. If they would, leave the sentence as it is. If they wouldn't, place **ne... pas** in the blanks. Then turn on the tape and check your answers by repeating the statements after the speaker. Pay particular attention to the pronunciation of the endings of the verbs in the conditional.

Moi, je (j') ______ éviterais ______ le tabac.

Toi, tu ______ prendrais ______ de repas copieux tous les jours.

Nous ______ irions ______ plus souvent au club de gym.

Vous ______ feriez ______ plus souvent des haltères.

Mes amis ______ mangeraient ______ beaucoup de matières grasses.

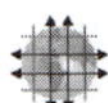

C. Résolutions. André has decided to improve his health. Here is what he told Rosalie he would do. Listen to each phrase, then stop the tape and fill in the missing verb in the conditional.

J'ai dit à Rosalie…

que je ______________________ les conseils de mon médecin.

que je ______________________ plus de fruits et de légumes.

que je ______________________ des plats plus sains.

que mes repas ______________________ moins copieux.

que je ______________________ tous mes repas par un dessert.

que nous ______________________ plus souvent au club de gym.

qu'on ______________________ de l'exercice ensemble tous les jours.

D. Prononciation: Les verbes en *-ir*. Stop the tape and complete these statements with the correct form of the logical **-ir** verb. Then turn on the tape and check you work by repeating the sentences after the speaker. Pay attention to the pronunciation of the verbs. When you have finished, circle the three sentences in which the verb endings sound the same.

CHOISIR maigrir *finir* RÉFLÉCHIR **grandir** réussir **grossir** ROUGIR **obéir** *vieillir*

1. Je prends du poids. Je ______________________ .

2. Tu deviens *(are becoming)* plus maigre. Tu ______________________ .

3. Ma fille devient plus grande. Elle ______________________ .

4. Nous faisons toujours ce que nos parents veulent. Nous ______________________ toujours à nos parents.

5. Vous avez beaucoup de succès dans vos études. Vous ______________________ à tous vos examens.

6. Mes parents sont au régime. Ils ______________________ des plats légers.

E. Rosalie et Rose préparent le repas. Listen as Rosalie **(mamie)** and Rose discuss the dinner they are preparing. Then stop the tape and answer the questions with complete sentences in French.

1. Qu'est-ce que Rose fait comme exercice?

____

2. Qu'est-ce que Rosalie voudrait diminuer *(cut back on)?*

____

NOM ______________________ COURS ______________________

CHAPITRE 9
En vacances

COMPÉTENCE 1 Talking about vacation

A. Que faire? Listen to what several people like to do on vacation. Write the person's name under the picture of the corresponding activity.

a. ______________

b. ______________

c. ______________

d. ______________

e. ______________

f. ______________

Now rewind the tape and listen again. This time, indicate where, according to the activities mentioned, the person named should spend his or her vacation. Place a √ in the appropriate column. You may choose more than one option. The first has been done as an example.

	À LA CAMPAGNE	DANS UN PAYS ÉTRANGER OU EXOTIQUE	SUR UNE ÎLE TROPICALE OU À LA MER	À LA MONTAGNE	DANS UNE GRANDE VILLE
1.			√		
2.					
3.					
4.					
5.					
6.					

B. Elle est dynamique! Suzanne is very active and prefers physical activities. You will be asked which of two activities she prefers. After a pause for you to respond, you will hear the correct answer. Verify your response and your pronunciation.

EXEMPLE	VOUS ENTENDEZ:	Préfère-t-elle rester à l'hôtel ou faire des randonnées?
	VOUS DITES:	**Elle préfère faire des randonnées.**
	VOUS ENTENDEZ:	Elle préfère faire des randonnées.

C. Une lettre de sa sœur. You will hear Daniel read Suzanne's response to his letter. Stop the tape and reread Daniel's letter on page 315 of the textbook. Then read these sentences. After reading the sentences, turn on the tape.

_______ Ma vie professionnelle n'est pas idéale.

_______ Il serait très satisfaisant d'aider des gens qui en ont besoin.

_______ Je trouverais la culture africaine intéressante.

_______ Je suis sûre que j'y serais heureuse.

_______ Je me sentirais peut-être isolée.

_______ La vie en Afrique serait peut-être trop difficile pour moi.

_______ J'ai l'esprit très aventurier.

_______ Je veux mieux connaître la région avant de prendre ma décision.

Now listen to Suzanne's letter. Which items in the preceding list does Suzanne say are true or would be true if she moved to Africa? Mark these items with an **X.**

Rewind the tape and listen again. Then answer these questions in complete sentences in French.

1. Est-ce que Suzanne réfléchit sérieusement à la proposition de son frère?

____

2. Est-ce qu'elle est contente de sa vie actuelle *(current)?*

____

3. Donnez une raison pour laquelle Suzanne aimerait peut-être rester en Afrique.

____

COMPÉTENCE 2 Making plans for a trip

A. Où vont-ils? You will hear a tourist describing his trip around the world. Starting in Paris, retrace his trip by drawing a line according to what he says. The first step of his trip has been done for you. Rewind and listen again as needed.

EXEMPLE VOUS ENTENDEZ: Je suis parti de Paris le 25 mai. D'abord, j'ai pris le train pour la Belgique où j'ai passé deux jours à Bruxelles…

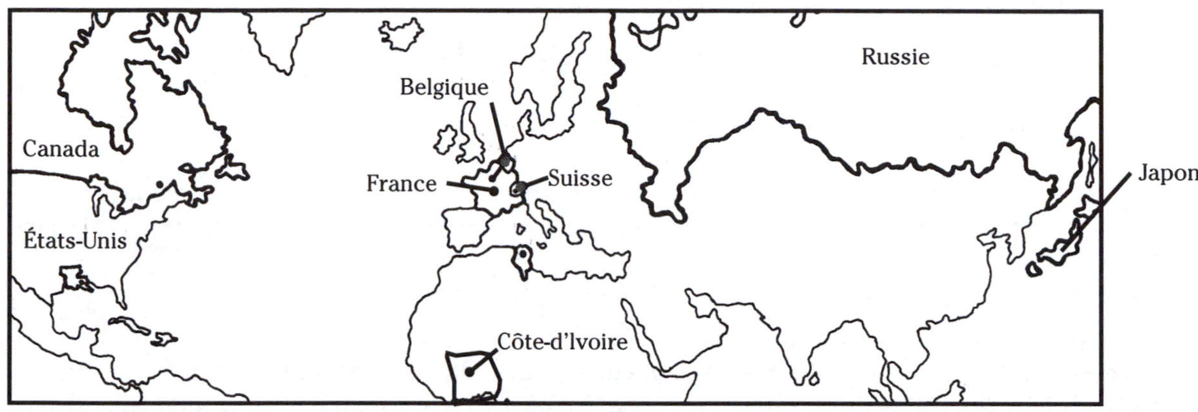

Now rewind the tape and listen again. Then stop the tape and complete these sentences with the name of the appropriate country.

1. Le 25 mai, il a pris le train de Paris à Bruxelles en ____________________.
2. Le 28 mai, il a pris l'avion de Bruxelles à Montréal au ____________________.
3. Après, il a visité la Louisiane aux ____________________.
4. Ensuite, il est allé à Tokyo au ____________________.
5. Après un séjour *(stay)* en Russie, il a pris le train pour Genève en ____________________.
6. Avant son retour à Paris, il a visité Abidjan en ____________________.

B. Prononciation: Le verbe *venir*. Several people are talking about when they will come back from vacation. Stop the tape and complete their statements with the appropriate form of the verb **revenir**. Then turn on the tape and verify your answers by repeating the sentences after the speaker. Pay attention to the pronunciation of the verb **revenir.**

1. Je ______________________________ dans deux semaines.
2. Tu ______________________________ deux jours avant moi.
3. Mon frère ______________________________ avec moi.
4. Nous ______________________________ le 2 août.
5. Quand est-ce que vous ______________________________?
6. Mes parents ______________________________ avec vous.

C. Prononciation: Le futur. Practice saying verbs in the future tense by repeating these sentences after the speaker.

_______ Je ferai un voyage en Afrique cet été.

_______ Tu viendras me chercher à Bondoukou.

_______ Le voyage sera assez long.

_______ Nous passerons beaucoup de temps ensemble.

_______ Mukala et toi, vous visiterez la région avec moi.

_______ Les gens seront très chaleureux *(warm)*.

Now listen as Suzanne talks to Daniel about how her visit will be. Then stop the tape and look back at the preceding sentences. Mark an **X** in the blank next to any statement that reflects what Suzanne said.

D. Qu'est-ce qu'ils deviendront? What will become of the various characters you have met in *Horizons?* Listen as you hear what will happen to them. After each item, stop the tape and fill in the missing words.

1. Annette ______________________________ à Nice où elle ________________________ professeur d'anglais à l'université de Nice. David et elle ______________________________.

2. Robert Martin ______________________________ ses études à l'université Laval au Québec. Après cela, il ______________________________ à Genève où il ______________________________ pour les Nations Unies.

3. Alice Pérez et sa famille ______________________________ à San Antonio et elle ______________________________ beaucoup de succès dans le commerce international.

4. Rosalie Toulouse et André Dupont ______________________________ le reste de leur vie en Normandie. Rose ______________________________ souvent des États-Unis pour voir sa grand-mère.

NOM ______________________ COURS ______________________

COMPÉTENCE 3 Discussing your trip

A. Vous travaillez dans une agence de voyages. Listen as someone orders a plane ticket on the phone. Fill in the form, checking off the options where appropriate. Rewind and listen again as needed.

Agence de voyages Explorado

Nom: ______________________ **Prénom:** ______________________

Destination: ______________________

Date: ______________________

Aller: simple ____________ **aller-retour** ____________

Vol: matin ____________ **après-midi** ____________ **soir** ____________

Classe: première ____________ **touriste** ____________

Fumeur: ____________ **Non-fumeur:** ____________

Paiement: chèque ____________ **carte de crédit** ____________

B. Prononciation: Les verbes en *-re*. Three of the conjugated forms of **-re** verbs sound alike. Repeat these sentences after the speaker and put an **X** next to the three forms that sound alike.

_______ Je réponds bien aux questions du prof.

_______ Tu réponds mieux que moi.

_______ Marc répond rarement aux questions.

_______ Nous répondons toujours correctement.

_______ Vous répondez souvent en classe.

_______ Les étudiants répondent toujours aux questions.

C. Prononciation: Le *e* caduc. Stop the tape and review the ***Prononciation*** section on page 326 of the textbook. Then read these questions and cross out the letter **e** where it is silent. Finally, turn on the tape and check your work by repeating after the speaker.

1. Tu peux me prêter ta voiture?

2. Tu vas me téléphoner demain?

3. Tu vas venir me voir ce week-end?

4. Tu n'as pas de devoirs pour demain?

5. Je peux te parler de mes problèmes?

D. Réponses logiques. Circle the logical response for each question you hear.

1. a. Oui, tu m'entends bien. b. Oui, je t'entends bien.
2. a. Tu vas venir me voir? Quelle surprise! b. Oui, je vais te rendre visite.
3. a. Oui, je te rendrai visite. b. Oui, je viendrai te chercher.
4. a. N'aie pas peur! Je ne vais pas t'oublier. b. Tu vas certainement m'oublier.
5. a. Oui, oui, je t'attendrai. b. Non, tu ne m'attendras pas.
6. a. Non, merci, je n'ai besoin de rien. b. D'accord, je t'apporterai quelque chose.
7. a. C'est très gentil! b. Oui, je te rendrai visite.

E. On se retrouve. Suzanne is picking up her friend, Alain, at the airport. Listen to their conversation, then stop the tape and answer the questions in complete sentences in French.

1. Est-ce que le vol est arrivé à l'heure?

____

2. Est-ce que Suzanne a dû attendre longtemps?

____

3. Qu'est-ce que les amis vont faire le lendemain *(the next day)?*

____

F. À vous maintenant! Answer the questions you hear with complete sentences. Stop the tape between items to allow enough time to respond.

1. ______________________________
2. ______________________________
3. ______________________________
4. ______________________________
5. ______________________________
6. ______________________________

NOM ________________________ COURS ________________________

COMPÉTENCE 4 Making preparations for a trip

A. Avant le départ ou à l'arrivée? Suzanne is preparing for her trip. Decide whether each sentence you hear concerns something she does **avant son départ** or **à son arrivée** at the airport in Abidjan. Circle your answers.

1. avant son départ à son arrivée
2. avant son départ à son arrivée
3. avant son départ à son arrivée
4. avant son départ à son arrivée
5. avant son départ à son arrivée
6. avant son départ à son arrivée

Now rewind the tape and listen to the sentences again. Decide which of the options would be the most logical thing for Suzanne to do next. Place a √ next to your answer. Rewind and listen again as needed. Stop the tape between items to allow enough time to respond.

1. Maintenant, elle devrait…

_______ montrer son passeport et passer à la douane.

_______ lire des guides touristiques et faire un itinéraire.

2. Maintenant, elle devrait…

_______ faire sa valise.

_______ emprunter de l'argent.

3. Maintenant, elle devrait…

_______ payer le billet.

_______ montrer son passeport et passer à la douane.

4. Maintenant, elle devrait…

_______ faire ses valises.

_______ montrer son passeport et passer à la douane.

5. Maintenant, elle devrait…

_______ téléphoner à l'hôtel pour réserver une chambre.

_______ écrire au bureau de tourisme pour obtenir des renseignements.

6. Maintenant, elle devrait…

_______ acheter un plan de la ville.

_______ changer un chèque de voyage.

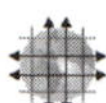

B. Prononciation: Les verbes *dire, lire* et *écrire*. Stop the tape and fill in the blanks with the correct form of the indicated verb. Then turn on the tape and verify your answers by repeating the sentences after the speaker. Pay attention to the pronunciation of the verbs.

DIRE	LIRE	ÉCRIRE
Je ____________ bonjour.	Je ____________ le journal.	J' ____________ une lettre.
Tu ____________ bonjour.	Tu ____________ le journal.	Tu ____________ une lettre.
Elle ____________ bonjour.	Elle ____________ le journal.	Elle ____________ une lettre.
Nous ____________ bonjour.	Nous ____________ le journal.	Nous ____________ une lettre.
Vous ____________ bonjour.	Vous ____________ le journal.	Vous ____________ une lettre.
Ils ____________ bonjour.	Ils ____________ le journal.	Ils ____________ une lettre.

C. Lui ou leur? Answer the questions you hear about your vacation trips and preparations. Use the appropriate form of the indirect object pronoun, **lui** or **leur**, in your responses. Stop the tape between items to allow enough time to respond.

1. ____
2. ____
3. ____
4. ____
5. ____

D. Suzanne organise son voyage. Listen as Suzanne makes some inquiries and arrangements for her trip. Stop the tape and indicate whether these statements are true or false by circling **vrai** or **faux.** Rewind and listen again as needed.

1. Il y a encore de la place sur le vol du 20 juillet. VRAI FAUX
2. Suzanne veut rester une semaine à Abidjan. VRAI FAUX
3. Suzanne dit à ses parents où elle va. VRAI FAUX
4. Suzanne a déjà un passeport. VRAI FAUX

Now rewind the tape and listen again. Then stop the tape and answer these questions.

1. Combien coûte le billet aller-retour?

____

2. Quelle est la date du vol que Suzanne va prendre? Quand va-t-elle rentrer?

____

NOM ____________________ COURS ____________________

CHAPITRE 10
À l'hôtel

COMPÉTENCE 1 Deciding where to stay

A. Quel genre d'hôtel? You will hear short descriptions of several hotels. Indicate the category of each hotel by circling **un hôtel pas cher** or **un hôtel de luxe.**

1. UN HÔTEL PAS CHER UN HÔTEL DE LUXE
2. UN HÔTEL PAS CHER UN HÔTEL DE LUXE
3. UN HÔTEL PAS CHER UN HÔTEL DE LUXE

un hôtel pas cher

un hôtel de luxe

Rewind and listen to the description of each hotel again. Fill in the blanks with the information about each hotel.

L'HÔTEL CARAYOU

1. Combien de chambres y a-t-il? ____________________
2. Il y en a combien avec salle de bains? ____________________
3. Est-ce que le petit déjeuner est compris? ____________________
4. Où se trouve l'hôtel? ____________________
5. Quel est le prix d'une chambre? ____________________

L'HÔTEL AMANTINE

1. Combien de chambres y a-t-il? ____________________
2. Il y en a combien avec salle de bains? ____________________
3. Est-ce que le petit déjeuner est compris? ____________________
4. Où se trouve l'hôtel? ____________________
5. Quel est le prix d'une chambre? ____________________

L'HÔTEL DIAMANT

1. Combien de chambres y a-t-il? ____________________
2. Il y en a combien avec salle de bains? ____________________
3. Est-ce que le petit déjeuner est compris? ____________________
4. Où se trouve l'hôtel? ____________________
5. Quel est le prix d'une chambre? ____________________

B. Dans la chambre. Listen as Suzanne talks to Daniel on the phone about her hotel room. Then stop the tape and indicate whether these statements are true or false by circling **vrai** or **faux.**

1. La chambre est grande.	VRAI	FAUX
2. Suzanne ne va pas passer beaucoup de temps dans la chambre.	VRAI	FAUX
3. Il y a une salle de bains mais il n'y a pas de douche.	VRAI	FAUX
4. Elle a une belle vue sur la ville.	VRAI	FAUX

C. Le ton de la voix. You will hear a conversation between two tourists, Sophie and Anne-Marie. Listen to what they say and their tone of voice and circle the best description of their emotions.

très satisfaites　　un peu surprises　　pas du tout satisfaites

Now listen as the conversation is read more slowly with pauses for you to write in the missing words. Rewind and listen again as needed.

ANNE-MARIE: Tu sais, je suis vraiment déçue *(disappointed)!*

Regarde ________________________!

Nous payons ________________________ la nuit et

________________________ est toute petite.

SOPHIE: Et nous avons seulement ________________________. J'aurais préféré avoir une baignoire *(bathtub).*

ANNE-MARIE: Ah, oui, moi aussi! Tu as essayé ________________________? Ils ne sont vraiment pas très ________________________!

SOPHIE: Écoute, demain on va ________________________. Tu as

________________________?

ANNE-MARIE: Oui, bien sûr. Et toi, tu as ________________________ ?

SOPHIE: Oui, elle est là. Alors, demain on cherche ________________________.

ANNE-MARIE: D'accord.

NOM ______________________________ COURS ______________________________

COMPÉTENCE 2 Giving directions

A. Qu'est-ce qu'il y a près de l'hôtel? You will hear a description of the neighborhood pictured. Imagine that you are standing on the **place,** facing the hotel. Write the name of each place in the appropriate blank. Stop the tape as needed.

EXEMPLE VOUS ENTENDEZ: En face de la place, directement devant vous, il y a un hôtel.
VOUS ÉCRIVEZ: l'hôtel

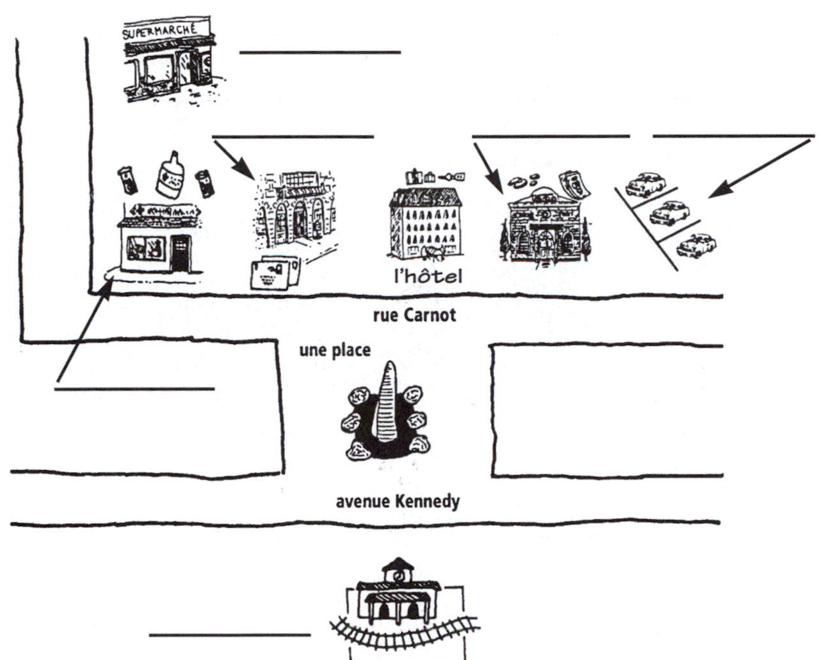

Now listen and repeat the name of each place from the top left to the right to the bottom after the speaker to verify your responses.

B. Où se trouve...? Stop the tape, look at the map in ***A. Qu'est-ce qu'il y a près de l'hôtel?*** and complete these sentences. Then turn on the tape and verify your answers by repeating the sentences after the speaker.

DERRIÈRE à côté de *au bout de* EN FACE DE **entre** de l'autre côté de

1. ______________________ l'hôtel, il y a une banque et un bureau de poste.
2. ______________________ l'hôtel, il y a une place.
3. La gare est ______________________ la place.
4. ______________________ la rue, il y a un parking.
5. La banque est ______________________ l'hôtel et le parking.
6. Au coin de la rue, il y a une pharmacie. ______________________ la pharmacie, il y a un supermarché.

C. L'impératif. A backseat driver keeps telling you how to drive. Let him know you don't want to do what he suggests. Write your responses.

EXEMPLE VOUS ENTENDEZ: Prends la rue Dupont.
VOUS ÉCRIVEZ: **Je ne veux pas prendre la rue Dupont!**

1. ______________________________
2. ______________________________
3. ______________________________
4. ______________________________
5. ______________________________
6. ______________________________
7. ______________________________

D. Pour indiquer le chemin. Stop the tape and open the textbook to the map of Abidjan on pages 354–355. Turn on the tape. Starting at **la poste,** follow the directions you hear. Write where you end up.

____

E. Prononciation: Les verbes *voir* et *croire*. Practice saying the forms of the verbs **croire** and **voir** by repeating them after the speaker.

CROIRE			
je	crois	nous	croyons
tu	crois	vous	croyez
il	croit	ils	croient
elle	croit	elles	croient
on	croit		

VOIR			
je	vois	nous	voyons
tu	vois	vous	voyez
il	voit	ils	voient
elle	voit	elles	voient
on	voit		

Now complete the statements you hear. Then circle **vrai** or **faux** to indicate whether each one is true or false for you and your family and friends.

Moi, je ______________________________. VRAI FAUX

Mes parents ______________________________. VRAI FAUX

Mon meilleur ami ______________________________. VRAI FAUX

Je ______________________________. VRAI FAUX

Mon meilleur ami et moi, ____________________ tous les jours. VRAI FAUX

Mes parents ____________________ souvent. VRAI FAUX

NOM ______________________ COURS ______________________

COMPÉTENCE 3 Giving advice

A. Encore des conseils. A friend is suggesting what you need to take on your camping trip. Write the number of each of his sentences below the corresponding picture. Not all the items pictured will be mentioned, so some spaces will remain blank.

B. Quelques conseils. You will hear a guide at the **Parc de la Comoé** giving directions to a group of tourists. Listen to what the guide says, then stop the tape and complete these sentences with one or two of the things mentioned for each.

Il faut mettre ______________________ pour se protéger contre les insectes.

Pour se protéger contre le soleil, on devrait mettre ______________________ et ______________________.

Il ne faut pas ______________________ ou ______________________.

C. Est-ce nécessaire? The tour guide is giving more instructions. Listen to each sentence and decide if the guide is expressing **une nécessité** *(one must)*, **une suggestion** *(it would be good to)*, or **une interdiction** *(one must not)*. Put a √ in the appropriate column.

	NÉCESSITÉ	SUGGESTION	INTERDICTION
1.	_____	_____	_____
2.	_____	_____	_____
3.	_____	_____	_____
4.	_____	_____	_____
5.	_____	_____	_____
6.	_____	_____	_____
7.	_____	_____	_____
8.	_____	_____	_____
9.	_____	_____	_____
10.	_____	_____	_____

D. Tu dois travailler! You will hear someone give advice to a friend who is not doing well in college. The first time, simply listen to the conversation at normal speed. It will then be repeated at a slower speed with pauses for you to write in the missing words.You will need to stop the tape during the pauses to have sufficient time to respond. When you are done, rewind and listen again to correct your work.

Voilà ce qu'il faut faire pour réussir à tes cours. D'abord, il faut que tu ____________________ toujours en classe et il ne faut pas que tu ____________________ en retard. Mais si le professeur est en retard, il faut que les étudiants l' ____________________. Il vaut mieux que tu ____________________ toujours les devoirs et que tu ____________________ tous les exercices. Il est important que tu ne ____________________ pas tes devoirs. Il est bon que les autres étudiants et toi ____________________ ensemble. Il est mieux que vous ____________________ les devoirs et que vous ____________________ les examens ensemble. Mais il ne faut pas que vous ____________________ au lieu de *(instead of)* travailler!

NOM ______________________ COURS ______________________

COMPÉTENCE 4 Finding out about jobs abroad

A. Quelle est leur profession? As you are asked, say what the people shown do as a profession. After a pause for you to respond, you will hear the correct answer. Verify your response and your pronunciation.

EXEMPLE VOUS ENTENDEZ: Qu'est-ce qu'ils font? Ils sont secrétaires ou infirmiers?
VOUS DITES: **Ils sont infirmiers.**
VOUS ENTENDEZ: Ils sont infirmiers.

EXEMPLE

1.

2.

3.

4.

5.

6.

7.

B. Professions. You will hear descriptions of what people do. Decide what their occupation is and write it in the space provided. For some, there may be more than one possibility. Stop the tape as needed.

EXEMPLE VOUS ENTENDEZ: Elle chante.
VOUS ÉCRIVEZ: *Elle est chanteuse.*

1. ______________________
2. ______________________
3. ______________________
4. ______________________
5. ______________________
6. ______________________

Now verify your answers by repeating the sentences after the speaker.

C. Prononciation: Les verbes *savoir* et *connaître*. Stop the tape and complete each sentence with the appropriate form of either **savoir** or **connaître.** Then turn on the tape and verify your answers by repeating the sentences after the speaker.

Je ____________________ une institutrice qui travaille pour le Corps de la Paix, mais je ne ____________________ pas dans quel pays elle est allée.

Est-ce que tu la ____________________? Tu ____________________ où elle travaille?

Elle ne te ____________________ pas, mais elle ____________________ qui tu es.

Nous ____________________ ce qu'il faut faire, mais nous ne ____________________ pas la région.

____________________-vous la région? ____________________-vous où on peut acheter un plan?

Les gens d'ici ____________________ toute la région.

Ils ____________________ où tout se trouve.

D. La négritude. You will hear the poem ***Préférence...*** by Claude-Emmanuel Abolo Bowole of Cameroon. The first time, simply listen as it is read at normal speed. It will then be repeated at a slower speed with pauses for you to write in the missing words. When you are done, rewind and listen again to correct your work.

Préférence...
de Claude-Emmanuel Abolo Bowole

Un message

À vous ________ **luttez,**

À vous ________ rêvez d'un monde meilleur;

À vous ________ avez le courage de dire

Ce que vous ______________ être la **vérité...**

À vous tous

______________________________...

J'adresse ce message d'espoir

Le monde ____________________

Est un monde de **haine,**

Qui ne le sait?

Le monde ____________________

________'en ferons-nous toi et moi?

__________ en faire

Un monde de paix,

Un monde de fraternité,

Un monde d'**amitié,**

Un monde de gaieté...

---

lutter *to fight* **la vérité** *the truth* **la haine** *hatred* **l'amitié** *(f) friendship*